Children and Play

Understanding Children's Worlds

Series Editor: Judy Dunn

The study of children's development can have a profound influence on how children are brought up, cared for and educated. Many psychologists argue that, even if our knowledge is incomplete, we have a responsibility to attempt to help those concerned with the care, education, and study of children by making what we know available to them. The central aim of this series is to encourage developmental psychologists to set out the findings and the implications of their research for others—teachers, doctors, social workers, students and fellow researchers—whose work involves the care, education, and study of young children and their families. The information and the ideas that have grown from recent research form an important resource which should be available to them. This series provides an opportunity for psychologists to present their work in a way that is interesting, intelligible, and substantial, and to discuss what its consequences may be for those who care for and teach children: not to offer simple prescriptive advice to other professionals, but to make important and innovative research accessible to them.

Children and Play

Peter K. Smith

with a chapter by Yumi Gosso

WILEY-BLACKWELL

A John Wiley & Sons, Ltd., Publication

Blackwell Publishing was acquired by John Wiley & Sons in February
2007. Blackwell's publishing program has been merged with Wiley's
global Scientific, Technical, and Medical business to form Wiley-Blackwell.

Registered Office
John Wiley & Sons Ltd, The Atrium, Southern Gate, Chichester,
West Sussex, PO19 8SQ, United Kingdom

Editorial Offices
350 Main Street, Malden, MA 02148-5020, USA
9600 Garsington Road, Oxford, OX4 2DQ, UK
The Atrium, Southern Gate, Chichester, West Sussex, PO19 8SQ, UK

For details of our global editorial offices, for customer services,
and for information about how to apply for permission to reuse the
copyright material in this book please see our website at
www.wiley.com/wiley-blackwell.

Library of Congress Cataloging-in-Publication Data

Smith, Peter K.
Children and play / Peter K. Smith ; with a chapter by Yumi Gosso.
p. cm.
Includes bibliographical references and index.
ISBN 978-0-631-23521-7 (hardcover : alk. paper) — ISBN 978-0-631-23522-4
(pbk. : alk. paper) 1. Play—Psychological aspects. 2. Play behavior in animals.
3. Child psychology. 4. Child development. 5. Psychology, Comparative. I. Title.
BF717.S56 2010
155.4′18—dc22

2008051208

A catalogue record for this book is available from the British Library.

Set in 10/12.5pt Sabon by Graphicraft Limited, Hong Kong
Printed in Singapore by Ho Printing Singapore Pte Ltd

1   2010

Contents

Contents

Series Editor's Preface

This book takes a broad perspective on play. In this respect, it differs from other recent writing on the topic, where the attention has been chiefly on symbolic play and its links with cognitive development. The perspective taken by Peter Smith raises a series of very different and interesting questions, and sets them within a wide framework. The chapters on the characteristics of play—especially on the history of ideas about play—are very welcome. The two chapters on animal play that follow are again unusual in texts on play in children, but the issue of relevance for students of human development is addressed clearly. Chapter 3 likewise stands out by virtue of the interest of many of the findings it describes: for instance, the results showing how food supplies affect the amount of play.

Cross cultural studies of play—the next topic addressed—are of great potential interest. The chapter makes some provocative claims that may surprise readers from a classical psychology background—for instance, the claim that children's play changes culture. Again, readers are provided with a wide range of examples to prompt them to reflect on the claim and ask themselves how well established it is. Chapter 6 examines another neglected topic—physical play. Here the question of how far physical play is significant for children's intimate relationships—their friendships—is raised. It is relatively neglected by research on relationship formation and maintenance.

Chapters 8 and 9 cover a topic that will be of great interest to most developmentalists—pretend play. Here the issue of the links between early pretend play and cognitive development (specifically theory of mind) is of special importance. The bidirectionality of the developmental links between pretend play and understanding of mind are of much current interest. Early skills in mindreading are associated with later sophistication in pretence and, importantly, *vice versa*. And the developmental significance of the social nature of shared pretence is fascinating. From John Gottman's work onwards there is evidence for the core place that shared or joint pretend experience has in children's friendships, similarly sibling research has established the emotional link between shared play and emotional/close relationships. Altogether this wide-ranging book is a very welcome addition to the literature on play.

Judy Dunn

Acknowledgments

I have worked on children's play for a number of years, and benefited generally from conversations with many colleagues. Tony Pellegrini, Jim Christie, and Peter Johnsen have been particularly helpful, and Brain Sutton-Smith always stimulating in his thoughts and comments. In regard to this book, I would like to particularly thank Yumi Gosso, who contributed the chapter on cross-cultural studies. Yumi herself would like to thank the Parakanã Program for permission to observe Parakanã Indians, the Conselho Nacional de Desenvolvimento Científico e Tecnológico for financial support, Thaïs R. A. Pinto Chaves for English assistance, and Francisco Simões for valuable comments and suggestions. I would like to thank Peter Blatchford, Chuck Corbin, Cheryl Dissanayake, Rachel Kelly, Karen Majors, Chris Jarrold, Vickii Jenvey, Mark Nielsen, Jaak Panksepp, and Dee Ray for providing recent articles and resources. Shenene Kara gave invaluable help with compiling the references. I am also grateful to the Series Editor, Judy Dunn, and to an anonymous reviewer, for their helpful comments on the first draft of the book.

Thanks to Jaak Panksepp for permission to reproduce Figure 3.2, to Frans de Waal for permission to use Figure 3.3, and to Lisa Riley for permission to use Figure 3.4.

As always, none of the above are responsible for my views. I am critical of some play research, but the community of play researchers has generally been a friendly and cooperative one, and I have enjoyed being part of it. I hope this book can convey something of the interest and excitement of studying children's play (and not only children's play, but animal play too) to a wider audience, and also contribute something to the ongoing debate on the importance that we should give to play in our modern societies.

Peter K. Smith
August 2008

Chapter 1

An Introduction to Play

Why Play?

Why play? Why a book on play in children? And, why do children play? It is clearly fun, but is it of any practical importance?

This is far from being the only book on children's play. There are many, including some good contemporary books. But this book does attempt to bring together a variety of perspectives—psychological theories, the cross-cultural evidence, and the evolutionary perspective including work on animal play. The focus, however, is on play in childhood.

Why do children play? Play certainly takes up an appreciable portion of many children's time budgets. It seems likely it is an important part of children's development, but views on this continue to be debated. We will review the evidence, and the theories they are testing. A lot depends on which kinds of play we are discussing; and what we mean by "important."

There are various definitions of what play is, and of various kinds of play. Some have had much more investigation than others. There is a rather vast literature on children's pretend play. By contrast, the research on children's rough-and-tumble play—which arguably is just as prevalent as pretend play—is much more sparse.

In this chapter, we will start with some examples of what is play, and what is not play, which most people would agree on, and then consider the characteristics and definitions of play. We will summarize the various main types of play. We will then look at the main methods of studying play. We will conclude with an overview of the plan for the remainder of the book.

Examples of What Is and What Is Not Play

Here are some short vignettes of behavior: some actually observed (and referenced), others typical of countless behavior sequences.

- Sultana (12 months) watches her mother. Her mother hides her face behind a floppy hat, then removes the hat and says "boo!". Sultana laughs. Her mother hides her face again, then removes it saying "boo!" Sultana laughs even louder. This is repeated, with Sultana reaching for the hat; and her mother saying "where's mommy" and laughing herself, before removing it.
- Jake (18 months) is banging two wooden blocks together. It makes a loud noise. Jake laughs and looks at his dad, and bangs the blocks together several times.
- A two and a half-year-old boy lies in his cot, babbling to himself: "One two three four. One two. One two three four. One two three. Anthony counting. Good boy you. One two three." [from Weir, 1962]
- Amanda and Lisa (4 years) are together. "I know what, I'll be a witch!" says Amanda. "Yes," says Lisa, "put my hat on." "I'll get my stick," says Amanda. "Oh yes, my stick" says Lisa. They "ride" on pretend broomsticks, and make monster noises at Emma and two boys. "Witches, witches, witches!" shouts one boy. "We are witches, we will spell you!" says Amanda. Amanda puts her arms around Laura. "We will spell you, we've got you, we are witches," she says. "I've tied her up" adds Lisa, pretending to tie her up. "No!" shouts Laura and pushes them away. Lisa goes off to where some books are on a chair. "These are special witch books you know!" she says to Amanda. "We are witches, we will turn you into a monster!" Amanda says to Laura, and "we are turning you into a nasty monster" to Stuart. [from transcripts by the author]
- Josephine (5 years) climbs up the ladder to the top of a slide, slides down on her back laughing, runs around, climbs up again, slides down again, runs around, climbs up, and now slides down on her stomach.
- Simon (6 years) runs up to Jared (7 years) in the school playground. He is laughing and kicks at Jared with his leg, and makes "kung fu" or boxing motions with his arms, repeatedly, but without making contact. Jared makes a few boxing motions back, then chases Simon briefly. He catches Simon and they roll on the grass, grappling with each other. After some 30 seconds they get up and walk off together, talking.

- "Arara'ywa, an 8 year old Parakanã (South American Indian) boy, throws his arrow and goes searching for it. He finds it and throws it again. He runs to the place he had aimed at. He looks for the arrow and laughs when he finds it. He runs to get the arrow and throws it once again, and returns smiling to get his arrow. He throws it again and goes to get it, followed by Ma'apyga, a 10 year old boy." [adapted from Gosso, 2005]

These vignettes describe different kinds of behavior, at varied ages, but most people would agree in saying that they were examples of play. Respectively, they could be described as social contingency play; sensorimotor play; language play; fantasy or pretend play; exercise play; rough-and-tumble play; and object play.

Now for some other vignettes:

- Edmund (15 months) is walking and crawling around a room in a friend's house. He is a bit tentative in his movements, looking around, touching a plant pot. He picks up a small box and looks at it, puts it down, and then goes on to a larger box. He stands up and looks inside it.
- Sarah (4 years) is sitting on the floor sucking her thumb. She is rocking backwards and forwards repeatedly, with little variation in her movements.
- Rupa and Shanette (aged 4) are collecting up toy cups and saucers and putting them away in a box. They have been asked to do this by Ms Patel, the nursery teacher. They make repeated trips to the play area, picking things up and putting them in the storage box.
- A group of boys are engaged in a game of soccer. They are kicking the ball about, trying to score in two makeshift goals. Maurice (aged 7) picks up the ball and runs with it. "No!" shouts Barach (aged 8), "you aren't allowed to pick it up!" The other boys agree. Maurice puts the ball down shamefacedly and kicks it with his foot to a team-mate.

What is happening in these episodes? It is likely that most people would not describe these as play. Respectively, they could be described as exploration; stereotypic behavior; work; and games with rules. But they share some features of play. Let's look at some of the characteristics proposed for play, and compare them with these examples.

Characteristics of Playful Behavior

The *Encarta World English Dictionary* (1999) gives many meanings for "play,", but the first two are those relevant for us: (1) to take part in enjoyable activity for the sake of amusement, and (2) to do something for fun, not in earnest.

This suggests a functional way of looking at play—it is done for its own sake, for fun, not for any external purpose. In fact, two different approaches to defining play were proposed by Robert Fagen, an animal ethologist, in 1974: the functional approach and the structural approach. In the functional approach, we look at what the purpose of the behavior is, or appears to be. By contrast, in the structural approach we look at the actual behaviors and the way that they are performed. A third approach is to think which criteria people actually use in deciding whether something is play, or not.

In the functional approach, it is suggested that play does not have an obvious end in itself or an external goal. This led to play being defined as having no clear immediate benefits or obvious goal. Symons (1978) advanced this sort of definition for monkey social play, but it can equally apply to human play. Thus, if an external goal is present (such as a need to eat, or to seek comfort, or to overpower another), then the behavior is not play. This can differentiate play from work, exploration, and perhaps stereotypy (if stereotypic behavior is seeking comfort in some way). Indeed, it can also differentiate play from games with rules, in that games such as football have an external goal. In fact, there are two goals in the proper game! But less facetiously, the general goal in games with rules is to win the game, and this can be a very serious business.

But there are difficulties with this definition. Many theorists, and many ordinary people, believe the child does get benefits from playing. However, perhaps they are not "clear, immediate benefits," but instead "unclear, delayed benefits"? One prominent school of thought is that the benefits of play *are* delayed; that the child is developing strength and skills now that will be useful in adolescence and adulthood. But some theorists believe that many benefits of play are more immediate (e.g. Pellegrini & Bjorklund, 2004); after all, strength and skills can be utilized now as well as in the future. Then, are the benefits clear? There is continuing disagreement about exactly what the benefits of play are; but we might hope to reach more clarity about this in the future. So, if some benefits are immediate, and some benefits are, or at least may become, clear, where does that leave this definition of play?

It may be helpful to think not so much of benefits or goals in the abstract, but from the point of view of the player. Even if (say) exercise play helps develop strength, or pretend play helps develop creativity (issues we consider later), children do not do exercise play in order to develop their muscles, and they do not do pretend play in order to be more creative. These activities are done for enjoyment, for their own sake. If exercise was done specifically in order to develop fitness—as, for example, an adult goes to a gym for a work-out—we would tend to call this work or possibly recreational activity, but not play.

The structural approach to defining play examines the behaviors themselves, and the way behaviors are organized or sequenced, in play as compared to non-play. As regards specific behaviors, the main examples that only occur in play are so-called "play signals" (described further in Chapter 3). In mammals they often take the form of an open-mouthed play face (as in monkeys grappling), or a bouncy gambol (as in puppies or kittens initiating a chase). An example in bonobos is shown in Figure 3.3. In children the corresponding play signals are laughter and the associated "open mouth play face" (Blurton Jones, 1967); see Figure 1.1. Such play signals are especially useful in rough-and-tumble play, where they can indicate that no aggressive intention is implied in a chase or wrestle (see Chapter 6). However a lot of play—especially human play—is not indexed by play signals. Often play is made up entirely of behaviors familiar in other contexts—such as running, climbing, manipulating objects, and talking.

Figure 1.1 A boy showing a play face
(Smith, Cowie, & Blades, 2003: p. 217, Figure 7.1(b))

But what about the ordering or sequencing of these behaviors? Another ethologist, Caroline Loizos (1967) argued that, according to the structural approach, we can think of a behavior sequence as playful, if the constituent behaviors are "repeated," "fragmented," "exaggerated," or "re-ordered." For example, a child just running up a slope may not be playing, but if she runs up and slides down several times (repetition), runs just half-way up (fragmentation), takes unusually large or small steps or jumps (exaggeration) or crawls up and then runs down (re-ordering), we would probably agree that it was playful. The structural approach is not in opposition to the functional one. After all, the child running up and down the slope has no immediate purpose, apart from enjoyment. The two approaches are logically distinct, however.

The third, criteria-based approach can build on both of the previous sets of insights, but is based on the point of view of the observer. It asks what criteria an observer might use to judge whether a behavior sequence is play or not play. A formal model of this was proposed by Krasnor and Pepler (1980), and is shown in Figure 1.2. They suggested there were four "play criteria."

- "Intrinsic motivation" refers to the idea that play is not constrained by external rules or social demands, but is done for its own sake; taken from the functional approach.
- "Nonliterality" refers to the "as if" or pretend element. Behaviors do not have their normal or "literal" meaning. This can also be seen as derived from the functional approach, but really comes into its own when we consider pretend play in children.
- "Positive affect" refers to the enjoyment of play, especially indexed by signals such as laughter. Specific play signals are taken from the structural approach.
- "Flexibility" refers to variation in form and content. This captures some of the sequencing aspects of the structural approach.

Krasnor and Pepler argued that no one criterion is sufficient to say something is play, but that the more criteria are present, the more agreement we will have that the behavior is play. Thus, rather than a rigid distinction between "play" and "non-play," we get a continuum from more clearly to less clearly playful behaviors (from the point of view of the observer). However Krasnor and Pepler did not actually try out their model on real observers. An empirical test of their model was subsequently made by Smith and Vollstedt (1985). They used the four criteria above, plus a fifth one:

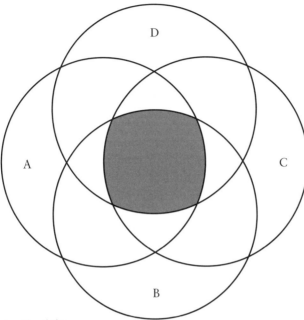

A - Flexibility
B - Positive affect
C - Nonliterality
D - Intrinsic motivation

Figure 1.2 Krasnor and Pepler model; shaded area is most playful
(Smith, Cowie, & Blades, 2003: p. 218, Figure 7.2)

- "Means/ends": the child is more interested in the performance of the behavior than in its outcome; another reflection of the structural approach.

To test out the model, Ralph Vollstedt and I made video films of nursery-school children in a purpose-built nursery class in the Department of Psychology at Sheffield University, where I then worked. We selected a number of short, discrete episodes and edited them into a film which we asked 70 adults to view. Some of the adults simply scored each episode as to whether it was playful or not; other adults were asked to judge the applicability of each of the five play criteria. We then examined the match between independent judgments as to applicability of the five criteria, and whether the episode was seen as playful.

We found that the episodes seen as playful were often seen as non-literal, flexible and showing positive affect. Means/ends also correlated with play, but did not add anything to the first three criteria. Interestingly, the intrinsic motivation criterion did not correlate with play judgments, despite its common occurrence in definitions of play. Observers often rated nonplayful activities (such as watching others or fighting) as intrinsically motivated; equally, some play episodes were seen as externally constrained—for example, by the demands of others in social play.

Further, the more criteria were present, the higher the ratings for playfulness. Taking the three criteria of nonliteralness, flexibility, and positive affect: If none of these were present only 24% of episodes were seen as playful; if one criterion was present, the figure rose to 47%; if two criteria were present, it jumped to 85%, and then to 100% if all three criteria were present. We concluded that if observers judge that any two of these three criteria are present, a judgment of play is likely to be made and that most episodes of play will fall into this category.

The play criterion approach does not attempt a one-sentence definition of play. This is unlikely to be useful: The boundaries are too blurred. It does acknowledge a continuum from nonplayful or less playful to playful behavior. It also identifies how observers actually decide to call a behavior sequence "play." The main criteria so far identified for young children are enjoyment, flexibility, and pretense. In Chapter 3, we will see how this criteria-based approach has been used to try to define animal play.

Types of Play

We will look at the various types of play in more detail in later chapters. There is not universal agreement on a typology. Thinking primarily of children's play, those listed below would be commonly recognized; they follow the vignettes presented above which are exemplars of them.

Social contingency play

This refers to simple games such as peek-a-boo, where there is enjoyment in the responses of others, often contingent on your behavior or on imitation of one person by another.

Sensorimotor play

This refers to activities typical of Piaget's sensorimotor period, that is up to around 2 years. It refers to activities with objects (or one's own body) that are based on the sensory properties of the object(s), for example sucking objects, banging blocks together, dropping them repeatedly.

Object play

Past the sensorimotor period, children take part in a lot of activities with objects; much of this being construction play. Fitting Lego blocks together, making block towers, using modeling clay, pouring water from one container to another, might count as object play.

Language play

Children can play with noises, syllables, words, and phrases. This can be the kind of babbling that Ruth Weir noted in her two-year-old son Anthony, as he went to sleep, or woke up, in his cot. Or it can be rhyming couplets, or repetitive statements, perhaps in a nonliteral context: "You be mummy!" "No, you be mummy!" "No, I'm daddy, you be mummy!"

Physical activity play

In general, this refers to gross bodily movements (rather than the smaller-scale bodily movements involved for example in sensorimotor play or object play. *Exercise play* is the main form of this—running, jumping, crawling, climbing, and so forth. Deserving separate consideration is *Rough-and-tumble play*. This is a vigorous social form of physical play, involving grappling, wrestling, kicking, chasing, and other behaviors that would be aggressive in a nonplayful context. This is often called play-fighting or play-chasing.

Fantasy or pretend play

Fantasy or pretend play is characterized by the nonliteral use of objects, actions, or vocalizations. A block becomes a cake, or a piece of paper becomes a bus ticket. Actions can mime pretend behaviors such as drinking a cup of tea, or turning the steering wheel of a car. "Vroom-vroom" signifies the car noise. A more complex version of pretend play is *socio-dramatic play*. This involves role play and more than one person participating. In the vignette above, Amanda and Lisa are engaged in role play as witches. They also mimed riding broomsticks and tying up a captive, in the absence of any object to represent the broomsticks or string.

These categories can overlap. Some object play may be pretend (building the Eiffel Tower); some language play may be in sociodramatic play ("You be mummy!"). Is pouring water from one bucket to another object play or sensorimotor play? However, they serve as prototypes and as a framework for discussion.

Things That Are Probably Not Play: Exploration, Stereotypic Behavior, Work, Rule-Governed Games

Exploration and play

A behavior that is sometimes confused with play is exploration. It is true that with very young children, during sensorimotor development, the distinction between exploration and play is difficult to make (see Chapter 7). For young infants, all objects are novel. However, by the preschool years the distinction is clearer. An experiment illustrating this was carried out by Corinne Hutt (1966). Hutt devised a novel toy (described in more detail in Chapter 7), a box that children could sit on, with a lever that could sound a bell or a buzzer. Children aged 3 to 5 years were rather serious when introduced to the toy, feeling it, touching and moving the lever—they were in fact exploring what the novel object could do. Fairly soon this changed. Typically, a child would relax and sit on the object making noises with the lever repeatedly or in different ways—which was seen as more playful activity. This illustrates how exploration of objects often precedes play with objects.

Stereotyped behaviors

Stereotypic behaviors are often seen in zoo animals, especially large animals penned up in relatively small enclosures. A tiger paces out its enclosure; is this exercise play? In a zoo, it is likely the tiger will follow the same path again, and again, and again, with no sign of enjoyment. Children can also show stereotypic behaviors. In small ways, such as thumb sucking, this may be normal; but repetitive rocking or self-stimulating movements can be an index of a deprived environment. Such stereotyped behaviors can be seen in institutionalized infants, for example in poorly equipped orphanages with little social or environmental resources or stimulation on offer.

Why is this not playful? There is no clear external goal, although presumably these stereotypic behaviors help modulate arousal in a very boring situation—they are more comforting than literally "doing nothing." Thinking of structural characteristics, there is also repetition here certainly, but little flexibility or reordering. Altogether, the lack of enjoyment and the lack of variation or flexibility put these stereotypic behaviors at the non-playful end of the continuum, despite the absence of external goals.

Work

Work refers to activity done for a clear external goal. This may be to earn money, to get food or resources, or to follow the instructions of someone in authority. Western children are rather sheltered from work. Only in later middle childhood or adolescence does it start to be common for children to earn some money by working, perhaps on a newspaper delivery round. Younger children may be asked to help do some household chores, tidy up their room, and so forth, although even these requirements are often not very high-profile. In modern western society, work is not strongly seen as part of childhood, at least up to middle childhood.

At school, of course, children are required to do some tasks and activities, but in the preschool and infant school, a lot of this is in playful mode. In the next chapter we will look at the "play ethos," and the view that "play is indeed the child's work" (Isaacs, 1929). A predominant educational view has been that children learn through play and that therefore "work" is not necessary for learning, up to perhaps the end of infant school. This view is not universally shared in western countries, of course, and it is considerably less prevalent in eastern cultures and in more traditional societies (see Chapter 5). In traditional subsistence cultures, children have a vital role in work-like activities such as protecting the crops from birds, caring for younger siblings, gathering firewood, and other useful tasks. These might or might not be enjoyable, and there may be playful elements embedded: for example, scaring birds from the crops can embody play chasing. But the external constraints to do these tasks do imply that they are not play.

Rule-governed games

"Games" can be distinguished from "play" by the presence of external rules: that means, rules that are established by convention, to a greater or lesser extent codified, and that provide constraints on what the game players can do. In our vignette above, Maurice broke the rules of soccer by picking the ball up, and the outcome was not enjoyable for him.

The existence of rules is not a clear-cut criterion to distinguish play and games. Peek-a-boo has a kind of rule structure, as has been described by Bruner and Sherwood (1975); they saw the developing expectations the child has (for timing, and repetition, for example) as being the beginnings of understanding rules to a game. The pretend play of preschool children often has some rule structure related to the roles adopted. For example, if someone is role-playing "doctor" to a "patient," there are some constraints on what he or she is expected to do, exerted by the other participants. Nevertheless, any rules or constraints are largely private to that particular play episode, and can be changed at any time ("I'm not the doctor now, I'm a policeman").

By the time children are 6 or 7 years old, rule-governed games like hopscotch, tag or soccer take up much more playground time. These are games with public rules, sometimes codified, with much less latitude for change. The transition from play to games is nevertheless a gradual one. As Jean Piaget showed in his classic study of boys playing marbles in Neuchâtel, Switzerland, the codification and stability of rules increases with age and the cognitive abilities of the players; there is not a clear boundary between play, and games.

This discussion is also relevant to the burgeoning area of video and computer games, and games on the internet. Since 1979, when Space Invaders hit the computer game market, there has been a rapid increase in the time children spend with computer games or in video arcades, and more recently on the internet. Is this "play"? In most cases, the games have definite rules to follow; if you don't follow them, you won't get far, let alone to the next level. It does indeed seem appropriate to refer to these activities as computer games, rather than computer play.

Methods of Studying Play

How have people studied play? The most obvious method, and indeed one often used, has been *observation in natural environments*. Another approach has been *observation in structured environments*. Some *experimental studies* have been carried out; these include enhancement and deprivation studies. It is also possible to use methods more traditional in the social sciences, such as *interviews and questionnaires*. Finally, there are a variety of *other sources*, such as toy inventories, pictures and photographic records, and other evidence relevant to children's play. We will look at these in turn.

Observation in natural environments

The most obvious way to find out about play is to watch children (or animals) playing, and describe and catalogue what they do. Besides simply describing, one can examine differences in play due to such factors as age, gender, ethnicity, and socioeconomic background. Also one can take account of natural environmental variations; for example, how play changes in different weather conditions or at different times of day.

It is worth remarking, however, that in many fields of psychology and child study, observation in natural surroundings has *not* been the major source of evidence. As an example, most studies of aggression and anti-social behavior in middle childhood and adolescence use questionnaires (self-report, or by parents, teachers or peers), or incident reports from schools, or (for delinquency) police records. In my own research on school bullying (Smith, 2000), I mainly used self-report questionnaires, peer nominations, and sometimes parent or teacher reports.

My own view is that it is rather regrettable, if at times understandable, that child study has not often used observation in natural surroundings as much as it might have done. It was certainly very much neglected for a period from around the 1950s to the 1970s. However, in the case of children's play, the incentives for this method are perhaps greater, and the disadvantages less, than in many other areas of child psychology. Regarding incentives, an important criterion for play is that it is unconstrained and done for its own sake. Therefore, artificial (constrained or experimental) situations are in danger of destroying an important characteristic of play. Regarding lack of disadvantages, play (unlike aggression or bullying) is approved of by adults (in most cases), so there is no need for children to conceal it from them. Also, the main age range for observing play is the preschool and infant school period (around 2 to 6 years), and children of this age do not seem to mind being watched. Anyone who goes to a playgroup or nursery class can easily watch lots of play going on, without their presence having much effect—something not so true in middle childhood or adolescence.

Is a playgroup a "natural environment" for young children? That is quite a deep question, which we can consider more thoroughly in Chapter 5 on cross-cultural issues. Free play in a playgroup is relatively unconstrained, but it might not be "natural" in terms of our evolutionary history. Certainly, the kinds of toys seen in them were not common until recent times. Even the composition of a playgroup—a large (20+) assembly of children of the same age, give or take 6 or 9 months—could be considered unnatural in terms of what children experienced in historical times or in nonwestern cultures (Konner, 1976).

The observation of play in natural surroundings has its strongest representation in the study of play in animal species by ethologists. Here, the "natural environment" is a meaningful term, as (apart from pets, farm and zoo animals) most animals live in environments not too different from those they evolved in. A classic example of such a study is Jane van Lawick-Goodall's (1968) observations of free-living chimpanzees in the Gombe Stream Reserve in Tanzania. She observed many fascinating behaviors, including infant chimpanzee play. The newborn infant is dependent on its mother for food, transport, and protection, but after 6 months or so begins to crawl around on its own while staying in the mother's vicinity. Soon it engages in tickling, wrestling and chasing play with mother, siblings, and peers. Many other studies of animal play will be considered in Chapters 3 and 4 (many, but not all, using such observational methodology).

During the 1930s, many researchers studying children used observation in the reasonably natural situation of a playgroup or nursery class to study typical behaviors, including play, in 3 to 5-year-old children. They (like the ethologists studying animals) developed categories and coding schemes, as well as time-sampling methodologies to record behaviors (Arrington, 1943). This research laid the groundwork for our knowledge of typical behavior patterns in western children in the 20th century. It was put to use in the child welfare institutes and the playgroups and nursery classes starting up in the USA, the UK and other western countries. Although this work had petered out by the 1950s, the observational approach was picked up again in the 1970s by child ethologists (Blurton Jones, 1972). Inspired by the animal ethologists, these researchers, often from multi-disciplinary backgrounds, sought to go back to basics in describing human, including child, behaviors. Some of this work reinvented the 1930s work; but, it had a more modern theoretical basis in evolutionary theory (Smith & Connolly, 1972). One notable outcome was highlighting rough-and-tumble play in young children, a topic neglected by the more educationally oriented psychologists and child study workers of earlier decades. Nicholas Blurton Jones, who had trained as an ethologist with Niko Tinbergen, used this research background to describe rough-and-tumble play and other play activities in an unstructured observational study of children in a nursery school.

The approach of the ethologists brought together two methodological aspects which, although often confused, are quite separable. One was the concept of a "natural environment," as discussed above. The other was the use of observational methods, often taken further by developing category lists of behaviors. Three category lists of play behaviors are shown in Table 1.1, one from the 1930s, one from the 1980s, one from the 2000s. Category lists can be combined with time-sampling methods—ways of recording the occurrence of categories systematically—to give quantitative measures of time spent in types of play, and sequences of behavior. It is then possible to examine how play varies by age, gender, or other individual characteristics; and by factors such as size and composition of group, location, and so forth.

Observation in structured environments

In this approach, observational methodology is used, but there is no attempt to have a "natural environment." For example, a child might be presented with a limited set of toys to see how he or she plays with them. This kind of approach was used in many studies of the development of pretend play. By imposing more constraint on the situation, some benefits are gained. For instance, it is possible to demonstrate age changes in how children can use the same set of objects while, in a natural situation, this opportunity could be difficult to realize. But there are also losses. As a natural home observation study showed (Haight & Miller, 1993), the majority of pretend play is social—between child and parent, or later between child and sibling or peer. The paradigm of a solitary child playing with a limited set of toy objects is a long way from how most children actually develop their pretend play capabilities.

Experimental studies

Experimental studies provide further control by explicitly placing children in different conditions: an experimental and control condition, or two or more experimental conditions. If all else is held constant, differences can be fairly confidently ascribed to the variables manipulated in the experimental conditions.

Often, experiments take place in constrained environments. For example, using the set of toys (as discussed above), a child's play behaviors might be compared at the same time and place but with slightly different sets of toys. Greta Fein (1975) looked at what 2-year-olds do

Table 1.1   Three Category Lists of Play Behaviors

1 (source: Manwell & Mengert, 1934)

Language frequency
Physical activity
Creative or constructive activity
Manipulative activity
Dramatic activity
Interest in stories
Interest in pictures
Interest in music
Self-responsibility
Attitudes in routines
Attention
Leadership
Group play
Independence of group

Watching others at play
Independence of adult
Kindness or sympathy
Conformity
Fair play regarding common property
Understanding of common property
Assuming responsibility
Laughing
Stability
Self-assertion
Mood
Ability to face a situation
Crying

Comment: this is taken from one of the early observational studies carried out in the USA in the 1930s, following the development of such methodology by pioneers such as Florence Goodenough and Ruth Arrington. Each of the categories above has several sentences of explanation/definition in the original article, which is good practice and obviously necessary in many cases (for example, Self-responsibility refers to taking a series of steps in getting ready for play, such as putting a cloth on a table and then getting clay to play with). Some categories (such as Manipulative activity, Dramatic play) are similar to ones we would use now; others (such as Ability to face a situation, Conformity) reflect prevailing concerns of nursery school teachers. The authors found only some categories to be reliable (in terms of inter-observer agreement), but they were able to examine types of group play at different ages from 2 to 4 years.

2 (source: Humphreys & Smith, 1987)

Passive-noninteractive: Sit; Stand; Lie; Eat; Watch person; Look at place; Sedentary; Musical
Passive-Interactive: Talk; With adult; Contact/comfort; Groom; Walk and talk
Observer-directed: Attend to observer
Adult-organized: Ordered by adult; Official sport
Locomotion: Walk; Run; Skip/hop
Nonlocomotor-active: Ball play; Climb; Roll, spin; Piggyback; Gymnastic; Dance; Support child
Object play: Quiet; Active

Role play: Quiet; Active
Rough-and-tumble: Tease/taunt; Hit/kick; Poke/maul; Pounce; Sneak up; Carry child; Pile on; Play-fight (stand); Play-fight (lie); Chase; Hold/grab; Push; Be chased/hit, etc
Aggressive: Argue/insult; Fight
Distress: Cry
Rule games: Skipping; Turn skip-rope; Chasing; Competitive; Clapping songs; Marbles; Count out; Football; Rounders; Throw/catch; Hopscotch; Other

Table 1.1 (*continued*)

Comment: These categories were designed to cover the range of behaviors seen in 7, 9 and 11-year-olds in school playgrounds in the UK in the 1980s. The larger categories were used to calculate time budgets for various activities; these are shown later in Figure 6.1. However, the main focus of the article was on rough-and-tumble play, hence the large number of individual categories within this global measure. The categories were influenced by the ethological perspective, and many are based on obvious behaviors, such as "run", or "turn skip-rope." However, the list would benefit from some definitional material, especially for categories like "quiet" and "active." The categories within the rule games section (as elsewhere) correspond to what was actually observed in the study, so might be expected to vary in different historical periods and in different cultures.

3 (source: Gosso, Morais, & Otta, 2007).

Physical exercise—play that involves various types of movements requiring gross motor coordination (e.g. running, jumping, and swimming), as well as activities that produce action-contingent effects (e.g. throwing or pushing objects);

Social contingency—games apparently motivated and reinforced by pleasure in producing contingent responses in others and in responding contingently to others (e.g. peek-a-boo, tickling, imitating gestures or verbalizations);

Rough-and-tumble—play-fighting, play chase, and play escape;

Construction—physical transformations in objects such as sand, clay, or Lego are produced, including molding, arranging objects in piles or rows, and making small baskets;

Pretend play—actions, objects, persons, places, or other dimensions of the here-and-now are transformed or treated nonliterally (analyzed in more detail by content of pretend play themes: *work*; *transportation*; *take care*; *animal actions*; *play fighting*; *daily life activities*; *entertainment*; *fantastic themes*).

Games with rules—those guided by explicit rules, often involving, at this age range, sensory-motor aspects, such as volleyball and soccer.

Comment: this study was used in comparing play from different groups of Brazilian children, including the Parakanã Indians (see Chapter 5). The main play categories are those broadly recognized now in most play research. In addition, these authors focused on pretend play in some depth, including the content of the play, plus other categories relating to the ideational scheme (nature of transformations) not reproduced above.

when they are given (a) miniature objects such as a plastic cup and a detailed horse model; or (b) less realistic objects such as a clam shell and a vaguely horsey-shaped object. After modelling by an adult, some 93% of 2-year-olds would imitate making the horse "drink" from the cup; however, only 33% would imitate making a horsey shape "drink" from a clam shell. The less realistic objects made the pretense more difficult; and the difference in behavior can be ascribed to the difference in the objects presented, on the plausible assumption that all other factors were equal.

Experiments can also be carried out in more natural environments. In a series of studies on preschool playgroups, Smith and Connolly (1980) observed the natural behavior of children aged 3 to 4 years with a large variety of toys. However they did vary aspects of the preschool environment in experimental ways. They looked at changes in the space available (by moving certain screens in the hall); they looked at the quantity of toys available (by having 1, 2, or 3 sets of all major items); and they looked at the size of the group (by having c. 10, 20, or 30 children attending). The different conditions were varied independently and on a large number of occasions, so that conclusions could be drawn about the effects of these variables. For example, a decrease in space produced less physical activity play, but did encourage more use of climbing frames (at the expense of running). Fewer sets of toys meant more sharing, but also more squabbling over possession.

Some experiments fall into the category of enhancement or deprivation studies. These are experiments that manipulate the overall opportunities for any, or certain, types of play. Some sophisticated deprivation studies of this kind have been done with animals such as rats (Hole & Einon, 1984). In children, there are a number of play training studies that have experimentally enhanced opportunities, mainly for types of pretend play. We will review these in Chapter 9.

Interviews and questionnaires

Children themselves can be asked about their play activities. In general, interviews are more useful with older children. Nevertheless, even 3 and 4-year-olds can give some useful information. For example, Takhvar and Smith (1990) combined observations of children's object or construction play with short interviews afterwards asking children what they were doing. Quite often, a child making what looked like just a pile or tower of blocks would describe it in pretend terms, as for example a "prison" or "space tower." In other words, what might have been categorized simply as construction play might be re-categorized as pretend play after these interviews were conducted.

More commonly, adults involved with a child—usually parents or teachers—might be interviewed or given a questionnaire. For example, there are questionnaires about imaginative or pretend play disposition that a parent can fill in to indicate the extent of such play they have seen in their child (Liebermann, 1977).

Other sources

There are more indirect sources of information we can use. One possibility is to make toy inventories—lists of all the toys in a child's home. Of course, this does not mean that the child actually plays with these toys, but it does indicate the range of opportunities that the child has.

Where past historical periods are concerned, we cannot make direct observations, experiments, or interviews. Nevertheless we can learn something from various kinds of records. First are artifacts—toys made for children in earlier times. Orme (2002, pp. 166–176) describes toys used by children in medieval times, such as rattles, tops, and dolls. These are known from the objects themselves or from descriptions. For example, John Florio (1598) described paper windmills: "A piece of card or paper cut like a cross, and with a pin put in at the end of a stick, which running against the wind doth twirl about. Our English children call it a windmill" (cited in Orme, 2002, p. 168).

A second source is records made by adults of children playing. Some are in diaries and autobiographies; others are in paintings. Hanawalt (1993) uses a range of such sources from medieval times to describe how London children then "played ball and tag, ran races, played hoops, and imitated adult ceremonies such as royal entries, Masses, marriages, and the giants Gog and Magog" (p. 78). Breughel's painting of 1560 *Children's Games*, now in the Kunsthistorisches Museum in Vienna, is a very famous example of its kind. It shows not only many games, but also play with objects such as with dolls, hoops, spinning tops, stilts, barrels, and windmills, and physical play in the form of riding piggy-back, playing leapfrog, play-fighting, and climbing trees. Edward Snow (1997), in his book *Inside Breugel*, gives a most detailed account of what is going on in this painting, which includes 46 kinds of play or game engaged in by some 200 children and young people in the painting.

Linda Pollock examined parent-child relations from 1500 to 1900 in her book *Forgotten Children* (1983). She used letters, diaries, and autobiographies, as well as newspaper reports. Her section on play (pp. 236–239) reveals a variety of attitudes to play on the part of parents, but again shows that the types of play we have described were common in earlier historical periods. For example John Dee (1527–1608) writes in his private diary, published in 1841, of "Arthur Dee and Mary Herbert, they being but 3 yere old the eldest, did make as it wer a shew of childish marriage, of calling ech other husband and wife" (cited in Pollock, p. 327); apparently an example of sociodramatic play.

Plan of the Book

In this chapter we have discussed what is meant by play, the main types of play, and the main methods of study. The next chapter reviews the history of the study of the topic of play from the eighteenth century to recent times, and outlines some major theoretical perspectives. There then follow two chapters on play in animals, one descriptive, and one examining theories of why animals play. Moving on to human play, Dr Yumi Gosso, who completed her doctoral thesis on the Parakanã Indian people of Brazil, contributes a chapter on cross-cultural studies of play, including a section on play in the Parakanã, one of few surviving hunter-gatherer peoples in the world today.

The next four chapters focus on particular kinds of play among children. We will look in more detail at physical activity play (exercise play and rough-and-tumble play); object and construction play; and pretend and sociodramatic play. The great majority of the research on which these chapters are based is on western children. The last main chapter considers some practical applications of play in today's world: the role of adults in play, play in education, the debate about "war toys," the role of recess breaks, and play therapy for children under stress. In some short concluding comments I attempt to sum up some main themes from the material that we will review.

Further Reading

A book with a wide remit embodied in its title is T. G. Power (2000), *Play and Exploration in Children and Animals*, Mahwah, NJ: Erlbaum. For a review of time-sampling methods in observing behavior, including play behavior, see P. Martin and P. Bateson (1991), *Measuring Behavior: An Introductory Guide* (2nd edition), Cambridge: Cambridge University Press. J. S. Bruner, A. Jolly, and K. Sylva (Eds.) (1976), *Play: Its Role in Development and Evolution*, Harmondsworth, Penguin, reprints over 70 classic articles or extracts on play, from 1896 (Groos) up to the 1970s. A. D. Pellegrini (2009), *The Role of Play in Human Development*, New York and Oxford, Oxford University Press, covers similar areas to this book.

Chapter 2

A Brief History of the Study of Play and of Play Theories

Throughout much of human history, children's play has probably been treated in a fairly matter-of-fact sort of way. The evidence we have from the history of childhood, and from studies of play in traditional cultures (see Chapters 1 and 5), is that a range of forms of play were seen as typical of young children and were to varying degrees tolerated or ignored. Adults might use play to distract children (e.g. from persistent demands for breast-feeding) or to encourage them into more work-like activities (such as preparing food, hunting, practicing weapon use). More rarely they might discourage play, if it interfered with other useful activities.

The first writings on the importance of play are related to education and may be dated back to Plato, in *The Republic* and *The Laws*. Plato had a hierarchical view of society and believed that the governors or guardians of his ideal state would be educated differently from the artisans or skilled workers. For the latter, however, play had a role in skills acquisition: "he who is to be a good builder, should play at building houses; he who is to be a good husbandman, at tilling the ground; and those who have the care of their education should provide them when young with mimic tools" (Plato, *The Laws*; cited in Rusk, 1967, p. 6). This remarkably foreshadows the later views of Karl Groos (1898, 1901) on play as practice in the acquisition of later skills.

When we come to writings about child-rearing, education and play in European society after the middle ages, the picture is quite complex (Pollock, 1983), and heralds a division of views which persists to the present day. The Puritan tradition in northern Europe and America tended to have a negative view of children. The concept of "original sin" suggested that children needed strict training and discipline so that they should not fall into evil ways. Play was seen as linked to the animal expression of instinctive behaviors and needed to be restricted or channeled into appropriate "civilizing" activities.

A more positive focus on play came from Rousseau's view that children were pure souls who would only be perverted by the ills of society (the opposite of "original sin"!). This assisted a view of play as a natural expression of childhood that should be fostered. It leads via educational thinkers such as Pestalozzi and Froebel, through to the play ethos of the twentieth century.

However, there remain a range of views on play: from the belief that it is vital for development, through to its being a useless discharge of excess energy. What distinguishes recent decades is that play has been actively debated and investigated as a serious research topic.

Early European Educators and the Role of Play

Concerns about children's education became important in Europe as societies modernized. John Comenius (1592–1670), a Czech educational reformer, wrote of his theory of education in *The School of Infancy* (1630). He argued that "whatever children delight to play with, provided that it be not hurtful, they ought rather to be gratified than restrained from it" (cited in Rusk, 1967, p. 17). However it was Jean-Jacques Rousseau's writings, and especially his book *Emile, ou Traité de l'éducation* (1762), that set up the most explicit alternative to the Puritan viewpoint; "The age of harmless mirth is spent in tears, punishments, threats and slavery. . . . Love childhood, indulge its sports, its pleasures, its delightful instincts" (Everyman translation, pp. 42–43). Rousseau (1712–1778), born in Geneva, was a French-speaking philosopher who proclaimed the innocence of childhood. (Unfortunately he did not always live up to his principles; he consigned his five illegitimate children by his maidservant to foundling hospitals!). *Emile* was a treatise on education according to "natural principles," advocating a child-centred view. It greatly influenced Pestalozzi and Froebel, although it outraged the political and religious establishment so that Rousseau had to flee Switzerland.

The practical application of such ideas was taken forward by Johann Pestalozzi (1746–1827), a Swiss educationist who emphasized the role of practical experience and contact with objects, rather than rote learning. It was the German educationist Friedrich Froebel (1782–1852), however, who more specifically advocated play as a means of learning. Froebel studied with Pestalozzi for two years; he opened his first kindergarten in Blankenburg in 1826 and is seen as a founder of the kindergarten system. "Kindergarten" translates from German as "child-garden," and this aptly sums up Froebel's ideas about play and development. He expounded his ideas in *Die Menschenerziehung* (*The Education of Man*) (1826), and *Die Pädagogik des Kindergartens, Gedanken Friedrich Froebel's über das Spiel und die Spielgegenstände des Kindes* (*Pedagogics of the Kindergarten*) (1861: a collection of his essays edited posthumously by Wichard Lange). These were influential in the start of the kindergarten and nursery school movement, not only in Germany and Switzerland but in other countries such as Britain.

Froebel wrote that "Play is the highest achievement of child development . . . it is the spontaneous expression, according to the necessity of its own nature, of the child's inner being . . . Play at this period of life is not a trivial pursuit; it is a serious occupation and has deep significance" (cited in Rusk, 1967, pp. 60–61). Play exemplified development from within the child, but could be nurtured by adult guidance and the provision of appropriate materials. Froebel's views encouraged a positive evaluation of the educational significance of play, as compared with the rote-learning approach which nevertheless became characteristic of many infant schools at the end of the nineteenth century (Whitbread, 1972).

Maria Montessori (1870–1952), the first woman to receive a medical degree in Italy, was another major influence in the education of young children (see Kramer, 1976). Like Froebel, Montessori saw the value of self-initiated activity for young children, under adult guidance. However, she put more emphasis on the importance of learning about real life, and hence on constructive play materials which helped in sensory discrimination and in colour and shape matching. Hence came the famous Montessori materials, still occasionally found in Montessori schools, with which children could practice these concept learning skills. Much of Montessori's work was with children from disadvantaged backgrounds; she opened the first Montessori school for children in the slums of Rome in 1907. This may help explain the value she put on actual skill development (which might be of more direct help to such children), than pretend activities. In fact she did not value pretend or sociodramatic play, seeing pretense as primitive and an escape from reality. She preferred to encourage children to actually serve meals, for example, and to clear up around the house themselves, rather than to play at mealtimes in a "play house." This particular aspect of her philosophy has largely been abandoned by contemporary Montessori schools; but it might have had some influence on Piaget (see below).

Evolutionary Theory and Play:
Darwin, Spencer, and Groos

With the advent of evolutionary theory in the latter half of the nine-teenth century, and its extension from animal to human beha-vior (Darwin, 1859, 1871), it was natural that play behavior should be a topic for evolutionary speculation in regard to its nature, origin and function. The English biologist Charles Darwin (1809–1882), the originator of the theory of evolution, did not write extensively on play (see Gruber, 1974), although he did make one of the earliest con-tributions to child psychology in his article "A biographical sketch of an infant" (1877), based on observations of one of his own sons' development.

Evolutionary theory has developed considerably since Darwin wrote *The Origin of Species* (1859) and *The Descent of Man and Selection in Relation to Sex* (1871). However, from its beginning and throughout, an evolutionary approach does lead us to predict that a behavior as common in mammals as play is, will have some functional significance —some benefits for the playing animal. We will look at modern evolu-tionary approaches to animal play further, in Chapter 3, but here we will continue tracing some historical developments.

One of the early trains of speculation from evolutionary theory actually challenged the ascription of a strong functional importance to play. Herbert Spencer (1820–1903) was an English philosopher who speculated on evolutionary theory even before Darwin's writings, and welcomed Darwin's work. He developed a particular take on this, emphasizing competition and the "survival of the fittest"—what has been called "social Darwinism." His book *The Principles of Psychology* was reprinted many times (final edition 1898), and in it he suggested that the evolutionarily higher animal species are better able to deal with the immediate necessities of life, and that their more highly developed ner-vous systems, rather than remaining inactive for long periods, stimulate play: "Thus it happens that in the more-evolved creatures, there often recurs an energy somewhat in excess of immediate needs . . . Hence play of all kinds—hence this tendency to superfluous and useless exercise of faculties that have been quiescent" (pp. 629–630). He proposed that play is "an artificial exercise of powers which, in default of their natural exercise, become so ready to discharge that they relieve themselves by simulated actions in place of real actions" (p. 630), and that play is carried out "for the sake of the immediate gratifications involved, without reference to ulterior benefits" (p. 632). Spencer's approach has been commonly labelled the "surplus energy" theory.

Spencer's view was attacked by the German writer Karl Groos (1861–1946). At the turn of the century, Groos published two influential works, *The Play of Animals* (1898), and *The Play of Man* (1901). These provide an integrative view of play, and one that ascribes greater functional significance to it. Groos criticized Spencer's theory on a number of grounds. He thought that surplus energy might provide "a particularly favourable condition for play", but was not essential.; a "superabundant nervous force is always . . . a favourable one for play, but it is not its motive cause, nor, as I believe, a necessary condition of its existence" (1898, p. 24; translated by Elizabeth Baldwin). He thought play had a much more definite function than in Spencer's theory.

Groos argued that play provided exercise and the elaboration of skills needed for survival, he wrote: "the utility of play is incalculable. This utility consists in the practice and exercise it affords for some of the more important duties of life" (1898, p. 76). This has been called the "exercise" or "practice" theory of play, and in its modern form it has many adherents. Groos argued that a main reason for childhood was so that play could occur: "perhaps the very existence of youth is largely for the sake of play" (1898, p. 76).

Hall and the child welfare movement

Another perspective from evolutionary theory was taken by Granville Stanley Hall (1844–1924), an American psychologist and educator who founded the *American Journal of Psychology*. In his book *Adolescence* (1908) and elsewhere, Hall argued that Groos's practice theory was "very partial, superficial, and perverse" (1908, p. 202). This was because Groos saw play as practice for contemporary activities. By contrast, Hall thought that play was a means for children to work through primitive atavisms, reflecting our evolutionary past: "we rehearse the activities of our ancestors" (p. 202), and "play is not doing things to be useful later, but it is rehearsing racial history" (p. 207). For example, "the sports of boys chasing one another, wrestling, making prisoners, obviously gratify in a partial way the predatory instincts." The function of play was thus cathartic in nature, and allowed the "playing out" of those instincts that characterized earlier human history. This became known as the "recapitulation theory" of play. In the form proposed by Hall, it has had little or no recent support.

While these views and quotations reflect the level of scientific knowledge at the time, and may appear dated, they raise important issues that still concern us. Does play have real functions selected for in evolution, or is it just a by-product of selection for other processes? Would any functions selected for in evolutionary history still apply in contemporary environments? Does play function for future skills, or for present circumstances?

After the promising beginnings around the turn of the 20th century, evolutionary perspectives on play were rather neglected between the 1920s and 1970s. Evolutionary theory continued to develop, of course, especially as it became integrated with genetic theory into the "modern synthesis" or "neo-Darwinian revolution" (Huxley, 1942). However, in the social sciences generally, and including psychology, the first decades of the 20th century saw a reaction against deterministic biological views, with (what may now be seen as) deterministic cultural views. This was noticeable in the work of cultural determinists in anthropology (including Mead's work on childhood in "primitive" societies), and Watson's behaviorist program in psychology, both of which argued that behavior was entirely determined by socialization and conditioning, and that any biological perspective on "human nature" was irrelevant.

A resurgence in evolutionary perspectives on play can be dated from the 1970s/1980s. There appear to be two strands to this. One was a return of observational methods to respectability, in the guise of human ethology. Following their decline in the 1940s (Arrington, 1943), observational methods used in natural surroundings were not in favor with psychologists, who espoused a supposedly "scientific" model of experimentation. I encountered this prejudice myself in the late 1960s when I was working on my doctoral thesis (Smith, 1970). This was based on natural observations of play behavior of 2 to 4-year-olds in day nurseries. This procedure was seen as "radical", and some colleagues criticized me for not having specific theories and hypotheses to test.

The other strand from the 1970s is the new evolutionary thinking coming from sociobiology. This reached a wider audience at the time, largely through Wilson's (1975) book *Sociobiology: The New Synthesis*, integrating the recent ideas about kin selection, reciprocal altruism, parent–offspring conflict, and similar insights into a comprehensive overview of animal and human behavior. We will look at this further in relation to animal play in Chapter 4.

So far as more practical applications of play research were concerned, although Hall's writings inspired a wave of interest in early childhood behavior, linked with the setting up of many child development or child welfare institutes in North America in the 1920s, the observational methods employed there were used simply to describe typical age and sex differences and ways of "managing" children's behavior, and lacked any evolutionary perspective (Smith & Connolly, 1972; and see the first example of category schemes in Table 1.1).

Psychoanalytic Perspectives on Play

Another major theoretical approach to understanding human behavior, developed some decades later than evolutionary theory, was psycho-analytic theory. This focused on the ontogeny of human development, and on the hypothesized repression of sexual desires for the opposite-sex parent in infancy, and the later consequences of this, promulgated in the writings of Sigmund Freud (1856–1939) and his followers. Freud's psychosexual stages take the infant through the oral, anal, and oedipal stages to the childhood latency period, where play most occurs, before the onset of puberty in adolescence reawakens the sexual urges that have lain dormant since infancy. Freud himself did not write a great deal about play, but it has come to have an important role within the psychoana-lytic movement, and especially in play therapy.

Freud thought that play provided children with an avenue for wish fulfillment and mastery of traumatic events. In a review of the role of play in psychoanalytic thought, Peller (1954) wrote that "play . . . is an attempt to compensate for anxieties and deficiencies, to obtain pleasure at a minimum risk of danger and/or irreversible consequences" (p. 180). Thus, play provides a safe context for expressing aggressive or sexual impulses which it would be too dangerous to express in reality. In addi-tion, play can, within limits, help achieve mastery of traumatic events; "Small quantities of anxiety are mastered in play, but anxiety of high intensity inhibits play" (p. 180). Both aspects are thought to be import-ant in play therapy (see Chapter 10). First, play expresses the child's wishes and anxieties; Peller relates the development of fantasy play themes to Freud's psychosexual stages. Second, play can help overcome such anxieties, by catharsis or by working through them.

The Play Ethos

Both the evolutionary and psychoanalytic traditions of thought did, on the whole, suggest important positive functions of play. From the

1920s, general educational thinking seems to show the beginnings of a "play ethos" that took a very strong and unquestioned view of the importance of play. As it developed and took hold, this play ethos may have distorted play research for several decades, especially in the 1970s and 1980s (Smith, 1988). The "play ethos" is a strong and unqualified assertion of the functional importance of play, namely that it is essential to adequate (human) development, and a series of quotes exemplifying it are given in Table 2.1.

Table 2.1 Quotes Illustrating the "Play Ethos"

Author	Year & page	Quote
Isaacs	1929 p. 9	"Play is indeed the child's work, and the means whereby he grows and develops. Active play can be looked upon as a sign of mental health; and its absence, either of some inborn defect, or of mental illness."
Norsworthy & Whitley	1937 p. 132	"Play is regarded by many as the most important educational factor of them all. . . . A child who does not play not only misses much of the joy of childhood, but he can never be a fully developed adult."
Wheeler & Earl	1939 p. 65	"Modern psychological researches into child development have reinforced the belief that play is the supreme psychological need of the young child. Consequently it is the one method of learning in the early years which is most likely to be conducive to the physical and mental health of the individual."
Gardner	1942 p. 9	"In fact the principle that young children are best educated through their play is very generally accepted by educationalists in this country and in America."
Jersild	1955 p. 501	"it is through play that much of the work of childhood is done . . . play is one of the most important means by which a child exercises his impulse to grow . . . play has tremendous importance in the progress of development and in the economy of daily life."

Table 2.1 (*continued*)

Tudor-Hart	1955 p. 10	Play is the very essence of life and the only means whereby the infant can learn anything. It remains the chief means of learning well into school years . . . it is through play that a child's physical, mental, emotional and social life grows and develops."
Department of Education and Science, UK	1967 p. 193	"We now know that play—in the sense of "messing about" with material objects or with other children, and of creating fantasies—is vital to children's learning and therefore vital in school."
Department of Environment Report, UK	1973 p. 31	"The realization that play is essential for normal development has slowly but surely permeated our cultural heritage."
National Conference on the Vital Role of Play in Learning, Development and Survival, Washington DC	1979	"Play is vital to the development of all so-called higher animals. Play is a biological imperative. Play heals, naturally and as a tool in psychotherapy with children. Play for your life: the stakes are survival."
Hetherington & Parke	1979 pp. 481–482	"Particularly in fantasy play through acting out roles, the child learns to understand others and to practice roles she will assume as she grows older. Finally, fantasy play permits the child to solve some of her emotional problems, to learn to cope with anxiety and inner conflicts in a nonthreatening situation."
Michelet	1986 p. 118	"for the child it [play] is the essential means of appropriating culture and gaining access to the techniques and skills of the world in which he lives."
Hewes	2007 p. 120	"Play is essential for optimal development."

The view that play is essential for both the emotional and cognitive growth of young children is strong in the British educational tradition, and this probably owes much to Susan Isaacs (1885–1948), Professor of Educational Psychology at the Institute of Education at London University, and a pivotal figure in the education of nursery school teachers; and to her successor at the Institute of Education, Dorothy Gardner. Isaacs combined a belief in the emotional benefits of play (deriving from the psychoanalytic tradition) with a wider view of its benefits for physical, social, and cognitive development generally, echoing the evolutionary perspective that animals that learn more, also play more. This is well embodied in her "Play is indeed the child's work" quote (the first in Table 2.1).

Such statements are often found in child development texts and teacher handbooks, and the cumulative effect is well stated in the UK government reports from 1967 and 1973 (see further quotes in Table 2.1). Recently, Isaac's saying has been taken up explicitly in a book on children's pretend play by Vivian Paley (2004), and reiterated in a chapter on the value of play in early learning by Hewes (2007, p. 120). We will consider the influence of the play ethos, and evidence for and against it, in subsequent chapters, especially Chapters 7 and 8.

Anthropological Perspectives on Play

Much writing on children's play has come from educationists and psychologists, but this has generally focused on play in contemporary western societies, such as the USA or UK. Nevertheless, writers such as Spencer, Groos and Hall certainly drew on evidence from other societies, often of an anecdotal nature. As anthropology developed as a discipline at the end of the 19th century and during the early 20th century, it was initially influenced by Darwin's evolutionary theory. But writers such as Franz Boas (the mentor of Ruth Benedict and Margaret Mead) espoused a contrary, cultural materialist view, in opposition especially to Spencer's "social Darwinist" writings. From around the 1920s to the 1970s, anthropological work largely (with some exceptions) avoided a biological/evolutionary perspective, and indeed rather little was written on children's play—a lack pointed out by Schwartzmann (1978) and Lancy (1980) when they came to review what literature there was in the later 1970s. We will review current literature on play in non-industrial societies in Chapter 5.

The anthropological work does put the western "play ethos" into a broader perspective. The conception that play is important for child development and therefore must be stimulated is most evident in industrial societies (Roopnarine & Johnson, 1994), in the middle and upper classes (Göncü, Mistry, & Mosier, 2000), and, for example, in European American families (Farver, Kim, & Lee-Shin, 2000). In such families, parents try to play with their children, and the children go to day care centers or schools where there are many objects to play with, and play is stimulated by the presence not only of toys, but also of caregivers who play with the children. The parents, when playing, think of the importance of that activity for cognitive development and for the social skills of their children (Farver et al., 2000; Roopnarine & Johnson, 1994). Also, in some societies like the USA, direct teaching is seen as inappropriate for very young children, and play is seen as preferable to promote competence and academic success (Bornstein, Haynes, Pascual, Painter, & Galperin, 1999). Therefore, educators and caretakers are encouraged to play with children and to use play as a means of teaching.

Psychological Perspectives: Vygotsky and Piaget

What about the main psychological theories and development, and the role of play? The play ethos assumed the educational importance of play, but without direct empirical evidence. Controlled experimental studies had to wait until the 1970s (see Chapters 7 and 8). Nor at the time was there much theoretical support from psychological theories of cognitive or social development. In the early/mid 20th century evolutionary thinking was neglected in psychology, as in anthropology, in this case due to the influence of behaviorism (Plotkin, 2004). Even observational methods fell out of favor in the 1940s, and the experimental paradigm of examining behavior predominated through to the 1970s–1980s, although such methods were not focused on play until the end of this period.

The primary psychological theorists on play during the 1930s–1960s are the Russian psychologist Lev Vygotsky (1896–1934), and the Swiss psychologist Jean Piaget (1896–1980). Both these major figures were born in the same year, but Vygotsky's life was cut tragically short by tuberculosis, so that he only had a decade of creative work in psychology. His writings remained little known in the English-speaking world until the 1970s/1980s. Piaget by contrast had a long creative life; after initial training in zoology he turned to psychology and spent over 50 years studying children's development.

In their writings (Piaget, 1951; Vygotsky, 1966) they discuss the nature of play, the immediate psychological mechanisms for playing, and the relationships between play, thought, and language. Their views differed as to whether play is primarily assimilating new experiences to existing schema (Piaget) or showing creativity through being liberated from immediate situation constraints (Vygotsky). Their work and writings, and indeed most psychological research on play through to the 1970s at least, concentrated on object and pretend play; these were more specifically human forms of play, and were perceived as educationally relevant. Physical activity play and rough-and-tumble play were virtually ignored in this psychological context.

Vygotsky

Vygotsky combined the affective and cognitive aspects of development in his approach to play (1966; from a lecture given in 1933). Like the psychoanalysts, Vygotsky saw the affective drive behind play as being the imaginary, illusory realization of unrealizable desires. He did not, however, consider this to be linked with very specific or sexual impulses, but as having to do in a much more general sense with the child's confidence and mastery (for example, in attitudes to authority in general). He stated that play is essentially wish fulfillment, not of isolated wishes but of generalized affects. Nevertheless, this affective drive related to wish fulfillment had strong cognitive implications, such that Vygotsky described play as being the leading source of development in the preschool years.

Vygotsky took this strong view of the cognitive importance of play because the nature of pretend play meant that the child was liberating him- or herself from the immediate constraints of the situation (e.g. the actual object), and getting into the world of ideas (e.g. what that object might become). A very young child cannot separate out an object from its meaning; but when he or she starts to engage in pretend play, and uses an object to represent another (for example a stick for a horse), then meaning begins to be separated from the concrete object; Vygotsky says that the substitute object (e.g. the stick) acts as a pivot, to separate the meaning or concept (e.g. of the horse) from the object itself. The child is thus liberated from situational constraints through his or her activity in an imaginary situation.

This is augmented by the demands of narrative scripts in social pretend play. Vygotsky cites the example of two sisters, aged 5 and 7 years, who played at being sisters! Normally these two girls did not dress alike, or hold hands a lot, but in "playing sisters" they did these things; they abstracted out the meaning, or concept, that sisters would be emotionally closer and more alike, than non-sisters.

Piaget

Piaget developed a theory of cognitive development in which the development of cognitive structures or schema in the child's mind depends on the two processes of accommodation and assimilation. In assimilation, a child fits a new experience into an existing schema. For example, a child may have learnt the word "dog," and for a while all animals are called "dogs" (i.e. different animals are assimilated into a schema related to the child's understanding of dog). This process is balanced by accommodation, in which the child adjusts an existing schema to fit in with the nature of the environment. For example, the child begins to perceive that cats can be distinguished from dogs, and develops different schema for these two types of animals. Through the twin processes of assimilation and accommodation the child achieves a new state of development. Assimilation helps the child to consolidate mental structures; accommodation results in growth and change.

Piaget's view of play was set out in his book *La formation du symbole chez l'enfant* (*Play, Dreams and Imitation in Childhood*) (original 1945, English translation 1951). In this he states that play "manifests the peculiarity of a primacy of assimilation over accommodation." Children act out their already established behaviors, or schemata, in play, and adapt reality to fit these. For example, referring to episodes such as his daughter Jacqueline's pretending to sleep, Piaget wrote:

> It is clearly impossible to explain this symbolic practice as being pre-exercise; the child certainly does not play like this in order to learn to wash or sleep. All that he is trying to do is to use freely his individual powers, to reproduce his own actions for the pleasure of seeing himself do them and showing them off to others, in a word to express himself, to assimilate without being hampered by the need to accommodate at the same time. (1951, p. 181)

Piaget's view of play embodies a criticism of some aspects of Groos's approach (play as pre-exercise), and of play as being important in learning. For Piaget learning was related more to accommodation to reality. This emphasis may be linked to Montessori's influence, for Piaget carried out his early research at a modified Montessori school, and for many years was president of the Swiss Montessori Society. He does not argue a strong role for play in learning. However he does see two possibilities for the functional significance of play. Play can consolidate existing skills by repeated execution of known schemas with minor variations. Also, he argued that play can give a child a sense of "ego continuity," that is, confidence and a sense of mastery. It does this because failure is largely circumvented in fantasy play, where the real properties of the materials are not at issue, and no external goal is aimed for.

The place of play in Piaget's theory of cognitive development has often been misunderstood (see Piaget, 1966; Sutton-Smith, 1966;). In fact, due to the play ethos, it has often been interpreted as more favourable than it actually is. For example, Golinkoff, Hirsh-Pasek, and Singer (2006, p. 8) write that "Piaget (1951), in particular, viewed pretend play as an adaptive behavior that was instrumental in furthering children's thinking . . . For Piaget and Vygotsky . . . play was an opportunity for children to learn more about their world, to stretch to accommodate new ideas, and to foster their imaginations". But in fact, Piaget and Vygotsky had rather diverging views, and Piaget saw play as assimilation, not accommodation!

Piaget and Vygotsky compared

Harris (2007) provides a good account of the origins of Piaget's ideas on play (especially pretend play), and the contrast with Vygotsky. Both were influenced by psychoanalysis (a very influential paradigm in the 1920s), but Piaget took from the psychoanalyst Bleuler the idea of the child being pre-rational, and showing what was then called "autistic thinking": setting aside objective reality, engaging in free association and wish fulfillment. Obviously, if carried too far and into adulthood, this would be a sign of mental illness. Piaget took the "autistic thinking" of the child—shown by pretend play and also by egocentric speech—as essentially negative (despite some minor positive aspects noted above), and something to be overcome by adaptive coping as the child gets older.

In contrast, "explicitly departing from Piaget's views, Vygotsky developed a more positive account of the status of pretend play" (Harris, 2007, p. 207). Pretend play conjures up alternatives to reality, which, however, presuppose a certain knowledge of reality, and are a liberating source of imagination and creativity. Rather than being suppressed as a child gets older, pretense (and also egocentric speech) changes form but continues to be progressive and having a positive role in the cognitive functioning of the adult. Vygotsky's views are influential on Harris's own views (2000, 2007) concerning the function of pretense and the imagination (see Chapter 9), and also on Göncü and Perone's (2005) presentation of pretend play as a lifespan activity (see end of Chapter 8).

Developmental Sequences in Play: Piaget, Smilansky, Rubin

Piaget (1951) was one of the first to describe a developmental sequence in children's play. This went from "practice play," through "symbolic play" (fantasy/pretend play), to "games with rules." Piaget saw these as overlapping stages through the childhood years, and they were linked to his cognitive developmental theory. By "practice play," he mainly meant early sensorimotor play in infants (as well as most animal play). "Symbolic play" became possible when the symbolic function was developed—the child was able to represent objects in the world around, internally. From this point, pretend or fantasy play becomes possible—a period Piaget saw as beginning from around 18 months. From around 6 years he saw symbolic play as being superseded by "Games with rules." Here the activity is governed by public rules, which must be followed, usually in co-ordinated play with other players, as in games of soccer, or hopscotch, or marbles (which Piaget studied, watching children in Neuchâtel, near Geneva).

Piaget's sequence remains useful in broad terms. The division between symbolic play and games with rules is not a sharp one, however. Socio-dramatic play sequences have local "mini-rules" for that episode, as we will see in Chapter 8; for example, players decide who will be in each role, and what certain objects represent, and these decisions can only be changed by negotiation. Equally, games with rules are not all as fixed as, say, Association Football. Indeed, as Piaget pointed out in his obser-vations of children playing marbles, they will negotiate the particu-lar rules of their game (whether a marble can be thrown or rolled, for example), and are beginning to understand cognitively that rules are a product of mutual agreement, and can be changed.

There is also an issue regarding the scope of Piaget's "practice play." If practice play means play that is neither symbolic nor rule-governed, then it can occur well beyond the sensorimotor period. Indeed rough-and-tumble play (Chapter 6) would seem to count as practice play, unless it has symbolic elements (as in monster play), or is rule-governed (as in games such as tag). The same would apply to exercise play generally (Chapter 6).

Table 2.2   Smilansky's 4-Sequence Developmental Model of Play

Functional	Simple body movements or actions with objects, e.g. banging bricks
Constructive	Making things with objects, e.g. building a tower with bricks
Dramatic	Acting out roles in a pretend game, e.g. pretending to be a doctor
Games with rules	Playing in a game with publicly accepted rules, e.g. soccer, hopscotch

Some time after Piaget, the Israeli psychologist Sara Smilansky postulated a fourfold sequence, from "functional play" (similar to Piaget's "practice play") to "constructive play" (making something, e.g. from Lego bricks), then "dramatic play" (like Piaget"s "symbolic play") and finally "games with rules" (Smilansky, 1968; see Table 2.2). She thus suggested that constructive play was intermediate between functional and dramatic play.

The sequential role of constructive play in Smilansky's scheme may appear dubious; constructional and overtly pretend play both seem to coexist through the preschool years. Also, Smilansky's scheme does deviate from the views of Piaget. Piaget (1951) had written that "constructive games are not a definite stage like the others, but occupy . . . a position halfway between play and intelligent work, or between play and imitation." He thought that the goal-directed nature of much constructive activity made it more accommodative than purely playful behavior. Either it was work-like, or else some symbolic element was present.

What is apparently constructive play may have fantasy elements. This becomes obvious when children are asked about their play. In her doctoral thesis with me, Mehri Takhvar asked 3 and 4-year-old children, who seemed to be engaged in constructive play, what they were doing. Sometimes, they answered that they were "making a spaceship," or "building a skyscraper," or made some similar response that indicated that the assembly of blocks or plastic pieces actually had a definite symbolic meaning for them (Takhvar & Smith, 1990).

The distinct, sequential nature of constructive play in Smilansky's scheme is thus questionable. Also, as with Piaget's scheme, there is no place for exercise or rough-and-tumble play (it is certainly not "constructive play"!). For that matter, language play or play with words (Kuczaj, 1986;

Weir, 1962) also does not fit into either scheme. Thus, both of these schemes or sequences have distinct limitations.

Rubin, Watson and Jambor (1978) nevertheless took the Piaget/ Smilansky sequence as part of a "play hierarchy." They combined it with categories of social participation, taken from the work of Mildred Parten, a psychologist working at the Institute of Child Development in Minnesota. Parten's doctoral dissertation in 1929, and subsequent publication (Parten, 1932), outlined how young children develop from solitary play, through parallel play, to associative and co-operative group play. Solitary play means the child is on his or her own, engaged in an activity. Parallel play refers to one child playing near another child, with the same materials (e.g. both are at a sandpit, or playing with wooden blocks at a table), but without substantial interaction. Associative group play means the children are playing together, but doing the same sort of activity (e.g. both putting sand into the same container). Co-operative group play is more advanced, as children play together with different roles (e.g. one child fetches containers, another fills them with sand). The full version of Parten's scheme (including "unoccupied" and "onlooker") is shown in Table 2.3; however many play researchers have focused on the four main categories where a child is actually playing with something.

Parten's developmental sequence has had some subsequent support from longitudinal research (Smith, 1978); however, solitary play need not necessarily be an indicator of immature behavior, as some older children may simply prefer playing alone sometimes (Roper & Hinde, 1978).

Table 2.3 Parten's Categories of Social Participation

Unoccupied	Child is not engaged in any activity
Onlooker	Child is just watching others, not joining in
Solitary	Child plays alone, away from others
Parallel	Child plays near other(s) with the same materials, but does not interact much—for example, playing independently at the same sandpit
Associative	Child interacts with other(s) at an activity, doing similar things—for example, each adding building blocks to the same tower
Cooperative	Child interacts with other(s) in complementary ways—for example, one child gets blocks and hands them to another child, who builds the tower

Table 2.4 Rubin et al's (1978) Nested Play Hierarchy

(source: adapted from Play Observation Scale Coding Sheet, 2001).

Name of Child:_____ ID_____ Cohort___ Age___
Free Play Session _____

Time Sample	:10	:20	:30	:40	:50	:60
uncodable						
out of room						
transitional						
unoccupied						
onlooker						
Solitary behaviors:						
Occupied						
Constructive						
Exploratory						
Functional						
Dramatic						
Games						
Parallel behaviors:						
Occupied						
Constructive						
Exploratory						
Functional						
Dramatic						
Games						
Group behaviors:						
Occupied						
Constructive						
Exploratory						
Functional						
Dramatic						
Games						
Peer conversation						
Double-coded behaviors:						
Anxious behaviors						
Hovering						
Aggression						
Rough-and-tumble						

Conversation/Interacting with:
1_____ 2_____ 3_____ 4_____ 5_____ 6_____

The Rubin et al. (1978) framework has been developed by Rubin (2001) into a Play Observation Scheme (POS); the coding sheet is displayed in Table 2.4. Here it is acknowledged that rough-and-tumble play is an additional play category, which extends the scheme beyond object-based play. The POS is useful as a descriptive device, although, given the limitations of the Parten and Smilansky categories, taking the measure to get an index of maturity of play would be more questionable.

More Recent Play Theorists

In recent decades, a number of theorists have tended to argue the benefits of play for cognitive development and creative thinking. The evolutionary background to children's play, and some refocus on exercise play and rough-and-tumble play, has been pursued by myself (Smith, 1982, 2004), and by my American colleague Tony Pellegrini (Pellegrini, Dupuis, & Smith, 2007; Pellegrini & Smith, 1998, 1998b). This will be reviewed in Chapter 6.

Jerome Bruner (b. 1915), reviewing both animal and human play, has argued for the role of play (primarily object and symbolic play) in problem-solving, especially creative problem-solving where the flexible nature of play comes to the fore. We will review his ideas and later developments on play and problem-solving, in Chapter 7.

Smilansky, besides extending Piaget's sequence, has also argued strongly for the developmental importance of fantasy and especially socio-dramatic play (Smilansky, 1968; Smilansky & Shefatya, 1990) and this has also been taken up by American psychologists Dorothy and Jerome Singer (1990); we will review this in Chapters 8 and 9, together with ideas from theorists such as Paul Harris (2000), an English psychologist, and Peter Carruthers (2002), an English philosopher, both now working in the USA.

A more critical perspective about play generally has come from Brian Sutton-Smith (1997), a New Zealander also now living in the USA. In his early writings, Sutton-Smith supported the importance of play for creative processes; but later (1986) came to argue against what he sees as the "idealization" of play. In contrast to many other theorists, he concludes that many theories about play, and even the way we define play, reflect the needs of adults in organizing and controlling children, rather than the actualities of children's behavior. These broader issues around how adults conceive of children's play will be examined further in our discussion of play in different cultures, in Chapter 5. In the next two chapters, however, we look at the evolutionary origins of play and animal play.

Further Reading

Good general texts on children's play, especially for those interested in educational relevance, are J. E. Johnson, J. F. Christie, and T. D. Yawkey (1999), *Play and Early Childhood Development* (2nd edition), New York: Longman; and W. G. Scarlett, S. Naudeau, D. Salonius-Pasternak, and I. Ponte (2005), *Children's Play*, Sage.

B. Sutton-Smith (1997), *The Ambiguity of Play*, Cambridge, MA: Harvard University Press, is an idiosyncratic and eclectic account of play in a broad, multi-disciplinary perspective.

Chapter 3

Animal Play: Definitions and Descriptions

Play is a very characteristic behavior of young mammals. As pet owners, people see kittens and puppies playing—chasing, play fighting and playing with objects. In fact, play behaviors seem almost ubiquitous amongst the mammals, although, certainly, it is more obvious in some species than in others. There is also evidence for play in birds, and possibly in other orders of animals. In this chapter we will look at the nature of animal play, and in the next chapter at the theoretical explanations of animal play, based on contemporary evolutionary theory. The study of animal play can provide important insights into understanding children's play. We can see what continuities and discontinuities there are in the forms of play, and the theories advanced to explain animal play may well be relevant in understanding why children engage in some forms of play (notably, physical play).

Possible Play in Birds, Lower Vertebrates, and Invertebrates

Criteria for recognizing play

Play is obvious in mammals, but less so in birds, and much less so in lower vertebrates (amphibia, reptiles, fish) or in invertebrates such as insects. One argument is that this might simply be because it is difficult to recognize play in species more distant from us. More likely, however, is that play has evolved as a useful behavioral strategy in the warm-blooded animals—birds and mammals—and especially in the relatively intelligent mammalian species. We will look at reasons for this in terms of life-history theory, later in the chapter.

To recognize play we need a definition. In fact, the kinds of structural definition advanced for example by Loizos (1967, Chapter 1) were based primarily on animal play, albeit in mammals. Burghardt (2005, pp. 70–78) has revised this to five main criteria for use in recognizing play in animals:

- Limited immediate function ["the performance of the behavior is not fully functional in the form or context in which it is expressed; that is, it includes elements, or is directed toward stimuli, that do not contribute to current survival"]
- Endogenous component ["the behavior is spontaneous, voluntary, intentional, pleasurable, rewarding, reinforcing, or autotelic ('done for its own sake')"]
- Structural or temporal difference ["it differs from the 'serious' performance of ethotypic behavior structurally or temporally in at least one respect: it is incomplete (generally through inhibited or dropped final elements), exaggerated, awkward, or precocious; or it involves behavior patterns with modified form, sequencing, or targeting"]
- Repeated performance ["the behavior is performed repeatedly in a similar, but not rigidly stereotyped, form during at least a portion of the animal's ontogeny"]
- Relaxed field ["the behavior is initiated when an animal is adequately fed, healthy, and free from stress (e.g. predator threat, harsh microclimate, social instability), or intense competing systems (e.g. feeding, mating, predator avoidance)"]

Burghardt then provides a one-sentence definition as follows: "Play is repeated, incompletely functional behavior differing from more serious versions structurally, contextually, or ontogenetically, and initiated voluntarily when the animal is in a relaxed or low-stress setting" (Burghardt, 2005, p. 82).

Play in invertebrates

Burghardt uses the above criteria to examine the evidence for play in animals other than mammals and birds. There is a very small literature on play in invertebrates. For example, some observations of what might be play fighting in ants, where they grab and release each others body parts, were cited by Groos (1898). However, these might be real fights. In his comprehensive review, Burghardt (2005, p. 379) concludes that "The occurrence of play in invertebrates that firmly meets all five criteria is not yet established with confidence in species other than the octopuses." The reference to octopuses refers to a study in which eight individually housed octopuses were presented with small floating plastic bottles (Mather & Anderson, 1999). Initial exploratory behaviors were followed by apparently more playful ones—such as squirting the objects with water—which were varied and repeated. Octopuses are amongst the most advanced invertebrates in brain development. However this play behavior—if it is play—was not seen in a natural environment, but an artificial one.

Play in fishes, reptiles, and amphibia

Play in fishes may not seem very likely either, but Burghardt devotes some 50 pages of his book to a discussion of this topic. He considers that there is some evidence for play in some fish groups, notably the sharks, and the teleosts (advanced fishes—examples are the herring, pike, carp, catfish, flying fish, needlefish). The kinds of possible play observed include leaping (over objects or other animals) and somersaulting. These appear playful, although other explanations include parasite removal or display. What may be object play has been seen in sharks, electric fish, and cichlids; and possibly social play, such as chasing, in cichlids. Some of these appear to fit all the five criteria above.

Amongst reptiles, apparently playful behavior with objects has been observed in monitor lizards, for example pushing around a bucket in a cage; and in turtles, pushing, shaking, and chewing hoops or balls in their enclosure. These actions appear to go beyond stereotyped or exploratory behavior and to have no obvious function. Turtles also show some precocious courtship type behaviors (display by thrusting and vibrating limbs) that might be thought of as social play. However there seems little evidence for possible play behaviors in crocodiles, snakes, or in the amphibia (frogs, toads, salamanders).

Play in birds

We are on relatively firm ground in describing play behaviors in birds. Although much less well treated than mammalian play, various kinds of play—locomotor, object, and social—have been described in a variety of species. The most frequent descriptions are in the parrot family, in crows, ravens, magpies, and jays, and in woodpeckers and hawks (Burghardt, 2005). These are among the more intelligent bird species, with much parental care, many of which are generalist feeders that need to exploit a variety of food sources.

Locomotor play includes soaring and diving by young hawks, and chasing and "mock fights" by falcons. Some of this play is solitary, some is social. There are anecdotal reports of ravens engaging in other kinds of locomotor play, such as sliding down slopes and pushing through snow.

Object play includes manipulating (tossing, tearing, shaking, etc.) and dropping sticks, stones, dead prey, or other small items, and sometimes catching them in flight. There is of course an issue about whether such activities are different from exploration. For example, a study by Heinrich and Smolker (1998) of young ravens, confirmed that they eagerly manipulated new objects (a great variety were introduced in the study), but that they soon ignored inedible objects. They seemed to be testing objects to see if they were edible, and did not engage in repeated or varied manipulation once this was established. However, more playful responses to novel objects have been seen in keas (large parrots native to New Zealand). One kea spent 20 minutes with a stick, chewing it, hitting it, jumping on it, and rolling under it; a stick is not edible and this is certainly repeated and varied manipulation! Pellis (1981) described object play in Australian magpies such as shaking an object with the head, pulling the object between beak and foot, and rubbing an object along the ground—distinguished from exploration by a longer duration and greater complexity of behaviors.

Social play mainly takes the form of chasing and fighting in a non-serious context. Pellis (1981, 1983) described play fighting and chasing as common in young Australian magpies, often with change of roles (attack/defence), and sometimes mixed with object play or precocious courtship play. Play fighting involved trying to peck another bird without being pecked back, and play chases involved running or flying after another. The magpies also showed possible play signals such as a "bouncy" walking gait, open bill, and a long soft guttural call. Play signals are a very strong indicator that the behaviors are play, and indeed are thought to act as a signal of playful rather than serious intent in play fights. They are also perhaps seen in the gentle play biting and foot clawing of young parrots. Aerial play fights have been described in hawks, crows, and magpies, and acrobatic aerial games in ravens. In keas, there can be complex social play involving several partners in play fights, and also in tossing and pulling objects. Burghardt (2005, p. 276) concludes that "we can accept without doubt the observation that birds with complex repertoires of behavior and big brains perform many playful acts."

Play in Mammals

In contrast even to birds, play in mammals is familiar and widespread. Play has been seen in most species of mammals that have been studied sufficiently, and, probably because we are mammals ourselves, it is relatively easy to recognize and accept it as play. As with birds, the main forms are locomotor play, object play, and social play (Fagen, 1981); in addition there is sexual play, and in primates "play mothering" in which a juvenile animal carries around an infant.

Locomotor play in mammals

Wilson and Kleiman (1974) coined the term "locomotor-rotational play" (or L-R play), which has been widely adopted. L-R play can be solitary, or social. It includes actual locomotor play in which the body moves elsewhere, as in chasing play; rotation of the whole body as in twisting or jumping; and movement of a body part, such as head shaking. Wilson and Kleiman described such play in rodents, seals, hippotamus, and the giant panda, and L-R play is now known to be characteristic of many mammals. For example, Kaufmann (1974) described rapid hopping back and forth in young wallabies—an apparently simple form of this kind of play. The gambolling of deer, or frolicking of kittens or puppies, would be well-known examples.

Object play in mammals

As with birds and other orders, object play in mammals is distinguished from exploration by repetition or duration, and by the variety or complexity of the manipulative behaviors involved. Some object play is seen in the young of predatory mammals—for example kittens grabbing and shaking objects, whether or not these are potential prey items. In dwarf mongooses, Rasa (1984) separated out investigative behavior with objects—mainly sniffing and scratching them—from playful behavior, in which up to 32 different forms of engagement with the objects were used, accompanied by different, more intense vocalizations. Whales and dolphins enjoy playing with objects, nosing, flipping, biting, or sucking them.

Social play in mammals

The most well-known examples of social play in mammals are play fighting and chasing, normally with one or more others of the same species. Play fighting can involve grappling, pushing, bouncing, biting, butting, and similar contact actions—varying obviously by species—that could be aggressive in a serious context. The playful context is indicated in various ways, and in some cases by a play signal such as an open mouth (e.g. bears, polecats), or a gambolling or bouncy approach (e.g. dogs), or laying the head on the back (e.g. seals). In play fights, the bites, pushes, or butts are not so hard as in real fights, a characteristic called "self-handicapping." There can also be role reversal—animals taking it in turns to be the attacker or on top. None of these characteristics are true of real fights, which are deadly serious—sometimes literally so; a real fight, although often ritualized and not resulting in much damage, can, if it proceeds further, result in severe injury or even death for one or other combatant.

Sometimes social play takes the form of chasing, something that could also be aggressive in a serious context. In addition, social play can involve non-serious forms of other behaviors, such as courtship (so-called pre-cocious courtship play) or sexual behaviors. It can also be combined with object play, for example, two animals tugging on the same object. Play mothering is described later in the section on primates.

Some Examples of Mammalian Play

To get a view of the range of kinds of play, and the kinds of research findings, it will be helpful to look at some case studies of accounts of play in particular species.

The meerkat (*Suricata suricatta*)

The meerkat is a social mongoose species, living in the desert and savanna of southern Africa, often in old termite mounds. Meerkats are mono-gamous, with little sexual dimorphism (little difference in size between males and females). They live in colonies of some 25 animals, normally comprising a breeding pair, their offspring, and some immigrant males. Mongooses become sexually mature by 7 to 11 months of age, and leave their natal group (home colony) at around 18–30 months; the domin-ant female expels her daughters from the colony forcefully by this time. Colony members go out foraging (they hunt for insects, small reptiles, and mammals), and cooperate in communal rearing of the young pups (some staying to "babysit" while the pack goes hunting).

Social play in a group of captive meerkats was described by Wemmer and Fleming (1974) as including: sniffing; grappling; wrestling; mounting; stiff-legged rocking gait; head-rolling; side-pressing; clasping; standing-on;

pawing; and biting. A young meerkat would typically approach, mount, or clasp another; they would grapple or wrestle; then one would depart, perhaps chased by the other. A young meerkat might also approach the adult male (father), who often mounted or clasped the young one and wrestled, although not bothering to chase on departure. The adult female (mother) seldom engaged in play. In another study of captive mongooses, Rasa (1977) describes playing with dead prey items, biting and shaking them. She also described a twittering "play call" often used to initiate social play.

A natural population of meerkats in the southern Kalahari desert was observed by Sharpe (2005a, 2005b; Sharpe & Cherry, 2003); she collected data on 55 individuals from 7 different colonies. She found the same patterns as described by Wemmer and Fleming in captivity. She found no sex difference in rates of play in young meerkats, with most youngsters sharing play bouts with around a third to a half of the colony members, especially same-age littermates. Most showed no preference for same-sexed or opposite-sexed littermates for play bouts; however, individual meerkats welcomed older play partners, more often refusing play invitations from younger ones. There was no relationship between preferred play partners and the individuals whom a young meerkat went foraging with or whom they dispersed (left the natal colony) with as they got older. Nor did frequency of play correlate with other activities such as grooming others, feeding pups (infants), cleaning the burrow, or acting as a sentinel for danger, or with actual aggression.

Bighorn sheep (*Ovis canadensis*)

Bighorn sheep live in the western mountains of North America, in loose herds usually segregated by sex except in the breeding season. They show pronounced sexual dimorphism: full-grown males weigh twice as much as full-grown females, and have much larger horns. Dominance hierarchies are established by fights involving butts and clashes. The young are called lambs (up one year) and yearlings (one to two years), after which they are adult.

Berger (1980) described play in bighorn sheep, observing them wild in British Columbia, Canada, and in the Colorado Desert, California, USA. Social play included butting and pushing; it occurred more in males. Locomotor-rotational play included neck twists, gambols, heel kicks, running, and chasing. Lambs started head-butting and pushing by about two weeks of age, preferring equal-age play partners. A typical sequence as play developed would be a running approach, with rotational movements (neck twists, jerky movements) acting as a play signal; followed by contact play (butting, pushing) and running off. Comparing the two study environments, Berger found less play by lambs in the Colorado desert, perhaps because of the danger and discomfort of running into cacti that were very prevalent there. Play was also less frequent in hot weather (and was not observed above 32°C).

Another natural observational study of bighorn sheep, in Montana, USA, was carried out by Hass and Jenni (1993). They described much the same behaviors as Berger, and pointed out that similar behavior patterns were used by adults in conflict and in courtship. Play bouts were short, usually just 1 or 2 minutes. Again, male lambs played more than females; and same-age partners were preferred. Play frequency peaked when lambs were 4 to 6 weeks old and declined after 12 weeks to low levels. Nevertheless yearlings and adults did sometimes play. One episode lasted 9 minutes and involved 18 animals: "lambs, yearlings of both sexes, and adult ewes raced up and down a steep roadcut, executing many heel kicks, neck twists, gambols, leaps, and exaggerated horn threats" (Hass & Jenni, 1993, p. 111).

The South American fur seal (*Arctocephalus australis/galapagoensis*)

During the breeding season seals live in large colonies called rookeries, with competition between males for access to females. Females give birth to single pups, which they suckle. The pup is weaned after a few months, starting to feed itself by swimming for fish; and the seal colony disperses until the next breeding season. Harcourt (1991a, 1991b) observed South American fur seals at Punta San Juan, Peru, at the main breeding beach. He especially watched 18 marked mother–pup pairs, to assess developmental trends.

Harcourt distinguished four types of play according to whether it was solitary or social, terrestrial or swimming in the water. Solitary terrestrial play involved shaking or biting objects such as seaweed or feathers or chasing penguins; when swimming, solitary play would consist in leaps or jumps in the water, or activity with seaweed or floating objects. Social terrestrial play involved chasing, mounting, or play-fighting with another pup on the beach or in the intertidal zone; when swimming, social play would consist in chasing or play-fighting another pup in the water. These four types showed quite distinctive time courses. Solitary terrestrial play emerged first, from day 1, and increased rapidly with age, peaking at 2 months and then declining rapidly. Social terrestrial play developed more slowly and was most prevalent from 2 to 4 months. Swimming play only became frequent by 4 months, and here social play came first, being most prevalent at 4 to 6 months. Solitary swimming play showed a lower but steadier frequency from 5 to 10 months. All forms of play were very infrequent after 10 months, although some social terrestrial play was seen in yearlings when they congregated again at the rookery in the following year.

Harcourt did not find significant sex differences in fur seal play; however, Arnold and Trillmich (1985), observing the closely related Galapagos fur seal, did find male pups more active than female pups, especially in play fighting. In Steller sea lions *(Eumetopius jubatus)*, a more sexually dimorphic species than fur seals, Gentry (1974) found such sex differences to be very marked.

The domestic cat (*Felis domesticus*)

The play of kittens of the domestic cat has been widely studied. Kittens are reared by their mother (the father playing no part in their rearing). West (1974) observed six kitten litters and described eight components of social play: belly-up; stand-up; face-off; vertical stance; horizontal leap; side-step; pounce; and chase. A typical sequence would be one kitten pouncing on another, followed by one kitten being belly-up, making treading and pawing movements, and the other being stand-up (over the other, directing "bites"); roles are very often reversed rapidly; one kitten may then make a horizontal leap away, and the other kitten may chase it. Of course, patterns are in practice very varied. The frequency of play increased from 4 weeks (when it started) to a peak at around 12 weeks, before declining, especially after 4 months when the kittens are approaching sexual maturity and becoming independent of the mother.

Barrett and Bateson (1978) observed 28 kittens from 13 litters, and independently produced somewhat different categories from West. They included object contact in their categories, finding more of this in male kittens. Mendoza and Ramirez (1987) observed 7 male kittens and found different developmental trajectories for social play and object play. Social play increased from week 4 to week 14, then declined rapidly, whereas object play only started increasing around week 9 and reached a peak at week 18, declining after week 21. These typical "inverted U" frequency curves, are shown in Figure 3.1. The shift from social play to

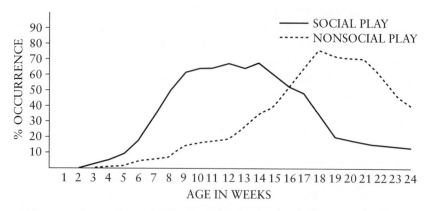

Figure 3.1 Changes in social and nonsocial play with age in kittens (adapted from Mendoza and Ramirez, 1987)

object play seems to occur at the time of weaning, and experiments by Bateson, Martin, and Young (1981) showed that simulating early weaning either by separating kittens from the mother early, or by injecting the mother with bromocriptine to inhibit lactation, resulted in an increase in play and especially object contact play.

A third category of play in kittens is predatory play, which can be seen with live or dead prey objects such as mice, or small birds. This kind of play does not decline as drastically as social play and can be seen in adult cats too. Caro (1979) examined predatory play in kittens by providing them individually with live mice or live canaries. He then assessed their actual prey-catching ability at 6 months, when they were hungry after no food for at least 15 hours. The findings were quite complicated, with a number of separate indicators of play and of later predator success; many correlations were not significant, but there were some positive correlations of predatory success with measures of both predatory play, and social play.

The Norway rat (*Rattus norvegicus*)

The Norway rat is a laboratory animal, bred over many generations for use in psychological experiments. It is not, therefore, a typical mammalian species (Pellis & Pellis, 1998), nor does it live in a "natural" environment. However, it has been very intensively studied. There have been many studies of play behavior in the rat, and in addition a range of deprivation experiments have been carried out.

An observational study of play in young caged laboratory rats was reported by Poole and Fish (1976). Social play involved charging, pouncing, wrestling, and inhibited bites; it was more common in males. There was often alternation between the roles of attacker and defender. Social play was usually with littermates; mother rats did not initiate play but would sometimes respond playfully. Rats that did more social play, also did more solitary play (solitary L-R behaviors such as jumping, jerking).

The differences between play fighting, and serious fighting in young rats as they got older, were described in some detail by Pellis and Pellis (1987). In play fighting, contacts (nosing, sniffing) were usually to the nape of the neck, and any bites were gentle or "inhibited"; movements were described as "erratic." By contrast, in serious fighting bites are often directed at the opponent's rump or backside; also, bites are not inhibited and successful bites can leave wounds.

Panksepp (1980) took "pinning" as a convenient index of social play. "Pinning" occurs when one rat is on its back, and another hovers over it in a dominant stance (see Figure 3.2). Rats that had been socially deprived (housed individually) engaged in much more social play. For both group-raised and individually raised rats, pinning (as a measure of social play) increased rapidly from 18 days of age to a peak at around 32–40 days, before declining again as they neared sexual maturity. Although there was role reversal, some stable dominance patterns (one

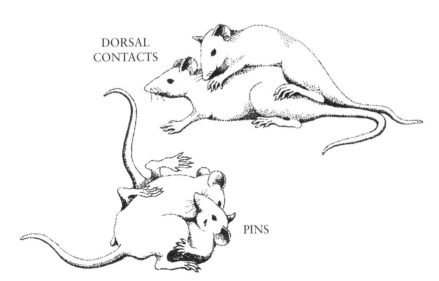

DORSAL
CONTACTS

PINS

Figure 3.2 An Illustration of "Pinning" from the Work of Jaak Panksepp

rat consistently pinning another, more than vice versa) did emerge over the course of the study. Pellis and Pellis (1991) argued that taking pinning as a sole index may confound playful and real fighting. Nevertheless, they too found changes with age; not only does play fighting become rougher and more complex, but there is an increasing asymmetry in roles and an increased possibility of playful fighting escalating to serious fighting. It appears that earlier play fighting does, in part, predict adult social status.

Socially isolated rats may play more when they get the chance, and this suggests that play is important to them. In fact, social deprivation when young rats are 20–50 days old—that is, during the period when most social play occurs—appears to have serious consequences for later adult behavior. Rats deprived of play fighting experience appear less tolerant of the approach of other animals. In some circumstances they are more aggressive, but they may also be more timid, or immobile after attack. These effects are not found if socially isolated rats are given one hour daily of play fighting experience with an agemate (Potegal & Einon, 1988).

Do All Mammals Play?

Play has been well described in a wide range of mammals. For a while it was thought that the mouse (*Mus musculus*) showed little or no play; but although mice are much less playful than rats, both social and solitary play have been described in them in semi-natural environments (Wolff, 1981). But do all mammals play? Here, we may need to distinguish the three main types of mammals, based on how the young are cared for:

- the monotremes are the most primitive mammals, laying eggs: the only surviving monotremes are the duck-billed platypus and two species of echidna or spiny anteater.
- the marsupials have tiny, helpless infants that are protected in a pouch where they can suckle from the mother. Even a large animal such as a kangaroo gives birth to an infant weighing less than one gram. Marsupials are restricted to South America (opossums) and Australasia (many species including kangaroos, possums, koalas, bandicoots, and wombats).
- the placental mammals are the great majority. Here the young develop in the mother's womb for a considerable time before birth. At birth the young may be relatively quick to develop (e.g. to run

independently), as in precocial species such as deer; or they may be relatively helpless, as in altricial species such as cats. But they are not nearly so helpless as marsupial newborns, and in evolutionary terms the womb has proved superior to the pouch.

Burghardt (2005) discusses this issue in detail. Regarding the monotremes, there are reports of both social play (playful biting and chasing) and solitary or L-R play (splashing, rolling) in the platypus, although there remain issues about whether these were definitely playful in the sense of being structurally different from non-playful behaviors. There are no observations of play in spiny anteaters, which have been relatively infrequently studied.

Play does clearly occur in many marsupials; the hopping, L-R play of wallabies was mentioned above (Kaufmann, 1974). Burghardt (2005) finds widespread evidence for L-R play in marsupials, in fact in almost all species (little if any play has been seen in South American opossums). In addition, there is a lot of social play, much of it play fighting, in species such as kangaroos and wallabies; and a few reports of object play.

In the placental mammals, Burghardt (2005) reports evidence for at least some form of play in all but two of the nineteen orders. All three forms (locomotor; object; social) have been described in 8 orders: proboscideans (elephants); rodents (rats, mice, squirrels); primates (monkeys, apes); carnivores (lions, wolves, bears); pinnepeds (seals, seal lions); perissodactyls (horses, tapirs), artiodactyls (pigs, deer, giraffes) and cetaceans (whales, dolphins). Both locomotor and social play have been seen in 3 orders: sirenians (sirens, manatees); lagomorphs (rabbits, hares); and scandentians (tree shrews). Social play has been clearly described in 3 orders: xenarths (sloths, armadillos); hyracoids (hyraxes); and pholidots (pangolins); locomotor play in 1 order: macroscelids (elephant shrews); and object play in 1 order: insectivores (shrews, tenrecs). There is some, but more equivocal, evidence for object and social play in 1 order: chiropterans (bats). Finally there is no evidence for play in 2 orders: tubulidentates (aardvark); and dermopterans (flying lemurs). These latter have few species (one species of aardvark; two species of flying lemur) and have been little studied, so the absence of play cannot be confidently stated.

In summary, the great majority of mammals show evidence of play, especially social and locomotor play. Many show object play. There are clearly substantial species variations in the importance of these different forms of play in behavioral repertoires. However, play is a characteristically juvenile form of behavior. While it may not be absent in adults (especially when interacting with young), it generally shows an inverted U curve of frequency with age, peaking as the young become mobile and interact with littermates or other young ones in a group or herd; then decreasing, generally, as sexual maturity approaches, stable dominance positions are being acquired, and the animal is typically engaged in serious competition for mates and resources.

Play in Monkeys and Apes

If play is common and nearly ubiquitous in mammals, this is especially the case in the primates. The order of primates includes prosimians (lemurs); new world monkeys (capuchins, spider monkeys, marmosets), old world monkeys (macaques, baboons, mangabeys, guenons, colobines), and the apes (great apes: chimpanzee, gorilla, orang-utan; lesser apes: gibbon, siamang). The primates generally have large brains for their size, good vision, and good manipulative abilities with their hands.

Social and locomotor play are common, as with other mammals. Social play is mainly play fighting, while locomotor play can be solitary (leaping, jumping, somersaults) or social, as in play-chasing. An interesting kind of play seen in primates is play mothering. Primate mothers generally carry young infants around with them; in play mothering, a juvenile (usually female), not yet old enough to be a mother herself, carries around an infant (Lancaster, 1971). Perhaps, the female learns something about mothering skills through doing this; for example, that one way to keep an infant from crying and fidgeting is to groom it. Play mothering is usually tolerated by the mother, and possibly mutually beneficial in that she gets a break from minding the infant! However, a dark side of this behavior pattern is that non-related animals may sometimes "kidnap" an infant, and mistreat it; the mother is more relaxed when an older sister or other kin is doing the "play mothering" (Hrdy, 1977).

Object play is particularly prevalent in many primates. Power (2000) summarizes the main types. These include what he calls transforming objects (tearing, twisting, wadding), relating objects (rubbing, rolling, wrapping, hitting, dropping, lining up), and other large motor behaviors with objects (waving, pushing, throwing). Following Torigoe (1985), he also lists the frequency of such play in different species of primate. Lemurs generally show the most limited range of object play, usually just using their mouths for this purpose. Most species use their fingers or feet as well as their mouth, and engage in some complex play (e.g. using one object against another or a surface or substrate), with object play being most complex in the great apes.

The literature on primate play is quite extensive. We will look in a bit more detail at the squirrel monkey (a new world species), the rhesus macaque (an old world species), and the great apes (chimpanzee, gorilla and otang-utan), our closest mammalian relatives.

The squirrel monkey (*Saimiri sciureus*)

Play in squirrel monkeys has been observed in natural environments (Baldwin & Baldwin, 1974) and in indoor and outdoor enclosures at an "animal farm" (Biben, 1986). Rudimentary play starts in infants at five weeks of age, and soon infants are sliding off their mother's back and wrestling vigorously with other infants. This rough-and-tumble play is a major form of peer social interaction, in the infant (first year of life) and juvenile (up to 30 months) stages; the main behaviors are grab, wrestle, roll over, tail pull, leap toward, chase, and acrobatics (Biben, 1986). Locomotor play (running, jumping, swinging from branches) also occurs but often culminates in a play fight. Object play occurs in the early months, but is not especially prominent in this species. In older animals, some elements of sexual behavior (mounting, thrusting) may get incorporated with play. Play declines rapidly by the end of the second year, but is not absent in older animals (and sometimes young animals attempt to play-fight with adults).

Biben (1986) describes two main types of wrestling play: directional and non-directional. In directional wrestling, one animal is on top of the other (similar to the "pinning" described in rats). This was preferred by males. Males did show role-reversal in their play fighting, but it was not complete; dominant infants also tended to dominate in play fights, though much less than in non-play contexts. In non-directional wrestling, both animals hang from a perch with forelegs clasped about one another. This was preferred by females, who got little chance of role reversal when playing with the generally larger and more dominant males. As a rule, young squirrel monkeys preferred to play-fight with a partner who was similar or subordinate in status, rather than a dominant one; but would still often play if a dominant partner initiated, or only such a partner was available.

Biben and Symmes (1986) also described two vocalizations—"peeps" and "cackles"—that particularly occurred during play fights. These occurred during the fight, not before or after, so they were not "play invitations" as seen in canids, for example. They were often given by the subordinate animal. Biben interprets the function of these calls as being motivational (signalling a willingness to continue play fighting), and/or (because the calls are quite loud) providing information for adults nearby that the fighting is playful and they need not interfere.

Studies by Baldwin and Baldwin (1974, 1976) have shown that the frequency of social play in squirrel monkeys varies greatly according to the environment they are in, especially the ease of availability of food. In some environments young monkeys play for as much as 2 or 3 hours a day, in others for only 10–30 minutes; and in one environment where food was very scarce, no play was seen in 261 hours of observation. Experimental studies varying ease of getting food showed that when it was very difficult to obtain, play rates fell to 1% of what they were when food was plentiful and easy to obtain. When more food was provided again, play levels rose or rebounded quite strongly. The inference is that social play has some benefits (a lot of time is spent, and monkeys "catch up" after deprivation), but as it not so evident when energy is concentrated on food acquisition, with animals still functioning within the normal range, the benefits can probably also be obtained in other ways (e.g. other forms of social experience and interaction).

The rhesus macaque (*Macaca mulatta, Macaca fuscata*)

The rhesus macaque is perhaps the most studied primate species. It is ground-living, with a complex social organization. There are separate male and female dominance hierarchies. Males usually disperse to other groups on reaching sexual maturity and have to compete in them. Females, however, usually stay in the natal group and inherit their mother's dominance ranking; in fact they inherit this in inverse order of age (the youngest daughter reaching the highest ranking amongst sisters), because mothers aid infants in disputes and it is mother's aiding or helping behavior that brings about the transmission of dominance.

A particularly detailed study of rhesus monkey play was made by Donald Symons (1974, 1978), based on his doctoral thesis. During this, he made 300 hours of close-range field observations of free-ranging rhesus monkeys in Puerto Rico. The great majority of rhesus monkey play is play fighting and play chasing; Symons documented 2,351 bouts of the former and 662 bouts of the latter. Play fighting can involve grappling, wrestling, tumbling, and mock biting in which one animal attempts to "bite" another and avoid being bitten. There are no specialized visual or auditory signals during play fights (Symons, 1974), but a play face (relaxed open-mouth face) often precedes a play fight and can be interpreted as a signal of non-aggressive intent. Correspondingly, a play chase is often initiated by a gambolling or staggering gait not seen in other contexts. Rhesus monkeys also engage in other forms of acrobatics, playful competition for objects, and if water is available, splashing and jumping play. However there is little solo object play (Fagen, 1981).

Besides spending a lot of time in play fighting, rhesus monkeys also show a rebound effect after being deprived of social play. Oakley and Reynolds (1976) brought about a severe reduction in social play in a rhesus macaque colony on a Stanford University campus pen, either by feeding them with unshelled sunflower seeds and birdseed (which took much longer to forage and eat than standard monkey chow), or by throwing food to distract them if they started to play. Both methods produced a significant drop in social play over a five-day period; followed by a rebound on the next day when the procedure was stopped. The frequency, and rebound after deprivation, suggests that play fighting is functionally important for young rhesus monkeys.

The great apes (chimpanzee and bonobo: *Pan troglodytes, Pan paniscus*; gorilla: *Gorilla gorilla*; orang-utan: *Pongo pygmaeus*)

The great apes have been studied both in the wild and in captivity. These species are highly intelligent compared to other primates. The infant and juvenile periods are relatively long, and mothers only give birth about every 3 or 4 years (up to 5 years in the case of orang-utans). Chimpanzees especially are noted for tool use and some tool-making abilities, and both chimpanzees and gorillas can learn some sign language.

In terms of social structure, the orang-utan stands somewhat apart as being the least socially complex; in their natural environment (forest areas in Indonesia), orang-utans live as solitary animals, except that a mother is accompanied by one or two infants or juveniles: young orang-utans remain with the mother until 7 to 10 years of age. Gorillas (there are three subspecies, all living in Africa) live in stable family groups, headed by a silverback male; group size may vary from around 2 to 20. The infant period lasts up to 3 years, and the juvenile period another three years, to age 6. Both the common chimpanzee, and the bonobo, or pygmy chimpanzee, also live in Africa. The common chimpanzee forms communities of some 40 to 60 animals that often split into smaller groups for foraging. Males form the core of the group and may compete for dominance; females may transfer, or even be kidnapped, into another group. Infancy lasts for 3 years, and the juvenile period for another four years, up to age 7. Females do not reach sexual maturity until 11 or 12 years.

Lewis (2005) has summarized the kinds of social play seen in the great apes. These include *play fighting* (aggressive movement patterns without threat gestures): wrestle; slap; jump at; jump on; play bite; cuff; pull; rough-and-tumble; roll; run towards; kick; sniff; chase; attack–withdraw; spar; drag; pinch; hit; *other less aggressive playful social interactions*: finger wrestle; peek-a-boo; gentle roll; grapple; tickle; play-walk; laugh; hair-tug/pull; *pseudo-sexual play*: mounting; genital inspection; licking; rubbing; thrusting; and *play mothering*: groom; carry; inspect (infants). The developmental trajectory of play in chimpanzees increases rapidly up to around 25 months, then starts to fall; in gorillas, it increases rapidly up to about 10 months, and then falls only slowly over the next 30 months. Although most social play, especially play fighting, takes place among infants and juveniles, pseudo-sexual play mainly involves older juveniles, subadults, and adults; and in addition, adults play with infant offspring (although rather infrequently), mainly using more gentle behaviors: tickling; gentle wrestling; peek-a-boo; nibble; grapple; embrace; sham bite; dandle; head-bob; shake-head; grasp; lift (Lewis, 2005, Table 1).

Chimpanzees do not show marked sex differences in their play. Infants play first with their mothers, but later primarily with other infants and juveniles. Forms of play are very varied. Bonobos are less well studied, but a relatively high frequency of sexual play has been noted in juveniles, subadults, and adults. Gorillas are a more sexually dimorphic species than common chimpanzees or bonobos, and their play too is more sexually differentiated, with males preferring play fighting, females preferring play mothering and quieter behaviors. Orang-utans seem to show less complex social play in the wild, mainly swinging, grabbing, and mouthing the partner. However all the great apes show some more varied play patterns in semi-captivity, and this is especially so in orang-utans which usually have little opportunity to mix in social groups in the wild (Lewis, 2005).

Despite some species differences, there are common features in play in the great apes. All have a play face, and this is especially obvious in chimpanzees, where the play face is accompanied by panting sounds, similar to human laughter; indeed, this "open-mouth play face" is seen as homologous to human laughter, with an ancestral origin in play (Panksepp, 1998; and see Figure 3.3). All show the characteristic inverted

Figure 3.3 The bonobo "play face"
(photograph courtesy of Frans de Waal)
When bonobos (close relatives of chimpanzees) play, they show an expression
thought to be homologous with human laughing. It is known as the "play face"
and usually accompanied by soft, breathy laughing sounds. Bonobos show this
expression when they tickle or hold each other, as here, or chase each other
around.

U age curve in frequency of play, with play tending to be replaced by
grooming as sexual maturity is approached; but adult play does
occur, notably between mother and offspring but also with other group
members.

Object play in the great apes has been reviewed by Ramsey and
McGrew (2005). In the wild, young chimpanzees may manipulate
branches and leaves in apparently playful ways. Adult chimpanzees do
make and use tools—for example leaf wads to sponge up water from
crevices, sticks to fish for termites—and young chimpanzees watch older
chimpanzees (often, their mother) doing this, and copy it, sometimes in
playful ways. They may throw stones in the air, and catch them; rake

around leaves to make a noise; and engage in a tug-of-war over pieces of vegetation. In a few cases, a chimpanzee has been seen cradling an object such as a log, or dead animal, as if play mothering. Studies of captive chimpanzees, who may be provided with a range of toys and unusual objects, reveal a correspondingly wide range of play with them.

Gorillas do not appear to use tools in the wild, and their object play seems correspondingly sparse; but they do play with objects when in captivity, sometimes in ways which suggest quite complex games—for example, catching different objects, or even pretense, as in "drinking" from an empty cup. Examples of possible "pretend play" in apes (especially captive apes) will be discussed in more detail in Chapter 8. Orang-utans are less studied, but some object play has been seen, including what may be the construction of play nests (nest building in trees being an important activity for adults). Again, in captive orangs, more complex games with objects may be seen: in one observation, two subadult orangs played with a shirt, taking it in turns to put it over the other's head and then charge and wrestle the "blind" partner, before reversing the roles. Figure 3.4 shows captive orang-utans playing with cloth materials.

Figure 3.4 Captive orang-utans playing with cloth materials at Twycross Zoo, UK
(photograph courtesy of Lisa Riley).

Having reviewed the evidence on play across different orders of animals, and especially in the mammals and primates, we are in a better position to examine contemporary ideas and theories about the evolution of play, and its likely functions in development, in the next chapter.

Further Reading

A landmark in the study of animal play was R. Fagen's (1981) book *Animal Play Behavior*. Shortly after that I wrote a review for *Behavior and Brain Sciences* (Smith, 1982) and edited a book *Play in Animals and Humans* (1984), Oxford: Blackwell. After what appears to have been a lull from the mid-80s to the mid-90s, research on play from an evolutionary perspective picked up again with an edited collection by M. Bekoff and J. A. Byers (1998), *Animal Play: Evolutionary, Comparative and Ecological Approaches*, Cambridge: Cambridge University Press. A. D. Pellegrini and P. K. Smith (2005) in an edited book *The Nature of Play: Great Apes and Humans*, New York: Guilford Press, focus on the evolutionary comparisons with humans to our nearest genetic relatives, the great apes. G. Burghardt, in *The Genesis of Animal Play* (2005), Cambridge, MA: MIT Press, gives the most thorough contemporary discussion of the origins of animal play and of its diverse forms in different species.

Chapter 4

Animal Play: Theoretical Perspectives on Function

Theories and Evidence Concerning the Evolution and Adaptive Value of Animal Play

Contemporary research on animal play

Contemporary research on animal play uses the explanatory framework of modern evolutionary theory and of sociobiology. Over quite a long period in the 20th century, animal ethologists conducted a generally well-balanced program of research that employed natural observations to describe behavior in a new species and to understand the full range of natural behavior, together with experimentation, as required, to test out hypotheses genuinely rooted in the natural ecology and behavior patterns of the species. Many of these earlier studies were broadly descriptive in nature; or in some cases they used and tested theories of causation, such as the hydraulic model of motivation developed by Lorenz (1956) or the instinct model developed by Tinbergen (1951).

Although modern evolutionary theory was already well developed, in the sense that Darwin's evolutionary theory had been integrated with genetic theory to form the "modern synthesis" (Huxley, 1942), the explanatory power of evolutionary theory for social behaviors (and thus for play, much of which is social) was not developed until the advent of sociobiology. This can be dated to the 1970s, the pioneering work by Hamilton (1964) and Trivers (1974) being expounded to a wider audience in Wilson's (1978) book *Sociobiology: The New Synthesis*. These integrated new ideas about kin selection, reciprocal altruism, parent–offspring conflict, and similar insights into a comprehensive overview of animal (and potentially human) behavior.

What does evolutionary theory say about play?

What is distinctive about a modern evolutionary approach to play? A fundamental perspective coming from evolutionary theory is that we generally expect behavior to be adaptive or to have a function. Animals are in the business of passing on their genes to future generations. From the "selfish gene" perspective (Dawkins, 1989), animals are vehicles for ensuring the survival and propagation of genes, which are the fundamental replicators. Animals which survive long enough to reproduce effectively have a better chance of passing on their genes. The behaviors, or behavioral strategies, of an animal can be assessed in terms of this. Any behavior will have plusses and minuses in this respect, or "costs" and "benefits." A related term used here is "fitness." *Individual fitness* refers to an individual's ability to survive and reproduce, itself. *Inclusive fitness* is a broader concept, embracing also the extent to which an individual's actions may help relatives (usually close relatives), even perhaps at some cost to itself (Hamilton, 1964).

The adaptive value, or benefits for fitness, of many behaviors is obvious. It is clear why animals eat, look after young, reproduce. But why should animals play? This is an obvious question for evolutionary theorists, and a number of suggestions have been put forward, which we shall review. But is it inevitably the case that behaviors have an adaptive function? Not always. For example, if an animal is in a new environment, different from the kind of environment its forebears evolved in, behaviors that were adaptive in the ancestral environment might still be performed even if they are not adaptive in the new one. Another possibility of non-functionality is that a behavior is a "spin-off" or by-product of another, adaptive, behavior. This has been referred to as a "spandrel" by Gould and Lewontin (1979). A spandrel is the triangular area between two adjacent arches, and the moulding or cornice above, in a building such as a church (Figure 4.1). It is often decorated; but this decoration is a spin-off from the functionality of the arches, not a function in itself.

Could either of these explanations apply to play? It may be relevant in explaining some infrequent kinds of play, or play only seen in artificial environments (e.g. object play in octopuses, see Chapter 3). But both are very unlikely in general terms. The vast majority of observations of animal play have been made in the animals' natural environments, which have not changed substantially for generations. Theories of animal play behavior do not rely on observations of play in zoos. The

spandrel

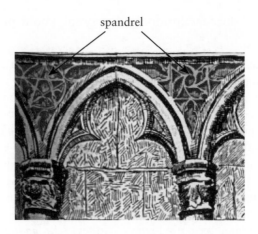

Figure 4.1 A spandrel

"spandrel" argument is most unlikely because of the ubiquity of play in many mammalian species, the rebounds found after deprivation, and because of the costs of play. A spandrel has no cost—it is an accidental by-product. But play has definite costs for an animal.

The main costs of playing are:

- Time: the time could have been spent doing other things—eating, watching, exploring, resting, etc.
- Energy: play is often quite vigorous, so there is an energy cost compared to resting.
- Risk of injury: especially in exercise play and play fighting, there is a greater risk of an animal falling from a branch, slipping off a slope, or getting hurt accidentally in a play fight.
- Neglect of predator danger: if an animal is absorbed in play, it may not be so vigilant in monitoring the approach of a predator.

There is plenty of evidence that these costs operate in mammalian play. We have seen how time is important, for example, in foraging for food: squirrel monkeys that had to spend more time foraging, spent less time playing. Energy expenditure is important for vigorous locomotor or social play, as these clearly use up more energy resources than quiet activity or resting. The exact amount has not often been calculated, but Martin (1984) found that kittens spent 9% of total time in play behavior, with a net daily energy expenditure in excess of resting metabolism of about

4% (Martin considered this a low figure, a point we will return to). We also saw how play may be reduced in very hot temperatures (for example, among bighorn sheep), when further energy expenditure would be costly in terms of maintaining body temperature.

Risks of injury have been documented in a number of species: for example, Byers (1977) observed ibex kids in vigorous locomotor play on varied and steep terrain, and found that one-third sustained some temporary injuries because of this. In bighorn sheep, less play occurred when there were many prickly cacti around. In social play, sometimes play fights can turn nasty and an animal get injured, especially as these fights get rougher as sexual maturity is approached. Evidence regarding reduced predator vigilance comes from Harcourt's (1991b) observations of South American fur seals. Young seals can be caught and killed by Southern sea lions, a larger species. Harcourt observed 26 pups being caught in this way; 22 were playing at the time, although play took up only 6% of the pup's time budget. Pups were distracted during play, and therefore less vigilant.

From an evolutionary perspective, these costs should be counterbalanced by some benefits. If they were not, animals that did not play would do better than animals that did, and play would disappear from the behavioral repertoire. The main arguments have been whether these benefits are major (more or less essential) or minor (optional extras); whether they are immediate (for the animal now, when playing) or deferred (for the animal when it gets older, for example a young animal acquiring benefits for adulthood); and just what kinds of benefits these are. All of these issues can be informed by a life history perspective.

A life-history perspective

Evolutionary theory encourages us to look at behavioral phenomena and the adaptive value of behavior in a life-history perspective—that is, thinking of costs and benefits through the lifespan, from conception to death. As we have seen, the "currency" of costs and benefits is, ultimately, inclusive fitness, of which a major component is normally individual fitness or reproductive success. Reproducing "successfully" may mean having lots of offspring, perhaps just once in a short lifespan (a so-called "r" strategy"); or it may mean having few offspring but providing them with a lot of parental investment (a so-called "K" strategy; Stearns, 1976). Frog spawn is an example of the "r" strategy—the mother frog has a massive explosion of eggs and then leaves them to their fate. Many (not all) insects and lower invertebrates follow an "r" strategy. By contrast, most birds and mammals follow more of a "K" strategy, having a small clutch or litter size, looking after the young for some time, and only then having a subsequent clutch or litter.

Two findings are particularly important in considering the relevance of life history theory to play. One is that play is mainly found in more encephalized species (species with larger brain size relative to body size), and mainly in more "K"-selected species with a lot of parental investment —birds, and especially mammals. It seems that the benefit-to-cost balance for play is greater in encephalized species. This makes sense if play is important for learning, in a general sense. There would not then be much (if any) benefit in playing, for species with largely instinctive or programmed behavior patterns (as in invertebrates, generally). In contrast, for species with flexible behavior patterns and a range of possible developmental pathways to follow, play could be valuable in exploring and practicing skills and behavioral routines that will be useful now or in the future.

The other finding important to consider in a life history perspective is that the frequency of forms of play characteristically follows an inverted U course in development (as in Figure 3.1), increasing rapidly in the infancy period as young animals become mobile, peaking, and then declining as the young approach sexual maturity. Admittedly, the rate and timing of decline varies, and adult animals do sometimes play; but this inverted U shape demands an explanation. The rising part of the inverted U is explicable in terms of very general developmental constraints, especially in altricial species; young mammals or birds are quite helpless and relatively immobile, so play is not really possible. But play typically increases very rapidly as young animals become mobile. The interesting question is why it declines later on, often around sexual maturity. While it must be acknowledged that adult animals sometimes do play, they generally do it much less frequently, and when play does happen, it is often with offspring and thus is potentially explicable in terms of benefits for the offspring rather than direct benefits for the adult player (benefits for the offspring also mean benefits to the adult player's inclusive fitness, if the player is a parent, or relative—a grandparent, uncle, or aunt, for example).

It would appear that the benefit-to-cost balance shifts decidedly against play as young mammals reach maturity. This could be because of a decrease in benefits, or an increase in costs—or quite likely both. As far as costs are concerned, we do know that play fighting often gets rougher as sexual maturity is approached. There is thus more risk of injury. At sexual maturity competition for mates becomes a prime issue for reproductive success, and it is understandable that an animal's time and resources need to be devoted more to this—for example, by defending a territory and competing directly or indirectly with others of the same sex for access to desirable mates. But do the benefits of play also decrease with age?

Immediate or delayed benefits

Changes in the benefits of play with age bear on the issue of whether any benefits are immediate or delayed. Traditionally, benefits have been viewed as delayed. It has been thought that young animals play so that, as adults, they are physically fit, good fighters, know how to exploit objects in their environment, and so forth. This tradition stems from early theorists such as Groos, but has maintained a central position in writings on play. For example, a juvenile learns fighting skills through play fighting, which it then puts to use as an adult in actual fighting. Presumably there might still be benefits to play fighting as you get older, but these would decrease with age, as your expected future lifespan decreased. There would be little benefit to an older animal playing, when it has few future years in which to harvest the benefits of play.

However, an alternative view is that play has important immediate benefits (Pellegrini & Bjorklund, 2004), a view that can be seen as stemming from earlier writers such as Hall (see Chapter 2). The argument here is that play might be beneficial straight away; after all, being physically fit and cognitively and socially skilled, will be beneficial now, during infancy and the juvenile period, as well as later. Indeed, given that infant and juvenile mortality rates can be quite high in many species (infants especially are vulnerable to predation and to lack of food), it could be especially useful for infants and juveniles to acquire such skills. Also, Pellegrini and Bjorklund (2004) argue, high mortality rates effectively devalue deferred benefits (you might never reach adulthood!), and put a premium on immediate benefits.

It is probably unnecessary to pit the immediate or deferred benefits viewpoints against each other too strongly. While some skills (e.g. physical fitness) need constant maintenance, others (e.g. awareness of the uses of objects) may not be easily lost, once acquired. In other words, some benefits of play may be rather short-term, others may be quite long-term and have both immediate and future benefits. We also need to be clear what is meant by "immediate" and "delayed." Many species have a relatively short lifespan—of only a few years—and play fighting during the first few months might have its main payoff just a few months later, at sexual maturity. This is neither immediate, nor a long time in the future.

Major or minor benefits

The frequency of play (at least in mammals) and the rebounds after deprivation suggest that play can have quite important, or major, functions. It may be that play is a vital or essential part of the development of a healthy and successful adult. However, there are counterarguments to this. One argument is that play has a lower priority than important maintenance activities. We have seen that play can virtually disappear (e.g. in squirrel monkeys) if obtaining food is arduous and time-consuming; yet, the monkeys suffer no obvious ill effects. Play may disappear in adverse weather conditions such as hot temperatures (e.g. among bighorn sheep), again with no obvious ill effects.

The other argument is that the costs of play are not very great. This was proposed by Martin and Caro (1985). They argued that the actual costs of play in terms of energy expended were not much greater than those of a resting metabolism. Paul Martin had researched play in kittens, and, as we noted above, calculated that the extra metabolic cost of play was only about 4% in that species. Martin and Caro argued generally that the costs of play had been overemphasized. They did not suggest that there were no benefits to play, but rather that the benefits of playing were minor (low costs, low benefits), and that the developmental outcomes from play could also be achieved in other ways (for example, you can develop physical fitness through exploration, foraging, fighting, etc., as well as through play). The latter point is often referred to as "equifinality"—the idea that there are different routes to the same developmental goal or outcomes. Play might only be one route or set of routes.

Martin and Caro's arguments provide an important antidote to the idealization of play. However, the argument is again one of degree. Few people dispute that play has costs, or that it can have benefits. Are the costs small? A figure of 4% extra metabolic costs may seem low, but, as in any economic analysis, it is the marginal costs that are important. An animal cannot avoid the basic metabolic costs of staying alive. The extra energetic costs of play do mean it will need more food. But energy costs are not the only costs. For some species at least (e.g. ibex, fur seals) the other costs of play (injury, predation) appear to really be quite high.

It may well be that the importance of the benefits of play—whether they are major or minor—varies greatly by type of play and for particular species. This would be fully consistent with the species variations in types and frequency of play. It is likely that play provides favourable opportunities for various kinds of skill development and learning (see below). There may, however, also be other ways of getting these outcomes, which, though perhaps less effective than play, sometimes have smaller associated costs. Depending on the benefit-to-cost balance, play will be a preferred option in many cases or circumstances, but it will decrease or drop out of the repertoire if costs rise too much, and developmental outcomes will be sought in other ways (Smith, 2005).

Sexual selection theory

Sex differences in play provide one important source of evidence about function. Sex differences link in to broader features of species difference in sexual organization and principles of sexual selection. Sexual selection refers to the competition amongst conspecifics (animals of the same species) for mates. Intrasexual competition refers to competition within members of one sex for reproductive access to the other sex. Generally, for sexually reproducing species, competition is seen as stronger among males. This is because females have a limited number of eggs, and, especially in "K"-selected species such as birds and mammals, normally need to either sit on eggs to hatch them or to provide milk for their young. Such a devoted strategy is more optional for males, who have a comparatively unlimited amount of sperm. In polygynous species, males choose to mate with a number of females, and intrasexual competition is high in males; in monogamous species, the differentiation between the sexes is less, but there will still be competition for high-quality mates. Competition is evident in body characteristics such as weapons and ornamentation (a peacock's feathers; a stag's horns), and in behavior, for example risky, aggressive strategies in males—which might include play fighting. Thus, gender differences in play fighting are predicted to be higher in polygynous species.

Different perspectives on play

The evolutionary perspective also leads to an awareness of different perspectives on play. If play has benefits, then benefits for whom? Trivers' (1974) writings on parent–offspring conflict provided the impetus for

this question. Trivers made it clear that there were conflicts of (reproductive) interest between parents and offspring, and also between siblings,
as they are not genetically identical (leaving aside the occasional case
of identical twins). Just as non-relatives are in reproductive competition, so are relatives, even if this is partially moderated by relatedness.
Parents are in a position to strongly influence or "manipulate" their offspring's behavior (and offspring can influence parents too, via crying,
demands for suckling, etc.); and thus we have to consider whether
juvenile play behavior, or lack of it, represents benefits for the juvenile
or for the parent.

Examining Possible Benefits of Play

How can we critically examine the possible benefits of play, or functional hypotheses? A number of methods are available:

- The form of the play behavior should be such as to make it a plausible candidate for the functions suggested.
- Cross-species differences should make sense in terms of types of play
  and proposed functions.
- Gender differences should be explicable within and between species.
- Within a species, age changes in the nature, frequency, and intensity
  of play should be consistent with postulated benefits.
- Individual differences in play frequencies would be predicted to lead
  to later developmental outcomes linked to the benefits of play. In
  particular, deprivation or enrichment of play experiences should
  result in measurable outcomes. Deprivation or enrichment can be due
  to natural circumstances (as we saw in squirrel monkeys), but they
  can also be experimentally manipulated, and for example many play
  deprivation studies have been carried out experimentally with rodents
  (Hole & Einon, 1984).

General Views on the Benefits of Play

Fagen (1981) considered different classes of effects of animal play, which
might be candidates for functional hypotheses. The one that he considered as the most supported was training of physical capabilities and
cognitive and social skills (for later use, although Fagen does not place
much emphasis on the immediate or delayed benefits distinction in this

context). In a review shortly after this, I (Smith, 1982) argued that most forms of play were selected for practice functions, when a lot of direct practice might be difficult or dangerous (for example, in fighting). Power (2000) saw the strongest case for an evolutionary function for play with rough-and-tumble play, but concluded generally that research on the developmental functions of play needs more conclusive results, and more studies of the social as well as the cognitive effects of play, before firm functional statements can be made. Bjorklund and Pellegrini (2002; see also Pellegrini & Bjorklund, 2004) however, reasserted a functional significance for play; documenting time and energy budgets and other costs of play (such as injury), they believe that physical, object and pretend play would not be so prevalent if they had not been selected for in our evolutionary history.

Locomotor play

Locomotor play in animals has been argued to have both immediate and longer-term functions. Stamps (1995) argued that an immediate function of such play is that the young animal becomes acquainted with the terrain it is in. This would be important if, for example, it is pursued by a predator; and could be seen as generally useful for survival. Another hypothesis for immediate functions, proposed by Barber (1991), is that play regulates the balance between food and energy intake, fitness and obesity. Play uses up excess energy to prevent obesity. This is similar to Spencer's surplus energy theory. Relatedly, animals may use up stored caloric energy to regulate body temperature (for example, to keep warm when the ambient temperature is low). Although this can explain some variations in play with food availability and with temperature, it raises other problems, such as why animals should routinely have excess energy (why don't they just eat less?); it also does little to explain the design features of play or its temporal course (why should play decline at sexual maturity?).

The more commonly argued view is that locomotor play functions as physical training. Fagen (1977, 1981) argued that there is a physiologically sensitive period in mammalian infancy, when exercise is most effective for strengthening muscles and enhancing general physical capacity —thus explaining the typical age curve. Fagen also argued that the design characteristics of locomotor play—typically, short, repeated bouts— were efficient for this, with high-intensity bouts exercising specific muscles, while low-intensity bouts exercised general physical capacity.

Lewis and Barton (2004) used a phylogenetic comparative method to examine social play behavior in relation to the cerebellum in nonhuman primates. They found that the frequency of social play and relative cerebellum size were positively correlated across species. As the cerebellum is strongly implicated in the coordination and control of motoric activity, this suggests that some aspects of social play (much of which is locomotor) have been selected for aspects of motor development.

Byers and Walker (1995) considered three aspects of the physical training hypothesis: strength, motor skill (efficiency of movement), and endurance. They examined the frequencies of locomotor play in mice, rats, and cats, in relation to growth of synapses in the cerebellum and muscle fibre differentiation, and found corresponding time curves. They argued that locomotor play has a long-term effect primarily on motor skill, as evidenced by these parallel changes. By contrast, they argued that effects on strength and endurance (not indexed so closely by the cerebellar and muscle fibre differentiation changes) would be temporary; such benefits would soon disappear, but could also be regained later. (An analogy here would be learning to swim or ride a bicycle; any strength or endurance benefits of swimming or cycling would be transient and could be gained equally well later, but the actual motor skills involved are arguably easier to acquire early in life, and once acquired are persistent—I have not ridden a bike myself for some 10 years but I am confident I could jump on one tomorrow and have no problems!). Byers (1998a) also argued that the short bouts and limited time spent in play, would just not be sufficient for effective endurance training.

Object play

Object play has generally been surmised to be practice or training for food extraction, prey catching, agonistic behavior, or tool use, depending, of course, on the species concerned. Thus Power (2000, p. 43) summarized that "object play in carnivores and birds of prey appears to be tied to prey-subduing and prey consumption behaviors, object play in other birds is tied to the use of tools in food attainment, and object play in primates appears to be tied to foraging practices and tool-use." Also, playful throwing of objects (for example in primates) might be practice for later agonistic or display behaviors—as seen for example in chimpanzees. This summary is consistent with the design characteristics of object play observed, and its species distribution. It is consistent with the general lack of gender differences found (i.e., food attainment and prey catching are generally characteristic of both males and females). However, as yet there is no strong longitudinal evidence linking individual experiences with object play to later outcomes. Caro (1979, 1980) attempted such work through experiments with domestic kittens. He correlated levels of play behaviors in kittens (such as pawing or biting) with adult predatory behaviors and capture efficiency. The results were complex, but generally non-significant. However, there are a number of drawbacks to the study; for example, some kittens were given extra object play opportunities, but the objects, two balls, were simple, and the kittens deprived of these objects still had other possible object experience, such as with wood shavings in their cages.

Social play

As we have seen, a lot of social play takes the form of play fighting or chasing. An obvious candidate for the function of such play is that it is practice for skills in later fighting. Using his detailed structural observations of rhesus monkey play, Symons (1978, Chapter 3) dismissed two such arguments that had been proposed, relating to communicative signals and dominance. He argued that rhesus monkeys are not learning the meaning of agonistic (aggressive, withdrawal) signals, because these do not occur in play fighting, only certain play signals specific to the play. He also argued that they are not learning dominance status, because of the role reversals in play fighting and chasing, and because a temporarily dominant animal does not take advantage of this and "cheat" in play fighting by hurting another.

However, Symons did argue that many of the actions in play fighting and chasing in primates (attempting to bite one another) are very similar to those used in real fighting, and therefore that the function of play fighting and chasing was practice for the skill and coordination needed to be a serious fighter when sexual maturity was reached. The play signals and avoidance of actual hurt make it a safe form of practice in infancy, before the serious fighting needed once sexual maturity is reached. The sex differences commonly observed in play fighting (more in males) is consistent with the greater role of fighting in intra-specific competition amongst adult males; and with the preferential selection of play partners of equal or possibly slighter greater strength to practice on. Consistent with Byers and Walker's (1995) views on locomotor play, play fighting might improve skilled motor performance in fighting rather than strength or endurance per se (which, on their argument, would only be temporary benefits). This training for fighting argument probably remains the most plausible function for much mammalian play, although direct evidence from individual differences is lacking.

However Pellis and Pellis (1998) argue that, in fact, the differences between playful and serious fighting render the practice function less likely; the targets of attack (the parts of the body the animal attempts to bite or play-bite) may differ, as does the sequence of movements (for example, animals allow alternation of roles and "counterattack" in play fighting, but try to prevent this in serious fighting). They argued that the functions of play fighting might be to overcome fear of retaliation in a fight or to get to know partner characteristics and changes in relationships. The Pellises worked with rodents and much of their argument is based on rodent play; but Biben (1998) has advanced broadly similar arguments based on squirrel monkey play (see Chapter 3). Advancing similar criticisms of the straightforward practice theory as Pellis and Pellis, she sees the likely roles of play fighting in this species as behavioral flexibility, becoming expert at reading intentions of others, reducing the stress of close bodily contact, experience in both the dominant and subordinate roles, and bravery in fighting.

In her work with meerkats (described in chapter 3), Sharpe (2005a) examined frequency of play fights in pups, juveniles, and subadults, and the likelihood of winning fights as an adult. She found no sex difference in play fighting; this is consistent with the design features prediction that play fighting is practice for real fighting, since in this species females do as much fighting as males. However, there were no correlations between frequency of play fighting and winning serious fights later; nor did role in play fights (e.g. chasing the other, getting the dominant position) predict this. Sharpe concluded on this and other evidence that "it seems most unlikely that the primary function of play in young mammals is the practice and refinement of adult motor skills" (p. 1028).

Panksepp (1993) has argued that play fighting is under the control of distinct neurophysiological mechanisms, and that "the main adaptive function of play may simply be the generation of positive emotional states" (p. 177). Lewis and Barton (2006), in a cross-species comparison of non-human primates, found that the relative volume of the amygdala and hypothalamus correlated with social play, but not nonsocial play, even after controlling for the size of other brain structures. The amygdala and hypothalamus become sexually differentiated by gonadal hormones, giving rise to sexually differentiated behaviors, which include play behaviors; the instinctive socioemotive aspects of play in primates appear to be regulated by the amygdala and hypothalamus. Lewis and Barton propose that behaviors such as social assessment, recognizing and responding to facial expression, and social response appropriateness, which are mediated by the amygdala, are developed through social play. The hypothalamus may regulate the motivation to engage in play through positive reinforcement of pleasurable activity.

Play fighting has also been thought of as a way of learning dominance status (as opposed to being familiar with dominant and subordinate roles). Poirier and Smith (1974) argued that through social play, "animals find their place in the existent social order." This was strongly argued against by Symons (1978), who pointed out that it conflicts with design characteristics such as inhibition of attack and role reversal. It also fails to explain the time course of play. Social play generally occurs before dominance ranks are established, or before an animal leaves its natal group to establish itself in a new one (Smith, 1982). Nevertheless, while this hypothesis is a poor candidate for most play fighting, it might be relevant for the rougher or intermediate types of play fighting seen in some species as sexual maturity is approached.

There are clearly unresolved issues about whether play fighting benefits an animal's subsequent fighting success. Another set of views is that play fighting and social play generally have a socializing function. The usual form of this hypothesis is that such play bouts result in social bonding. A variant is that it allows learning of social signals (e.g. for submission). A problem with such hypotheses is that they do not explain the prevalent sex differences found: social bonding and understanding social signals are just as important for females as for males. Nor do they explain partner preferences related to strength, familiarity or kinship. In primates, social grooming seems to be the main vehicle for bonding, rather than play.

Play as "training for the unexpected"

Play occurs in safe and familiar environments during the extended and protected juvenile period and in the presence of adequate resources (Burghardt, 2005). One theme occurring in the play literature (both animal and human) is that, when faced with a relatively unfamiliar, but safe, environment, play affords opportunity for behavioral and cognitive innovation and the subsequent practice of newly developed behaviors and strategies. Bruner (1972) emphasized the variability in play, and the possibility that play facilitated creative problem solving (a theme taken up in Chapter 7).

The role of play in the development of innovation was formalized by Špinka, Newberry, and Bekoff (2001) in what they labeled as the "training for the unexpected" hypothesis. This was applied to the locomotor and social play of animals, which was hypothesized to help them prepare for unexpected and novel environmental and social circumstances. They argued that, in the safe context of play, animals appear to place themselves into unconventional and often disorienting positions. Moreover, play behavior in itself can bring about new situations where learning can occur. These novel behavioral situations give them opportunities to experiment with a variety of routines in relatively safe circumstances and generate novel, and possibly adaptive, responses. With practice in play, animals become better at using these routines in other situations and generally more adept and flexible in coping with new circumstances which they are likely to encounter as adults.

Pellegrini, Dupuis, and Smith (2007) took this further by hypothesizing that because play affords opportunities for the generation of new, and possibly adaptive, responses to novel environments, it is an excellent candidate for an example of how behavior can affect evolutionary processes. Play behaviors are a low-cost way in which to develop alternative strategies to a new and challenging environment. The ease with which play and play-related behaviors spread through the population should relate to them being naturally selected for. The innovative outcomes of play could bring about changes in gene frequencies through processes of organic selection.

Organic selection refers to processes that allow environmentally acquired behaviors to influence the genotype, without invoking discredited Lamarckian ideas of evolution. Ideas of what are broadly called organic selection date back to at least Lloyd Morgan (1896) and Baldwin (1896). In modern terms, the idea is that environmental challenge activates or deactivates certain genes or alleles responsive to that challenge. But individuals with different genotypes may acquire or learn this new behavioral response with varying ease or efficiency. Although in each generation the new response is socially learnt, or at least environmentally acquired, nevertheless over a number of generations natural selection will favor those genotypes that more readily acquire this new behavior. Innovative behaviors associated with play during the juvenile period should be especially prone to this process because of the protection and provisioning associated with play during the juvenile period. Adolescence and adulthood are not typically characterized by this protected environment, so at these later stages of the life cycle it would be less effective to use play in skill learning than a more direct strategy, such as observational learning (Bateson, 2005).

One version of how the innovative behaviors developed in play might impact evolutionary processes was described by Waddington (1957) as genetic assimilation. Waddington's experiments were with fruit flies, and involved developmental modifications to adult flies as a result of early stressors (such as heat shock), and subsequent artificial selection; but more naturalistic examples of this effect are available (see also Bjorklund & Pellegrini, 2002). At least in Waddington's prototypic experiments, genetic assimilation involved delayed phenotypic response and rapid genetic change. However, organic selection as described by Bateson (2005) is seen as distinct from genetic assimilation. It involves rapid concurrent phenotypic change to a stressor, and delayed genetic change via the occurrence of mutations. Mutational change can allow an adaptive, acquired characteristic to be expressed more easily. In either case, however, characteristics that are acquired extra-genetically (including via play and learning processes) may in the long term bring about genotypic change.

The Possible Relevance for Human Play of Studying Animal Play

The sociobiological revolution (Wilson, 1975) reinvigorated animal ethology, providing a strong theoretical framework for understanding social interactions between conspecifics.

The core ideas of sociobiology have become widely accepted as central to understanding animal behavior. The ideas are also likely to have some relevance to understanding human behavior (Wilson, 1978). This has met considerable initial resistance and hostility; and, of course, as with any program, there has been some loose writing and loose theorizing. The debate now is generally a more reasoned one about the extent of the influence of evolutionary theories on understanding human behavior, and the terminology has changed from that of sociobiology to that of evolutionary psychology and, notably, evolutionary developmental psychology (Bjorklund & Pellegrini, 2002), with an explicit realization of the interplay of genetic predispositions and environmental influences in development.

One inference from animal play to human play would be that play has benefits. This could especially be made for locomotor play, object play, and play fighting, which show homologies to play in human children. By contrast, pretend or fantasy play appears more specifically human. But, interestingly, the two arguments for the non-functionality of animal play made at the start of this chapter (lack of adaptiveness in a new environment; and a non-functional spin-off of adaptive behaviors) might apply to human play. First, we do live in a very different environment from the one in which we evolved (arguably that of nomadic hunter-gatherers—see Chapter 5); we now mostly live in a "human zoo" (Morris, 1969). Adaptive functions of play might be "skewed" in this new kind of environment (play fighting is an obvious candidate for such consideration). Second, it is at least a plausible argument that particularly human forms of play (such as pretend play) are spin-offs from our generally high intelligence and curiosity (see e.g. Lancy, 2007). Where appropriate these ideas will be taken up for human play in subsequent chapters.

However a consideration of how human life-history differs appreciably from that of other mammals and primates (Bogin, 1999; Kaplan, Lancaster, Hill, & Hurtado, 2000), can provide a counterargument for the importance of play. Human infants are very immature and helpless at birth. Relative to brain size, the human gestation period is short when compared to other primates, probably because a longer pregnancy would have led to larger neonatal head size and severe birth complications, given the evolution of bipedalism and concomitant constraints on the size of the birth canal (see Trevathan, 1987). As a result, there is a long period of helpless infancy. There is also a long period of childhood from around 3–7 years (the child is weaned but still dependent on adults for food and protection), and there is what has been described as a separate juvenile period from around 7 years to adolescence, in which individuals are no longer dependent on parental care but are not yet sexually mature. In addition, there is a longer adolescent period before full adult stature and strength are reached (Bogin, 1999; Pereira, 1993). Comparatively, whereas growth is complete at around age 11 for chimpanzees and gorillas (our closest genetic relatives), this is at around age 20 for humans.

Lancaster and Lancaster (1987) argued that the long period of immaturity in humans was adaptive for an environment in which extensive parental investment could pay off in terms of skill acquisition by offspring, in a situation in which immediate productive activity by children might be difficult due to hazards (e.g. hunting) or the difficulty of extracting resources (e.g. foraging). "Skill acquisition" here could include both physical-growth-related capabilities (strength, general coordination) and cognitive and social learning. It involves acquiring competences useful for later life (but not necessarily very much later, bearing in mind that both subsistence responsibilities and reproductive opportunities would have started much earlier in traditional societies than is common in modern western societies).

The parental (and also grandparental) investment envisaged by Lancaster and Lancaster (1987) and others (e.g. Hawkes, O'Connell, Blurton Jones, Alvarez, & Charnov, 1998; Kaplan et al., 2000) might take the form of allowing or encouraging play activities, a view consonant with the hypothesis that play was broadly selected for when practice would be dangerous or ineffective (Smith, 1982). This view of play as especially important as a characteristic of human childhood does not necessarily go so far as Groos' (1901) view that childhood largely existed so that play could occur; but it does see play as part of a package of adaptations involving prolonged immaturity, opportunities for learning (in a broad sense), and parental investment in such learning (Lovejoy, 1981).

Further Reading

Major sources for animal play were given in Chapter 3.

Chapter 5
Play in Different Cultures
Yumi Gosso

Play is found in all human societies; no matter where they live or what language they speak, children spend time in playful activities. Playing is such a common phenomenon, and so naturally expected in children, that some cultures consider play to be the "job" or "work" of childhood (Takeuchi, 1994; and see Chapter 2). But although play has been observed in all societies where children have been studied, there is a lot of cultural variation. Each culture sees play in a distinct way, and the reaction of adults to play also varies. Play can be seen as an effect of culture, as adult culture influences the play that is seen; but it is also a cause of culture, as children's play reproduces but also changes culture over time (Carvalho & Rubiano, 2004; Roopnarine & Johnson, 1994). When children represent events which are common in adult life, they are bringing part of that culture into their play: for example, when pretending to herd cattle or pound rice (in traditional societies), or mimicking soap opera characters or playing at birthday parties (in modern societies). But when children create arbitrary rules (e.g. "only my pistol shoots"), or propose their own rules (e.g. "If the person doesn't throw sand on you, you can't call him 'silly.' If the person does throw sand on you, you can call him 'silly'!"), or create their own rituals, they are not just reproducing the adult culture, but also adding their own elements to it (Sutton-Smith, 1997).

Most people nowadays live in urban, technological societies. Most studies of play are based on observations of Western urban middle-class culture, although there are certainly variations by social class, and differences between Western and Eastern cultures. But even nowadays, many children do not live in cities or towns but in agricultural societies, where people subsist by being farmers or pastoralists. There are also still a few peoples who do not have permanent settlements and live predominantly by foraging: hunting animals and gathering plant foods.

Although the people who still practice it are now very few in number, the foraging way of life, also known as hunter-gathering, is of particular interest and importance. It is commonly argued to be the environment of evolutionary adaptedness for humans. This way of life was prevalent for more than 90% of the time that *Homo sapiens* has been in existence. The ancestors of modern humans led a hunter-gathering way of life for perhaps 2 million years. *Homo sapiens* appeared somewhere between 150,000 and 200,000 years ago. The advent of agriculture and animal husbandry, which had scarcely begun some 5,000 years ago, is unlikely to have played a large role in shaping the modern human genotype. Evolutionary psychologists consider that our basic psychological mechanisms were shaped in the context of the hunter-gathering way of life to solve specific adaptive problems (Bjorklund & Pellegrini, 2002; DeVore & Konner, 1970; Eibl-Eibesfeldt, 1989).

For this reason we start this chapter by describing the play of Parakanã Indian children. The Parakanã still live in a hunter-gatherer environment, so they may give us some idea of how our hunter-gatherer ancestors used to play. Following this, we will look at some general influences on children's play across different cultures, based on anthropological work. These include the time available for play, the companions and available objects for play, the social and physical environment, and the involvement of adults in children's play. These influences can help us understand the differences found amongst hunter-gatherer, pastoralist, and urban societies of various kinds.

Parakanã Children

The Parakanã Indians live in the north of Brazil, in a reserve in the municipalities of Novo Repartimento and Itupiranga in the state of Pará. They were first contacted in the 1970s, and since 1987 they have been helped by the Parakanã Program, a contract between the National Agency for Assistance to Indigenous People (FUNAI) and the Northern Electric Company (ELETRONORTE). The Parakanã Program offers health assistance, education, support for farming, and protection of reservation boundaries. According to the Parakanã Program census, in 2000 altogether 502 Indians were living in five villages, in a 21,858 square-mile reserve. The Parakanã Indians, who call themselves "awaete" (the real people), have little contact with "torias" (non-Indians). They do not have television or telephones. Women, children, and the elders in the villages only communicate through the Parakanã language; only the younger men speak Portuguese.

Parakanã Indians mainly live by hunting wild animals and gathering fruits and seeds, although they also grow manioc for their own consumption. They gather Brazil nuts and some palm fruit like *açaí* and *bacaba*; and they hunt land turtle, deer, alligator, tapir, peccary, armadillo, curassow (a big black bird), guans, paca, agouti (types of rodents), and several species of fish. Hunting is a male task, while cooking is a female task. Another important activity for women is preparing manioc flour. Women also make baskets with straw, and in ceremonies they do chanting and body painting. These activities are part of a woman's routine after the age of 25, but it is common to see girls taking the paint used by their mothers to paint their own arms.

Age stages in the Parakanã

Parakanã Indians divide individuals into age stages, and there are socialization patterns characteristic of each stage. From 0 to 3 years old, children are called *konomia pipi*, which means "little child." Most children are nursed until they are at least three years old. Up to this age, they stay close to their mothers or older siblings and, when the mother goes out to gather food, she usually carries her child up to age two. The end of this stage usually coincides with the birth of a sibling; that is when a change of status happens.

From 4 to 6 years old, children are named *konomia ete*, which means "those who are children." They now play in groups without adult supervision. They spend a lot of their time in the village and its vicinity, not only playing but also helping adults in their tasks, taking care of younger children, or searching for fruit to eat. Older children take care of younger ones when adults are not around. Even 5-year-old children can be seen carrying younger siblings or newborn cousins. It is common to see 6-year-old children carrying other 3-year-old children on their backs and jumping into the river, playfully diving and swimming, away from the eyes of adults. At this stage, the child is not given as much attention as "little children," and may be relatively ignored by adults and older children. The child, in turn, may react with fits of rage and bad mood, which are usually ignored. In this way the child soon learns that no one is special or superior. Among the Parakanã, a child can cry for several minutes without receiving any attention from adults.

From 7 to 10 years old, children are called *otyaro ere*, which means "the one who is growing up." The girls at this age begin to do some domestic work, while the boys start to join their fathers in hunting and fishing. From 11 to 15 years old, the Indians are named *otyaro*, which means "the one who is grown up." At this age some girls are married, and the boys go hunting by themselves.

At all of these age stages, there is no area which is strictly reserved for children. They have free access to every place in the village, go in and out of other people's houses, listen to and observe adult routines, and know everything that is happening in the village. They are excellent informants. There is no scolding or punishment for Indian children (Chaves, 2000; Cohn, 2002; Gosso, 2005), maybe because the adults believe that the children still can not understand or "hear" them. Xikrin Indians believe that children do not know certain things, because they cannot know them, "they still have weak ears" (Cohn, 2002). Yet, the children somehow understand which activities are appropriate for boys and girls, just as children from other cultures do.

Activities of Parakanã children

Young Parakanã girls observe and participate in their mothers' activities when they pound and toast flour. The pestle is used to prepare manioc flour, as in many Brazilian Indian cultures. In play, girls use the pestle to pretend they are pounding flour in an empty mortar. Another common form of play among Parakanã children involves collecting fruit in the woods. By 5 years, girls like to make baskets out of palm leaves in their play, but they also carry their mothers' straw baskets on their backs, and a large blade, and go to the woods in groups (Figure 5.1). There, using the blade, they collect non-edible fruits and use them to play.

Parakanã Indian children also mimic the festivities of their communities, singing and dancing like their parents do. Figure 5.2 shows a group of Parakanã boys singing and dancing, after pretending they were in a men-only meeting (a common activity in the village).

Parakanã boys also play with bows and arrows. Gosso and Otta (2003) observed three variations on this play among Parakanã boys: (1) throwing arrows upward, without a target; (2) practicing on a static target (e.g. a potato); and (3) following and hunting a living animal (e.g. a lizard or rat). Variations (1) and (2) were seen among 8-year-old boys, and (3) among 10 and 15-year-old boys. In one observation, some Parakanã men captured a wild cat in a trap. While the men were careful not to let the wild cat escape, they allowed some 7 to 11-year-old boys to kill the wild cat with their small bows and arrows (the ones they used in their play). The boys stood around the cat with their bows and arrows

Figure 5.1 Four to eight year-old Parakanã Indian children leaving for the woods with their mother's baskets

Figure 5.2 Parakanã Indian boys dancing like their fathers

in their hands and with very serious faces. When an adult said "go on," the boys began to shoot their arrows. The wild cat was killed by many little arrows, and all the men laughed, observing the boys' seriousness.

As we can see, the way of life and the behavior of adults toward children in the Parakanã society are very different from what we are used to observing in Western urban societies. Parakanã children represent their parents' activities in their play, as happens in other societies in which children have free access to all adult activities. Of course, the Parakanã are just one example. In the Brazilian context, Gosso, Morais, and Otta (2007) compared Parakanã children, children living by the seashore, and urban children of low, mixed, or high social status, and found appreciable differences in their play patterns. Many other studies in different societies find differences, but there are also some common themes. What factors contribute to the differences and similarities between cultures?

Factors Contributing to Cultural Similarities and Differences

The time available for play

One important aspect is simply the time available for play. Children in rural or agricultural societies, or who belong to low-income families, especially girls, often have less time available to play (Göncü et al., 2000; Larson & Verma, 1999). In such societies, children must do domestic chores in order to help the adults. Gaskins (2000), writing about Maya children, states that adults expect children to contribute to the work. From the age of 6 years on, they help their older siblings in domestic chores and take care of their younger siblings. The same is observed among Indian children (Gosso, 2005). As they grow, these children take on more responsibilities and more chores, and so the time available for play decreases.

Even though they need to work, children from those communities do not abandon play. Often, they find ways of amusing themselves in the task itself. For example, they may have the task of scaring birds from the crops; using a sling or improvised drums can be a fun way of doing this, combining work and play. Children may also intersperse some playful activity with the task; for example, they may play marbles with their friends on their way to the grocery, or chase birds when going out to search for water. Superimposing or interspersing work and play makes the chores less boring and adapts them to the status of the child (Punch, 2003).

Socio-economic circumstances are relevant, as pressure for children to help with work is more marked in lower-income groups. However, gender differences are actually more marked. Girls have less free time than boys, because they are given more domestic chores and it is they who primarily take care of younger siblings (Bock & Johnson, 2003; Edwards, 2000; Gosso, 2005; Larson & Verma, 1999; Maudin & Meeks, 1990). Larson and Verma (1999) compared findings from several studies, in non-industrial and industrial societies, on the time budgets of children and teenagers. They found that in nearly all non-industrial, rural societies, boys have 4% to 32% more free time than girls, because girls are required to carry out domestic chores more than boys.

In communities formed by groups of extended families where people help each other, as in some Indian communities, the boys also have more play time than girls (Gosso, 2005). Among Parakanã Indian children, Gosso observed that boys spend about 60% of their waking time in play, but girls only 48%. This difference was smaller in 4 to 6-year-old children (boys 59%; girls 51%) but increased in 7 to 12-year-old children (boys 61%; girls 45%). In literate industrial societies, differences in free time are smaller, but they still exist and in the same direction: boys have more free time than girls (Larson & Verma, 1999; Maudin & Meeks, 1990).

Companions and the available objects

Most studies in different cultures find that children prefer play companions of the same gender, even when it is possible to play with children of the opposite gender. This gender segregation is extensively documented in the literature and arises at around 3 years of age (Harlow, McGaugh, & Thompson, 1978; Maccoby, 1990; Serbin, Moller, Gulko, Powlishta, & Colburne, 1994). Boys and girls also tend to imitate the activities of their own gender in play, even when they are not encouraged to (Eibl-Eibesfeldt, 1989). The initial preference for companions of the same gender can be partly explained by the differing preferences of boys and girls for various play styles (activity level, play objects). It is also widely thought that children are establishing a social identity and a gender identity through involvement with reference groups in social situations (Tajfel & Turner, 1985); the better the understanding about sexual identity, the higher the preference for companions of the same gender (Erwin, 1993).

Harris (1995) argues that the division of children into gender-specific groups is universal. This is clearly not an absolute, but a significant

Table 5.1   Mean Percentage of Time Spent in Different Types of Play
Shown as a function of the gender and age group of the play partner

Focal child		Play companions								Solitary play
		Parallel play				Group play				
		Male		Female		Male		Female		
Age range		4–6	7–12	4–6	7–12	4–6	7–12	4–6	7–12	
Male	4–6	22.8	5.7	10.4	4.9	27.9	6.0	11.1	1.6	9.6
	7–12	8.5	28.4	4.3	6.3	2.4	39.7	1.0	5.3	4.1
Female	4–6	8.2	2.3	33.5	6.8	9.2	1.9	24.1	9.6	4.4
	7–12	2.1	3.0	1.7	10.9	5.1	12.5	16.3	38.5	9.9

tendency. Even if the number of children in a given community is very small, there will often be two groups: a group of boys and a group of girls, of varied ages. As the number of children increases, the groups will be divided by gender and also by age. Gosso (2005) observed this in a group of 29 Parakanã children aged from 4 to 12. Table 5.1 shows the percentage of time spent in parallel play and group play, according to the gender and age group (4 to 6-year-olds, and 7 to 12-year-olds) of the focal child and primary play companion; the frequencies highlighted in the table show the highest values. Clearly, children tended to play with companions of the same age and gender. Also, gender segregation increases with age.

There are very consistent data showing gender differences in play style, regardless of culture. In general terms, boys occupy more open spaces (Bichara, 2003; Levy, 1994), go farther from their houses to play (Edwards, 2000), play in larger groups (Sinker et al., 1993), spend more time in rough-and-tumble play (Beraldo, 1993; Goldstein, 1995; Gosso, 2005; Humphreys & Smith, 1987; Morais & Otta, 2003; Pellegrini & Smith, 1998a), prefer vehicle toys and blocks, and get more involved in activities that require gross motor movements (Bichara, 2002, 2003; Bloch, 1989; Smith, 2005). Girls correspondingly tend to occupy internal or smaller places, and play in smaller groups, often in twos, with a stricter selection of companions, prefer to play with dolls or other forms of domestic play (Bichara, 2003; Smith, 2005), and tend to act out social activities more often (Bjorklund & Pellegrini, 2000; Draper & Cashdan, 1988).

Explanations for those gender differences involve both biological and cognitive-developmental factors (Smith, 2005). There is clear evidence of the influence of sexual hormones in play behavior. Excessive exposure to male hormones during fetal development can highly increase the preference for activities or objects considered typically masculine, as compared to groups of children who were not exposed to those hormones (Bjorklund & Pellegrini, 2002; Humphreys & Smith, 1984; Pellegrini & Smith, 1998; Smith, 2005). But while the hormonal explanation may contribute to the more generic differences, there is also evidence of a strong cultural influence in the activities considered more appropriate for each gender. There are cultural differences in the understanding of which types of play are typically masculine or feminine by adults. For example Carvalho, Beraldo, Santos and Ortega (1993) found that Brazilian children from more traditional and less cosmopolitan cities, or from lower income families tended to classify fewer kinds of play as "for both sexes" than upper-middle-class children in large cities. This tendency increased with age.

In some, mainly traditional, societies, gender roles are very well defined. For example, Gikuyu children from Kenya use objects and carry out activities according to the practice of adults of the same sex (Leacock, 1978). Boys play making axes, knobkerries, spears, shields, slings, and bows and arrows. Girls play making pottery for cooking imaginary food, with clay or reed dolls, and mats or baskets of plaited grass. Another example is that of South American Indian children: boys play bows and arrows and girls make baskets (Clastres, 2003; Gosso & Otta, 2003; Gosso, 2005). From the age of 4 or 5, a boy receives a small bow from his father and a girl tries to weave her own basket or imitates her mother, doing body painting on her companions, all in a playful context, together with older sisters (Gosso, 2005). An Indian child will seldom do play activities which are typical of the opposite gender (Clastres, 2003).

Gender differences are less closely prescribed in some modern societies. Gosso, Morais and Otta (2006) observed the use of miniature domestic utensils (pretending to prepare food) in pre-school children's make-believe play in São Paulo, Brazil. The usual gender difference in favor of girls for this activity, was not seen in upper-middle-class children. There may be a decrease of gender stereotypy amongst higher socio-economic level parents and educators in technologically more advanced societies.

In another study (Carvalho, Smith, Hunter & Costabile, 1990), British and Italian children gave their opinion about five activities: rough-and-tumble play, catch, fights, football, and rope skipping. In general, the older the child, the more activities were considered "for both equally." Also, although rough-and-tumble play and football were seen as typically masculine activities, more girls stated that they were "for both equally," perhaps reflecting an increase of opportunities and activities for females in modern urban societies.

The social and physical environment

Usually, children represent in their play the sorts of activities that they see adults doing, and the values that are important for their society. The more the child can live close to adults in daily life, without many restrictions, the more contact he or she will have with the routines of the society, and the more realistically he or she will be able to represent it in play activities. In hunter-gatherer societies, as seen above with the Parakanã, children have free, unrestrained circulation in the village or community, accompanying adults from a very young age. They observe others attentively, play in groups of mixed ages, and the older children take care of the younger ones (Gosso, 2005).

Studies with children from hunter-gatherer societies show that their types of play are very similar to the activities of the adults in the group (Gosso, Otta, Morais, Ribeiro & Bussab, 2005; Kamei, 2005; Konner, 1972; Leacock, 1978). The children are in frequent contact with adults and their activities. Their play, often imitative of adult subsistence activities, can be interpreted as training for adult life and as a substitute for formal education (Kamei, 2005; Leacock, 1978; and see Chapter 9). For example, Baka hunter-gatherer children, living in the African tropical forest, predominantly play at hunting, collecting, house, and music and dance. Boys make guns from the stem of a papaya, attack animals with stones, shoot plants and inanimate objects with bows and arrows, mimic the forest spirits with songs, and play a flute made of a papaya stem. Girls play with dolls, play "aita" (a guitar with seven strings), play with a miniature bunch of bananas, etc (Kamei, 2005). Children also imitate the festivities of the community in play. !Ko children (Eibl-Eibesfeldt, 1989) and !Kung children (Shostak, 1981) have been observed playing trance dance. Mehináku Indian children represent the daily scenes of the community with a profusion of details, such as marriages, bet-rayals, gift-exchanging between tribes, and the healing of the sick (Gregor, 1982).

In pre-industrial cultures generally, the education of children is a more natural and casual process, through observation and imitation of adult behavior. In the make-believe (Neé-pele) of the Kpelle children from Liberia, 4 to 11-year-old boys and girls represent some of the routine activities of adults. For instance, Lancy (1996) observed a Kpelle boy with a bell, chasing two small girls who ran around the kitchen. The boy was pretending he was a dog, and the girls, antelopes. Kpelle men, when hunting antelopes, use small dogs with bells around their necks. Another type of play observed among 4 to 6-year-old Kpelle girls was to pound rice in dirt mortars. They use pestles which are nearly 1 metre long to pound, and several girls pound together at the same time. In a rural community from Nyansongo, Kenya, children were observed helping the adults in work activities, such as taking care of the animals and of smaller children. The adults did not encourage play, neither did they offer help or toys for playful activities. The children played with their siblings and cousins in mixed-age groups, and, in general, combined play with their tasks (Edwards, 2000). A'uwe-Xavante Indian children also combine play with domestic tasks (Nunes, 2002).

Morais and Otta (2003) observed the play of 19 children aged around 5 years in a school located in Itamambuca beach, on the north coast of São Paulo state. Most of the fathers of the children were tenants or gardeners, and most of the mothers were house cleaners. These children had a large free area to play in, formed mainly by a football field surrounded by native woods. The children pretended to ride horses or to be dogs, introduced imaginary snakes into the play scene, did small purchases in grocery shops, swept the garden, swam in the river, and bathed in waterfalls. These types of activity were not found in the play of urban children. These plays represented the adult routine in the local beach community.

The modern urban situation is very different. In places where television is available, children spend less time playing than children who do not have television (Van der Voort & Valkenburg, 1994). Takeuchi (1994) found that the time spent in play outside the house by Japanese boys was inversely proportional to the time spent on video games. By contrast, children who live in rural places, even with some access to the media, often have more freedom, little adult intervention, large spaces, and many available companions; all factors that favor the occurrence of play.

In industrial societies, children typically see a more restricted range of adult work activities; but they have more access to manufactured toys and to the mass media. Children do imitate daily life activities in their play, such as cooking, showering, talking on the phone, going shopping, taking care of baby dolls; but they also engage in play outside of this range such as space travel, magic carpets, super-heroes, ghosts (Edwards, 2000). Morais and Carvalho (1994) recorded 237 episodes of make-believe play among 4-year-old children in free play in a pre-school in São Paulo, Brazil. There was a lot of influence of media characters in the choice of pretend themes, more markedly among boys than among girls.

This gender difference was also noted in a review by Van der Voort and Valkenburg (1994) of the influence of TV on symbolic play. While girls played food, domestic scenes (mother, daughter, maid), house and castle building, and imitated animals such as butterflies and birds, boys played superheroes, fighting with and without weapons (swords, revolvers), police chases, war, planes, skyrockets, and trains, and imitated animals such as lions and dinosaurs. The greater media involvement in boys' play themes can be explained by the absence of contact with a male role in daily life, carrying out common activities, and also because most of the main characters in hero, action and war movies are male.

In large urban centers, when both parents work, usually children stay with a caregiver or in an institution such as a day care center. Either way, the caregivers are usually female, and this provides children with more contact with female role models; relative to girls, boys lack role models of their own sex for realistic activities. Morais and Carvalho noted that when the father was represented in symbolic play, he was shown driving the car, leaving for work or coming home from work, without any concrete activity in the intervals. In the context of a large city such as São Paulo, "the father tends to be a distant and not very accessible model for the boy" (Morais & Carvalho, 1994, p. 24).

The involvement of adults in children's play: three kinds of society?

The way adults from a given culture see play has an important influence in several ways: the interactions between parents and children, the stimulus given to the children, the availability of toys or spaces for play. We saw in Chapter 2 how the "play ethos" developed in modern western societies, placing a high value on play and the role of play in learning. The conception that play is important for child development and therefore must be stimulated is much more evident in societies with more access to information, in the middle and upper classes (Göncü et al., 2000), in industrial societies (Roopnarine & Johnson, 1994), and in European American families (Farver, Kim & Lee-Shin, 2000). Gaskins, Haight and Lancy (2007) describe three types of societies with differing prevailing attitudes to play. They call these "culturally cultivated play," "culturally accepted play," and "culturally curtailed play."

Culturally cultivated play refers primarily to urban, middle-class Euroamerican families. Such families emphasize individuality and self-expression, and (following the play ethos, Chapter 2) "believe that 'play is the child's work' " (p. 181). In these kinds of families, parents try to play with their children, the children go to day care centers or schools where there are many objects to play with, and play is stimulated not only by the presence of toys, but also by caretakers who play. The parents, when playing, think of the importance of that activity for the cognitive development of the children and increasing their social skills (Farver et al., 2000; Roopnarine & Johnson, 1994). In some societies, like the USA, direct teaching is criticized as inappropriate for very young children from the developmental viewpoint, and play is preferable to promote competence and academic success (Bornstein et al., 1999); educators and caretakers are encouraged to play with children and to use play as a means of teaching.

A study by Göncü, Mistry, and Mosier (2000) in urban areas of Kecioren, Turkey, and Salt Lake City, USA, found that child activities are segregated from adults, and children remain under the care of a care-taker while their parents work. In these societies, where the availability of children of the same age to play is restricted, children play with adults more than with other children. Caregivers often carry out activities in a playful manner, and value play, as they believe that play contributes to the development of the child and prepares the child for school. There are of course variations within this range of attitudes. In Taiwan, for example, mothers typically encourage pretend play, but also use it to practice proper conduct, for example, when addressing others, and appro-priate social routines (Haight, Wang, Fung, Williams, & Mintz, 1999).

Culturally accepted play refers to societies where parents typically expect children to play and do not disapprove of it, but neither do they invest much time or energy in supporting it. Lancy's (1996) work with the Kpelle people in Liberia is cited as an example; Bock's study in the Okavango Delta (see Chapter 7) would likely provide another. Children, especially by around 6 years, start to be seen as useful in looking after younger siblings and performing subsistence tasks, but adults see play as harm-less and and a means of keeping children busy and out of the way until they are old enough to be useful.

Generally in non-industrial societies (Roopnarine, Hossain, Gill, & Brophy, 1994), rural societies, or low-income families (Göncü et al., 2000), adults do not encourage play, neither do they try to dedicate time to playing with their children. Play is definitely not a concern of the adult in these societies. The play partner of the children, most of the time, is not an adult. Adults are concerned with their daily tasks and delegate play to other children. That way, children play more with other children, without constant adult supervision, in spaces which are not especially structured for play, and with objects which are naturally available (rather than manufactured toys).

In these societies, when an adult plays with a child, there is no concern about the benefits of play for the development of the child, as happens in industrial western societies. In India, for example, when parents play with their children, they play for the pleasure of the play itself and to make their children happy (Roopnarine et al., 1994). Martini (1994) observed children in the Marquesas Islands, Polynesia. When the men leave the house early to fish, the women are busy with several domestic chores; the children get up, make their own breakfast, care for smaller siblings, do small domestic tasks, and go to school. Children play in groups, away from adult supervision, and do not usually ask them to solve conflicts that arise in play. After observing hunter-gatherer children, and other societies in which play is not considered important for the cognitive development of the children, Gosso et al. (2005) argued that one of the functions of play is to keep children busy so that the adults can carry out their chores.

In some agrarian subsistence communities, such as in San Pedro, in Guatemala, and Dhol-Ki-Patti, in India, where children participate in adult activities and contribute to the family economy from a very early age, play is also seen as a child activity, and the adults leave the children free to play among themselves. The caregivers in those communities think object exploration is appropriate for the child alone, without adults. Often, the play groups are formed not only by relatives of the child (siblings and cousins) but also by other children in the community. There is a low frequency of play in adult–child pairs, and there is a higher frequency of play in complex groups, formed by relatives and neighbors (Göncü et al., 2000).

Culturally curtailed play refers to societies where adults will tolerate only miminum amounts of play. Gaskins' (1996, 1999, 2000) study of the Yucatan Maya people of Mexico is cited as an example. Children are busy running errands, accompanying parents etc, from 3 or 4 years. Parents believe that children need to acquire skills through observation and imitation; play has no privileged position. Indeed, play is seen as "having little purpose beyond being a distraction for children when they cannot help with the work to be done and as a signal that the children are healthy," and "extensive pretense in particular is of questionable appropriateness. Adults believe that one should not lie even in jest, and fiction, written or oral, is not a valued genre" (Gaskins et al., 2007, p. 192). The Maya only value play in so far as it distracts children and allows adults to finish their tasks, and also because it is a sign of health (Gaskins, 2000).

The physical environment

Different adult conceptions of play can be seen not only through adults' behavior towards children's play but also through the objects offered. The objects made available to children have meaning, and indeed can be loaded with cultural values from the society to which they belong. Toys are chosen to entertain children, to satisfy their physical and socio-emotional needs, but also because they are social symbols which make explicit reference to cultural attitudes and practices (Gosso et al., 2006).

For example, the type of object offered to the child may encourage certain types of play. In American and European societies which value play (Haight et al., 1999) and in upper-middle-class schools in Brazil (Gosso et al., 2006), children are offered many miniature objects which favor symbolic play. In other societies, where the available objects are natural materials such as stones, sand, water, and other objects that have no specific function or are little structured (boxes, cardboard cylinders, etc.), children more often play alone or in parallel with other children (Rubin & Howe, 1985).

In many South American Indian communities, boys receive toy bows and arrows from their father, while girls receive baskets from their mother (Clastres, 2003; Gosso, 2005). Here, the Indian parents are simply reproducing what their parents did for them before; they are following a tradition, without explicitly teaching or encouraging gender roles. A person who observes an Indian village notices that the adults are, apparently, not worried about the children's development. The meaning of the objects that are given to the children, however, is very important for such communities (Gosso, 2005). The Indian girl does not expect to receive a bow and arrows, nor does the boy expect to receive a basket! Similarly, in other cultures it is not expected that a boy receive a doll or the girl, a toy car. Toys are symbols that transmit explicit meanings to the child, but they are also the tools used by the children to express their imagination in an autonomous way, as well as their socio-emotional growth (Sutton-Smith, 1986).

Societies that value cognitive development and symbolic and abstract thought, often offer toys whose function is to stimulate the child's cognitive, symbolic, and linguistic skills. By contrast, there are other cultural groups that, adopting cooperative values and emphasizing practical reasoning, encourage play that involves physical and practical activities and cooperative games (Gosso et al., 2005; Morais, 2004). The choice of objects and activities offered to the child is more conscious in those societies which play that their children in order to develop specific skills. In societies where this concern is not present, the objects and opportunities are offered as they have always been, following tradition, without a conscious purpose; nevertheless, when play is observed carefully and in detail, it can be seen that play reproduces the adult culture, filtered by the child's view, and the values which are important for that culture will be present in that reproduction (Gosso et al., 2005).

Similarities and Differences across Cultures

Children everywhere play, regardless of culture and place, and everywhere a child playing is a sign of healthy development. But play does vary greatly in different cultures, and through the study of children's play, we can not only understand important psychological processes but also learn more about the socio-cultural dimension of societies. Play has universal dimensions, but also culture-specific aspects.

Cross-cultural studies show that, both in subsistence and industrial societies, girls seem to have less free time to play than boys. This is mainly due to the higher demand for girls to perform domestic tasks and take care of younger siblings. Also, the domestic chores usually given to girls, such as house cleaning, care of younger siblings, and food preparation are carried out inside the house, while the chores usually given to boys, such as gardening and running errands, are done outside the house (Larson & Verma, 1999). Boys are not as closely observed by adults, and maybe have more opportunities to intermix tasks with play than girls.

Another similarity observed in play across cultures is the gender difference, and the gender and age segregation of play groups. Gender segregation has been extensively documented, as well as the difference between boys and girls in their play. From a very early age, children grow up approaching other children of the same gender and age. There seem to be common interests that naturally bring them together, regardless of the place in which they are raised. Beliefs that boys should play in a certain way, while girls should play in a different way also exert an influence, more strongly in some cultures than in others.

Among the differences in play, growing industrialization has changed some aspects of family organization, which, in turn, have altered child rearing and also the availability of companions. In non-industrial, more traditional, extended-family societies, parents trust their relatives, close friends, and even older children to help take care of their children. Children play with their peers, who may be cousins, siblings, and friends, not necessarily of the same age, in a rich and complex environment from the viewpoint of social interaction. In most of those societies, adults are busy with their subsistence tasks, and playful activities seem to be "children's business." According to Lancy (1996), children simply imitate their parents, and so learn about the main tasks and routines of their socio-cultural group.

At the other extreme, in industrial, nuclear-family societies, children start going to day care centers from a very early age, spending more time with children of the same age than with children of different ages, as their mothers are in work and can not count on help from relatives or friends to take care of their children. Also, the time spent with children of different ages is limited. In these societies, there is more concern with play and its implications for the healthy development of the child. More stimulus is given through playful interactions between adult and child, and the activities offered to the child take that concern into account, as well as being informed by child development research.

This concern with play and more playful interaction between parents and children in modern societies may be a consequence of losing some of the opportunities for play with peers that naturally occur in non-industrial societies. But, adult–child play is different from child–child play, and the play among peers in a school or day care center environment is different from the play among children of different ages in environments without adult supervision. In schools and day care centers, the caretakers are responsible for the children, and must make sure that the child is not in danger. Any problem is the responsibility of the institution. This concern, sometimes excessive, and the constant supervision that results from it, may hinder the child from learning the limits of his or her own competence, as well as that of his or her companions, during play.

American Indian children (Cohn, 2002; Gosso, 2005; Gosso et al., 2005) and children from the Marquesas Islands (Martini, 1994) play in rough places without any adult supervision; there are also sharp and dangerous objects within their reach, and yet they do not get hurt very often. Among the Parakanã children studied by Gosso (2005), there are no records of accidents involving sharp objects. Somehow, there must be some informal instruction, perhaps from older peers, which efficiently transmits information on how to deal with the dangers of the environment, and how to properly use dangerous objects. Perhaps in modern societies our education is not as efficient at teaching these limits in a natural way, as happens in other societies; therefore, we must constantly watch our children.

The interaction with children of other ages may also have unique functional importance. This type of interaction may provide a better understanding of the other, both in the sense that older children accept the limitations of younger children, and that younger children learn to deal with older children, while, in general, the children learn to negotiate play without much adult interference. The socialization of children of different ages usually results in more opportunities for the care of younger children by the older ones, called "mothering" by Carvalho and Beraldo (1989), who define it as the "precocious presence of the capacity of recognizing and assuming the other's perspective, and of reacting empathically" (p. 59).

The lifestyle in modern societies has limited the opportunities to play with children of varied ages in diverse environments; at the same time, and maybe as a compensation for that limitation, it offers alternatives such as very elaborate toys, electronic games, and much more frequent adult–child interaction. Comparing this scenario to that of non-industrial societies in which children are free to play with whatever and whomever they want, it seems that modern societies are more focused on children than non-industrial societies, where the child was just another member of the society, with no special status. This does not mean that children are more important in modern societies than in traditional ones. In general, children are loved; for example, there are reports of great care and affection towards the child not only among Brazilian Indians in the 16th and 17th centuries (Chaves, 2000), but also more recently among Xavante Indians (Maybury-Lewis, 1956; Nunes, 2002).

An important difference between subsistence communities which live in extended family groups (e.g. Indians, hunter-gatherers, rural societies) and the nuclear families of modern societies may be that in the former, when a new child is born, the older child loses his or her status and becomes just another member of the community. From then on, life changes, and so does the intensity of the attention given to that child. This happens around the age of 3 or 4, after weaning, and when the child can already walk along with older children, who then take care of the younger ones.

In modern societies, couples have fewer children; many have an only child; children usually receive much the same level of attention until adulthood. When another child is born, the older child does lose some of the parents' attention, but they are typically concerned to not make the first child feel rejected. The difference in the change of the child's status can be largely explained by the number of children per family. In subsistence societies, couples have many more children than in modern societies, so parental investment per child is less.

In a general way, regardless of the society, all studies indicate that children play with the reality that they are allowed to observe, creating their own culture. Children who live freely among adults, with no media and not much supervision, and children who have some access to adult activities even with some presence of the media, can represent quite well the adult activities of their communities. Children from large urban centers also represent the activities of adults in their communities, when they play shopping, and when they imitate their father leaving for or arriving home from work. That is the reality that they are usually able to see. Also, as a great part of their time is spent observing media characters, there is an influence of those characters in their play activities.

Children from all societies create their own ways of representing the world, not only through the observation of the adults, but also through interaction with other children. They mix components from their own reality, their creativity, and their imagination to alter and create new rules, or to insert new elements into play. All of this is more readily understood when shared with other children from the same social group.

Further Reading

H. Schwartzmann, *Transformations: The Anthropology of Children's Play* (1978) is a thoughtful and wide-ranging book, that provided an impetus for anthropologists to returen seriously to the topioc of children's play. For an anthropological perspective on play in a specific culture, D. F. Lancy 1996: *Playing on the Mother-Ground*, New York: Guilford Press, is an account of play in the life of the Kpelle people of Liberia.

Chapter 6

Physical Activity Play: Exercise Play and Rough-and-Tumble

The majority of discussion of children's play in both books and research articles relates to play with objects, pretend play, and sociodramatic play—topics we will examine further in Chapters 7, 8, and 9. Indeed, the two major classificatory schemes of play by Piaget and Smilansky, which we reviewed in Chapter 2, basically focused on these, and paid no attention to physical activity play or rough-and-tumble play. Object, pretend, and sociodramatic play also capture the interest of teachers, because they appear to have important benefits and functions for learning skills that teachers and educators believe to be useful. Various theorists and researchers have argued that such forms of play foster problem-solving skills, creativity, language use, social skills such as role-playing, and cognitive skills such as conservation ability (e.g. Bruner, 1972; Dansky & Silverman, 1975). While these claims may have been overenthusiastically embraced, once the research evidence is considered carefully (Smith, 1988), it is certainly plausible that object and pretend play give useful and enjoyable experiences in which many skills can be acquired. Also, such forms of play are usually quiet and "well-managed" in a classroom or playgroup environment.

Perhaps as a result of these factors, physical activity play has been relatively neglected in the research literature and by educators. But we know that children actually spend a lot of time running around, jumping, climbing, skipping, and play fighting—often just for fun, though sometimes as part of games such as "tag." Such play might involve objects (trees, a skipping rope, etc.) but often does not. This chapter will review these kinds of play, including play-fighting or rough-and-tumble play. What kinds of play are involved? What age and sex differences do we find? What do children gain from these kinds of play, and what function might they have in development? Some implications for parents, teachers, playground supervisors and playworkers are returned to in Chapter 10.

Stages in Physical Activity Play

Pellegrini and Smith (1998a) provided an extensive review of the research evidence regarding physical activity play. They argued that physical activity play (defined as involving large muscle activity) has three main types following overlapping but sequential time courses. First were "rhythmic stereotypies": bodily movements that are characteristic of babies such as kicking legs and waving arms. This is followed during the preschool years by "exercise play": running around, jumping, climbing—whole body movements which may be done alone or with others; this increases in frequency from toddlers to preschool and peaks at early primary school (childhood) ages, then declines in frequency. Overlapping with and succeeding this is "rough-and-tumble play," play fighting and play chasing; this increases in frequency from toddlers, through the preschool and primary school ages, to peak at late primary or middle school ages, and then declines.

Rhythmic stereotypies

Rhythmic stereotypies have been discussed in detail by Thelen (1979), who made longitudinal studies of this during the first year of life. She defines them as gross motor movements without any apparent function, such as body rocking and foot kicking. These were also described by Piaget in his writings on sensorimotor play. The onset of rhythmic stereotypies is probably controlled by neuromuscular maturation. They are first observed at birth and peak around six months of age. Infants spend about 5% of their time on average doing these rhythmic stereotypic behaviors (Thelen, 1980), but this can rise to about 40% at peak periods. Although this is usually a solitary activity, similar physical play opportunities can occur in the context of adult–child interaction. For example, parents bouncing infants on their knees and throwing them in the air (Roopnarine, Hooper, Ahmeduzzaman, & Pollack, 1993; Thelen, 1980) provide vestibular stimulation and gross body movements.

Exercise play

Exercise play is gross locomotor movement, such as running and climbing, in the context of play. It is physically vigorous and may or may not be social. Exercise play can start at the end of the first year, as toddlers become mobile, and initially much of it (like the later aspects of rhythmic stereotypies) may take place in the context of adult–child interaction. This is sometimes referred to as "rough physical play," in which, for example, an adult (usually a parent, and often the father in such cases) chases the toddler, or throws, rolls over, or tickles him or her, such that the toddler (as well as the adult!) experiences gross locomotor movements. MacDonald and Parke (1986) reported that this peaks at around 4 years. Some of these play forms appear to be precursors if not examples of rough-and-tumble play, which we come to in the next section. Indeed many studies do not differentiate exercise play from rough-and-tumble or pretend play, with which it co-occurs. Thus, it may be underreported in the literature.

In the toddler years, exercise play is reported to take up some 7–10% of time in day care settings (Field, 1994; Rosenthal, 1994). It appears to increase in frequency with age, and (like other forms of play) follows an inverted-U developmental curve, peaking at around 4 to 5 years (Eaton & Yu, 1989; Routh, Schroeder & O'Tuama, 1974). For example, in work I carried out observing 3 to 4-year-olds in playgroups (Smith & Connolly, 1980), vigorous physical activities (such as running, chasing, climbing) occurred in 21% of the samples of behavior I recorded (some of this might have been non-playful; and some might have been rough-and-tumble). A very similar level, 20%, was reported in a study by McGrew (1972).

As children move into primary school the rates of exercise play decline. Opportunities for such play are less, being restricted mainly to break times in school playgrounds. In 6–10 year olds, Pellegrini (1995a) found that exercise play accounted for some 13% of observations of outdoor play during playground breaks (and of course it would be much less indoors). Simons-Morton, O'Hara, Parcel, Huang, Baranowski, and Wilson (1990), in a study of children's exercise and physical fitness in 9 to 10-year-olds, obtained self-reported frequencies of moderate to vigorous physical activity across a three-day period. They found that children exercise more before and after school than during school. Over the course of each day, they engaged in one or two bouts of moderate to vigorous physical activity (of 10 minutes or longer).

A number of factors affect exercise play. One is simply the amount of space available. In a series of experimental studies I carried out with Kevin Connolly in the 1970s (Smith & Connolly, 1980), we ran two preschool playgroups and varied aspects such as the amount of toys available and the amount of space. Generally, toy availability had much more impact on children's behavior than space availability; but a clear exception was physically vigorous activity, much of which was exercise play. We had three conditions of space availability, produced by moving large curtain screens in a very spacious church hall. These were either 25 sq. ft per child (the recommended minimum), 50 sq. ft per child (probably typical of many playgroups or nurseries), or 75 sq. ft per child (this last condition feeling more like an outside play area, although all were held indoors). Physically vigorous activity showed a clear increase as more space was available. It is obviously easier to move around quickly in a place with lots of space than in one that is restricted. Interestingly, although there was less vigorous physical activity in the more confined conditions, there was some shift from running to climbing (usually using some climbing apparatus provided). While not sufficient to balance out the reduced opportunities for running around, this could be interpreted as an attempt to "compensate" for this, vertically rather than horizontally!

In fact, young children do seem to need opportunities for physical exercise more than older children. They are more likely to get restless after long sedentary periods and to run around when released from them. This has been shown by naturalistic "deprivation" studies. The first of these was carried out by Theresa Hagan and myself (Smith & Hagan, 1980). We looked at the amount of physical activity play shown by 3 and 4-year-olds in an outdoor playground after varying lengths of time indoors (30 minutes or 90 minutes). There was much less space available indoors, and vigorous physical activity was discouraged. Irrespective of length of session indoors, the outdoor sessions started with high rates of physical activity play, falling off over time, but the initial and overall rates were significantly higher after the longer indoor period (see Figure 6.1).

It seems that when children are deprived of an opportunity to exercise and then given an opportunity, the intensity and duration of exercise increase. This was also found by Pellegrini, Huberty, and Jones (1995) in a study in the USA with 5 to 9-year-olds. They replicated the finding of higher levels of physical activity after a longer indoor "deprivation" period, although this was especially marked for boys compared to girls.

It may be the case that during the period of childhood, when skeletal and muscular systems are maturing quite rapidly, the body overcompensates for lost opportunities to exercise these rapidly developing systems.

Besides the available space, what is in the space is important too. Soft surfaces encourage more physical activity play than hard ones. And the provision of a certain amount of interesting equipment, such as climbing frames and rope ladders can provide more opportunity for a variety of exercise play. In a study of two adventure playgrounds in

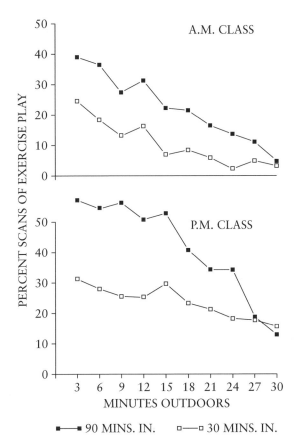

Figure 6.1 Changes in outdoor physical activity levels in preschool children, over time, after a shorter or longer period of sedentary indoor activity
(from Smith & Hagan, 1980)

London, Hughes (2007) filmed and recorded relatively low levels of loco-motor play in what he called "dead areas"— areas that were underused as of little interest. By adding a rope bridge in one playground and a series of rope runways in the second, locomotor play increased from 42% (playground one) and 18% (playground two) to about 70%, in both playgrounds. This increase was not just a temporary effect due to explora-tion of the new items, as Hughes waited one month before filming at the post-test. Rather, the equipment provided scope for fantasy and chasing games, involving vigorous motor activity, that had not been facilit-ated before.

Malnourishment is another factor that inhibits exercise play. When short of food, the body probably uses valuable nutrients for physical growth, rather than exercise play. Finally, low levels of exercise play are observed in tropical climates (Cullumbine, 1950), just as in playgrounds lower levels of exercise play are observed during warm periods, compared to cool periods (Smith & Hagan, 1980; Pellegrini et al., 1995).

Rough-and-Tumble Play

Play fighting, or rough-and-tumble play, is a common form of peer interaction throughout the school years. It involves wrestling, grappling, kicking, tumbling and rolling on the ground, and chasing (see Figure 6.2). Although rough-and-tumble play (often shortened to R&T) was neglected

Figure 6.2 Rough-and-tumble play
(author's photo: Plate 7.2 in Smith, Cowie, & Blades 2003: p. 215)]

Table 6.1   Percentage Responses by Boys to Questions Regarding Play Fighting
(adapted from Smith, Hunter, Carvalho and Costabile, 1992, and Smith, Smees, Pellegrini and Menesini, 2002)

	Do you ever play-fight?	Do you ever play-chase?	Do you like play fighting?	Can you tell if children are just play fighting rather than real fighting?	Can a play fight lead to a real fight?
5 yrs N=33 Smith et al. 1992	70	91	58	82	79
5–8 yrs N=44 Smith et al. 2002	70	81	56	93	88
8 yrs N=24 Smith et al. 1992	50	83	50	75	79
10 yrs N=24 Smith et al. 1992	58	83	67	96	79

for a long time by psychologists, there is now a reasonable body of literature on this form of play in children, which is very common (as also, as we saw in Chapter 3, in many mammals). Table 6.1 shows responses to questions put about play fighting, to children aged 5 to 10 years. A majority say they take part in it (especially play chasing, which is more common in girls than play fighting), and a majority say they enjoy it, although not all do. When children are asked why, the most common response is that "it is fun." If they do not enjoy it, the most common reason is that "you might get hurt" (Smith, Smees, Pellegrini, & Menesini, 2002).

R&T tends to increase through the preschool and early school years. Early on parents may get involved in "rough physical play," but from 3 and 4 years onwards it takes place predominantly between peers. The frequency of R&T seems to increase from around 3–5% of free time behavior in preschoolers, to 7–8% in 6 to 10-year-olds, and 10% in 7 to 11-year-olds, before declining to around 5% in 11 to 13-year-olds and 3% in 14-year-olds (Pellegrini & Smith, 1998a). Figure 6.3, showing time budgets for the playground activities of 7 to 11-year-olds (Humphreys & Smith, 1987), gives a figure of about 10% at this peak period, compared to about 1% of time spent in real fighting. Obviously the 10% figure, like the others cited, is quite variable; for example, it

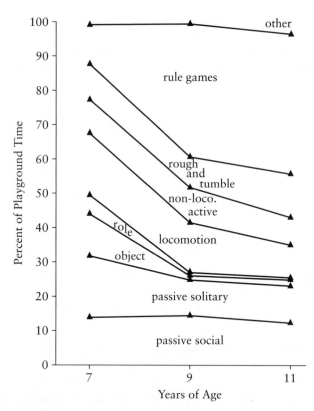

Figure 6.3 Playground time budgets of 7, 9 and 11-year-old children. (from Humphreys and Smith, 1987)

depends on factors such as how soft or hard the play surface is! Children do much more on soft grassy areas than on hard concrete, especially play fighting. Nevertheless the inverted U curve with a peak in the pre-adolescence years seems well established.

Partners in R&T

Children sometimes chase or wrestle in pairs, but also in larger groups, with children joining in a melee for shorter or longer periods. Pellegrini (1993) found groups of three or four children to be very common in this activity. In addition, friends are often chosen as R&T partners. This is the case at nursery school (Smith & Lewis, 1985), and through the primary school years. Humphreys and Smith (1987) observed R&T play partners in 7, 9 and 11-year-olds, and found that at all ages friends were preferentially chosen. In this latter study we also assessed dominance ranking in children—who they think is tougher or stronger. This did not bear any relationship to choice of play partner in R&T episodes, for 7 and 9-year-olds. However, it did for 11-year-olds: we found a statistically significant tendency for 11-year-olds to choose play partners close in dominance ranking to them, but on average slightly lower.

Telling play fighting and real fighting apart

Play fighting superficially looks like real fighting; after all, similar behaviors (chasing, hitting, kicking, wrestling) are involved. But a number of criteria, established by ethological observations, and confirmed by live and video-based playback interviews with children (and adults) differentiate the two.

Unlike real fighting, play fighting is characterized by positive facial expressions (as shown by a "play face," laughter, or smile), self-handicapping (a stronger child does not necessarily "win"), restraint (in play, kicks and blows are not hard or do not make contact at all), role-reversal (children may voluntarily take it in turns to be "on top" or be "chased"), and how the encounter starts and finishes (in play, starting by an invitation and ending with continued play or activity together; in real fights, starting with a challenge and ending in separation) (Boulton, 1991; Fry, 1987; Pellegrini, 1988, 2002; Smith, 1997). A full table summarizing such differences is presented in Table 6.2.

When asked, most children do indeed say that they can tell play fighting from real fighting (see Table 6.1). This can also be assessed by playing children sections of videotape showing either play fighting or real fighting, and asking them to say which they think it is, and why. Most children can do well at this task, and from 8 years they give reasons in terms of criteria similar to those in Table 6.2: for example, "it was only a play fight because he didn't hit him hard"; "it was a real fight because they were both angry"; "that was a play fight as the other boys didn't watch them." Even at 4 years, some cues are recognized and can be explained by many children (Smith & Lewis, 1985). In one study English and Italian 8 to 11-year-old children were found to be accurate in judging videotapes of play fighting and real fighting, irrespective of whether they were watching children of their own or the other nationality (Costabile, Smith, Matheson, Aston, Hunter, & Boulton, 1991)—and, when asked, they responded in terms of many of the criteria given in Table 6.2.

Table 6.2   Main Ways in Which Play Fighting and Real Fighting Episodes Can Be Distinguished

Criterion	In R&T	In real fighting
Circumstances leading to an encounter	No conflict over resources	Frequently conflict over resources such as space, toys, equipment
How an encounter is initiated	One child invites another, who is free to refuse	One child frequently challenges another, who cannot fail to respond without losing face
Facial and vocal expression	Usually preceded or accompanied by smiling and playful expression	Often staring, frowning, red face, puckering up, and crying
Number of participants	Sometimes two but often more children in an episode	Seldom more than two children primarily involved
Reaction of onlookers	Little interest for non-participants	Attracts attention from non-participants; often a crowd gathers around to watch
Self-handicapping	The stronger partner will often not use maximum strength	Self-handicapping normally absent
Restraint	Contact between partners is usually gentle; blows are not hard	Restraint occurs to a lesser extent or is absent
Reversal of roles	Participants may take it in turns to be on top/underneath, or to chase/be chased	Turn-taking not usually observed
Relationship between participants immediately after an encounter has ended	Participants often stay together while moving to another activity	Participants usually separate

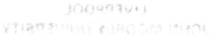

As we were all children once, and most of us will have taken part in R&T, it is a surprising finding that many teachers and playtime supervisors say they have difficulty distinguishing them and often make mistakes. Smith et al. (2002) found that 41% of primary school teachers said they sometimes have difficulty telling them apart, with 18% saying they could not do so (worse than most children, see Table 6.1). In fact, teachers and playground supervisors do sometimes mistake them, and intervene to break up what they think is a "fight" only to be told "We were only playing, Miss!" (Sluckin, 1981; Schafer & Smith, 1996).

Why should this be? It may be relevant that many primary school teachers and playground staff are female, and perhaps did not engage in so much play fighting (as opposed to chasing) when young. Also, school staff tend to value quieter forms of behavior and thus quieter types of play. Finally, many teachers and playground staff believe that play fighting often leads to real fighting—an issue we look at in a following section. What is perhaps even more surprising is that even some psychologists have confused and conflated play fighting with aggression; but this has been much less the case following the explicit writings and research about R&T in the 1980s and 1990s.

Participants and non-participants in R&T

In the videotape studies described above, children were asked to assess episodes that they were not personally engaged in. However, in one study we took this further, to compare the perspectives of participants and non-participants in filmed R&T bouts (Smith, Smees, & Pellegrini, 2004). We used videotaped episodes of play fighting in a primary school playground, with children aged from 5 to 8 years. We edited episodes quickly and played some back on the same day to both participants and non-participants. We found that participants had insights into what was going on in an episode, which outside observers, whether adult or child, often did not have. Participants were able to give more criteria to explain their judgments as to why an episode was playful or not. They also cited criteria that were likely to be useful and to which they as participants had more privileged access—whether a hit or kick really hurt, and whether an apparently aggressive act was within a pretend or game framework previously agreed by those involved.

For example, an episode between Jahred and Jonathan was described by both as playful when they watched it on the videotape. Jahred (a participant) said "it's a game, we're trying to learn karate"; Jonathan (a participant) said "it's a game about fighting and pretending kicking, but only soft." It was more difficult for non-participants. Tomas said "they real fight in karate, but I think it's just playing—it's real fighting when you lie down and cry, but they didn't, so it's not real fighting," while Cheryl said "I can't tell," and David thought it was a real fight although he could not tell why.

In judging whether something was playful or not, non-participants made more use of general statements about emotion or intention, for example, "it was a real fight because they were both angry," or "that was a play fight because it probably didn't hurt him." They also relied more on facial expressions, for example "it were a mess about [playful] because he were smiling." These criteria use the kind of information that can more readily be seen or inferred from the video clips. For example, in one episode, Duane (participant) said it was playful as "they are taking him to prison, and I'm the jailor," and David (participant) said "we are getting Mark to put him in prison." However Stephen (non-participant) judged it as playful because "they are all smiling" and Awil (non-participant) because "they were not fighting, he was smiling."

Does play fighting turn into real fighting?

Sometimes playground supervisors clamp down on play fighting, because they think it often leads to real fighting. But how often does this actually happen? It certainly can happen, and when asked, most children say it can happen (Table 6.1). It is one reason why some children say they don't like play fighting. But it does not seem to happen very often, and certainly not often in primary school children.

A number of observational studies have been made of play fighting, making use of the criteria in Table 6.2 to distinguish it from real fighting. A play fight turning into a real fight is consistently found to be a rare occurrence, taking account of the many play fights that actually occur. During the primary school years, these studies suggest that only about 1 episode in 100 or 1% of play fighting episodes turn into real fighting. But when we asked primary school teachers what proportion of play fights they thought turned into real fights, while there was a wide variation (from 10% to 80%), the average was about 30% in each of two separate studies (Schafer & Smith, 1996; Smith et al., 2002). This is clearly a misconception.

How has this misconception arisen? I can think of one good reason, though there may well be others. This is that, although the great majority of play fighting is really playful, occasionally things can go wrong and a fight does develop or someone gets hurt. According to a study by Pellegrini (1994), this is much more likely in sociometrically "rejected" children—those who are disliked by many peers and seldom liked much. He found that these children often respond to rough-and-tumble aggressively (in around 25% of episodes, compared to 1% as the usual norm); indeed, this behavior could contribute to their being disliked by classmates. It seems possible that teachers or lunchtime supervisors are making general judgments about play fights turning into real fights in children generally, based on experiences with these "rejected" children who may be taking up a lot of their supervisory time.

Why should some play fights turn into real fights, especially when "rejected" children are involved? This could happen for two main reasons. One has been called "honest mistakes" and refers to a lack of social skills: a child lacking appropriate social skills incorrectly responds to a playful initiation, such as a playful punch, as if it were hostile. The other would be deliberate manipulation or "cheating"—a child, sophisticated in understanding and manipulating playground conventions, deliberately misuses the expectations in a play fight situation to hurt someone or display social dominance while "on top" (Fagen, 1981; Pellegrini, 1988; Smith, 1997).

Changes in R&T with age

We saw earlier that one study (Humphreys & Smith, 1987) found a developmental shift in choice of play partners; approaching adolescence (11 years), dominance first appears to be a factor, with initiators often choosing someone near them in strength but slightly weaker. In fact this finding is one of several studies which suggest that approaching or in adolescence, some R&T can lose its largely innocent or purely playful quality.

Up to around 11 years, most evidence suggests that the great majority of R&T is purely playful, and that when play fighting does turn into real fighting, this is due to a lack of social skills and not conscious manipulation. For example, Smith et al. (2004) found virtually no evidence for manipulation of play fighting to real fighting in their videofilm and interview work with 5 to 8-year-olds. There are a few possible examples of such manipulation, at this age range, in the ethnographic literature (Sluckin, 1981; Oswald, Krappman, Chowduri, & Salisch, 1987), but in general quantitative research suggests that these are rare (Pellegrini, 1988, 1993).

From around 11 years, the picture does appear to change. Neill (1976) first observed how some play fighting could be manipulative, in 12 to 13-year-old boys. He stated that R&T could be a "means of asserting or maintaining dominance: once a weaker boy has registered distress the bond can be maintained by the fight taking a more playful form, but if he does not do so at the start of the fight, the stronger boy may increase the intensity of the fight until he does" (Neill, 1976, p. 219).

Pellegrini (1995b) extended the work on the dominance status of R&T partners, with a longitudinal study from 12 to 13 years (first and second years at US middle schools). His findings suggested that R&T was sometimes used to establish dominance, in the first year (when pupils meet many others they do not know, moving up from primary school). By the second year, rates of R&T declined, and also rates of real fighting, as a hierarchy had been established.

Boulton (1992a, p. 322) found that interviewing 15-year-old adolescents provided insight into possible uses of play fighting for dominance. For example, Craig, a boy, says:

> Craig: . . . we're only playing but you can still tell who's the hardest.
> MB: How can you tell?
> Craig: Well, you try and get them down, or try and hold them down, or get them round the neck, things like that.
> MB: So how can you tell who is the strongest?
> Craig: It's the one who can do those things. Like, the other day, Peter came up to me from behind and grabbed me round [my] neck, so I tried to get him off and get him down. We were only messing around, but I still got him down.
> MB: So what does that show?
> Craig: It shows that I'm harder than him. I could probably win him in a fight.

This example shows how a play fight can give indications of strength and dominance, even while staying playful. The next extract, with Peter, (p. 324) shows how at this age the borderline between play fighting (here called a "toy fight" in South Yorkshire dialect) and real fighting, can become blurred when dominance is involved:

> MB: If two people were play fighting to see who was the strongest, what would happen if one of them did not give in?
> Peter: That happened last week. Craig and Imran were messing about, and it went on for ages. Imran got Craig down but he wouldn't give in, so

Imran got Craig round the neck and got it tighter and tighter until Craig couldn't talk. He wouldn't let go. He was right mad.

MB: Is Imran always like that?

Peter: No way, I think he wanted to show Craig that he was [the] hardest.

MB: Was it a real fight?

Peter: Sort of. They know each other and don't fight, but it came close that time. It started off as a toy fight, but Craig wouldn't give in.

Cultural differences in play fighting

Play fighting has been seen in a very wide range of societies, including hunter-gatherer communities such as the Kalahari San, South American Indian communities, as well as a range of modern industrial societies. It thus appears to be a cross-cultural, universal aspect of human behavior.

However, it's expression can vary by culture. A particularly clear example of this was described by Fry (1987) amongst the Zapotec people of Mexico. Fry made observations of children's play (and adult behavior) in two villages, which he called San Andrés and La Paz. In San Andrés, children engaged in more play fighting, and there was also more real fighting and aggression in this community; in La Paz, fighting was avoided amongst adults, and in children too there was both less fighting and less play fighting. It seems that in so far as fighting and aggression are valued or not valued, children's play fighting may also be encouraged or discouraged.

Sex differences in Physical Activity Play

Boys more frequently engage in all forms of physical activity play (Pellegrini & Smith, 1998a), with the possible exception of rhythmical stereotypies in infancy (Thelen, 1980). This is probably related to a more general sex difference commonly found in physical activity. In a meta-analysis of 90 studies, Eaton and Enns (1986) found that physical activity was higher in boys than girls, and that this difference increased from infancy to mid-adolescence.

Boys and girls obviously differ substantially in play and social behavior, especially in the school years. This is obvious by the preschool years. Although many activities do not show a sex preference at this age, by 3–4 years children tend to select same-sex partners for play, and by the time children are getting into team games at about 6 or 7 years, sex segregation in the playground is much greater. Boys tend to prefer out-door play and, later, team games, often of a vigorous nature; girls prefer indoor, more sedentary activities, and often play in pairs (Lever, 1978). Maccoby (1998) has summarized these sex differences into three main phenomena: segregation (a strong tendency for children to play with others of their own sex from 3 years onwards); differentiation (different styles of interaction in boys' and girls' groups); and asymmetry (boys' groups are both more cohesive and more exclusionary than girls' groups).

Boys more frequently engage in physical activity play generally, and especially in play-fighting (as well as in actual fighting). Boys, more than girls, engage in rough-and-tumble play in virtually all human cultures where systematic observations have been made (DiPietro, 1981; Humphreys & Smith, 1984). These differences hold for both parent–child play (Roopnarine et al., 1993) and peer play, and are found more consistently for play fighting than for play chasing.

These sex differences can be explained in part by social learning. Fathers engage in rough-and-tumble play more with sons than with daughters, and more than mothers do (Parke & Suomi, 1981; Carson, Burks, & Parke, 1993). In schools, girls' play is supervised more closely than that of boys (Fagot, 1974), and this may inhibit physically vigorous play, which teachers consider inappropriate for girls. In addition, peer group processes are important, as emphasized by Maccoby (1998). Boys and girls have clear ideas of what is gender-appropriate behavior, and peer pressure will increase the tendency to conform to them.

There are also hormonal influences to consider. Hormonal influences on physical activity and play typically center on the role of androgens on neural organization and behavior. Normal exposure to androgens during fetal development predisposes males, more than females, towards physical activity generally, and exercise play and rough-and-tumble play more specifically. It has been suggested that excessive amounts of these hormones during fetal development lead to masculinized play behavior in females (Collaer & Hines, 1995). "Natural experiments" in which human fetuses are exposed to abnormally high does of androgens, support the androgenization hypothesis, as androgenized girls prefer male activities and more vigorous activities such as play fighting, than matched control girls (Berenbaum & Snyder, 1995; Hines & Kaufman, 1994).

Pellegrini (2002) relates the sex difference in R&T to sexual selection theory. In a polygamous or culturally imposed monogamous mating system (as humans can be argued to have), there is competition among males for access to "choosy" females, rather than *vice versa*. This greater competitive imperative on boys means that they will benefit more from

investing in dominance-related activities, especially as they approach reproductive maturity; by doing so, they compete against other boys, and also
impress girls (Pellegrini & Long, 2003). Of course, not many 12 to
14-year-old boys will become fathers in the near future. However, our
reference point here might more appropriately be ancestral human popu-
lations, hunter-gatherer or foraging peoples, who characterized 90% or
more of the duration of human evolution.

Fry (2005) has documented how, in many foraging societies, adolescence is a period of male physical contests. These are quite ritualized
—the intent is not to kill the other or even to harm them severely—but
also quite serious in their intent and outcome. Male skill in contests seems
to predict prestige and standing in the community, and therefore probably reproductive success. For example, Gusinde (1931, quoted in Fry,
2005, pp. 76–77) writes of the Ona Eskimo people:

> The example of the adults often spurs them on, for, when an opportunity
> presents itself, they also valiantly fall to and never tire in their rivalry to
> down an opponent . . . They choose soft earth, preferably dry mossy
> ground, where women and children and watching men form a large
> circle, in the inner space of which the wrestlers step. . . . Although the two
> opponents seize each other resolutely and gradually increase their efforts
> to the utmost, the wrestling never degenerates into ill-feeling, even though
> the stronger one finally knocks the weaker one to the ground with such
> force that he can sometimes get up only with difficulty. Many a man may
> be badly hurt, to be sure, but in the long run he may not escape further
> fights, but must venture on to increasingly stronger opponents in order
> not to get the reputation of a weak coward. For a very long time after-
> wards such a performance stimulates constant discussions, comparisons,
> and various opinions.

Fry (2005, p. 78) argues that the rougher kinds of R&T we see in present-
day adolescents in Western societies may be analogous to these ritualized
contests in foraging peoples, and that "If so, we may have a convergence,
in adolescence, of practice and dominance functions of R&T."

Functions of Physical Activity Play

Physical activity play has been hypothesized to have a number of
functions, and/or benefits. However, we need to distinguish the different types of physical activity play: rhythmic stereotypies, exercise play,
and rough-and-tumble play.

Rhythmic stereotypies

As we saw in Chapter 4, Byers and Walker (1995) proposed that exercise play in animals supports neural maturation and synaptic differentiation at important critical periods in development. Pellegrini and Smith (1998a) argued that this applies especially to rhythmic stereotypies in human infancy. These probably are functional. Thelen (1980) found evidence for deprivation effects, although she could not use the kind of experimental design used with older children. She observed more spontaneous rhythmic stereotypies in infants who got less vestibular stimulation from caregivers, and (when released) in those infants who were restricted in movement by for example being placed in infant seats. She concluded (op. cit., p. 148) that "deprivation of active as well as passive movement may . . . promote stereotypy". Thelen (1979), in a longitudinal study, found correlations between the age of onset of specific kinds of stereotypies (e.g. involving arms, legs, hands, knees) and the age of passing neuromuscular items in the Bayley Scales of Infant Development. It appears that infants engage in rhythmic movements involving particular body parts, shortly before gaining voluntary control of them (such that they pass the Bayley test items). Thelen (1979) suggested that these activities are part of a general neuromuscular maturational process, at a time when aspects of neuromuscular development are going through a sensitive period.

Pellegrini and Smith (1998a) postulated that rhythmic stereotypies provided immediate benefits to infants in terms of improving control of specific motor patterns. These spontaneous behaviors, fitting most definitions of play, may modify or eliminate irrelevant synapse formations and help the development of motor control in more goal-directed ways. As they point out, this is consistent not only with the age course of rhythmic stereotypies, and the evidence for deprivation rebound, but also with the lack of gender differences: There is no reason to suppose that this very basic level of motor control will be more important for boys than girls.

Exercise play

As with the theories concerning locomotor play in animals, exercise play in childhood can be hypothesized to enhance physical training of muscles, for strength and endurance and skill and economy of movement. This is consistent with the nature of exercise play and with the findings of the deprivation studies, which show that children engage in longer and more intense bouts of exercise play after being confined in smaller spaces and/or prevented from vigorous exercise (e.g., in classroom settings). Such rebound effects appear more important in the childhood and juvenile periods, when children are more likely to get restless after long sedentary periods, than in adulthood (Pellegrini, 1995a).

Byers (1998a; Byers & Walker, 1995) argued that in some mammal species, locomotor play has a long-term effect primarily on motor skill, but its effects on strength and endurance would be temporary; such benefits would soon disappear, but could also be regained later. However, in reviewing the literature on children's play, Pellegrini and Smith (1998a) argued differently. They acknowledged that exercise play could improve skill and economy of movement, but found no direct evidence to support this. However, they argued, there was good reason to suppose that exercise play would function in improving strength and endurance in a more substantial way than Byers argued. They pointed out that the age course of exercise play corresponds to the period when arm and leg muscles and bones are growing rapidly. Children engage in a lot of exercise play, sufficient to provide benefits of exercise. Finally, there is evidence from sports psychology that children who engage in physically active sports do get fitter. As one example, Lussier and Buskirk (1977) looked at the outcomes of a 12-week endurance training program, involving long distance running, on 8 to 12-year-old boys and girls. The training decreased heart rate during submaximal workloads and increased maximum oxygen intake; in other words, their bodies were coping better with the exercise demands.

Byers (1998b, p. 600) argued in reply that "the getting into shape hypothesis is likely incorrect." One of his counterarguments was that training effects are short-lived. His other argument was that if such training is important, we would expect a different age distribution of such play from the inverted U curve actually found; adults would benefit from such play as well. Pellegrini and Smith (1998b) had a riposte for the second argument, namely that adults get exercise in lots of other ways; traditionally (e.g. in hunter-gatherer and forager societies) adults would get plenty of exercise through hunting, gathering, foraging, herding, cooking, making houses, tending infants, and many other subsistence activities. (This may not apply so much to some contemporary urbanized adults, who need to go to fitness clubs to compensate for sedentary working lives; but this is not relevant when considering the function of exercise play in an evolutionary perspective). Thus, "it is not that exercise play is more important for juveniles, but rather than play may be the only way to get sufficient exercise training, at least before organized games and sports in human societies" (Pellegrini & Smith, 1998b, p. 610).

There is still plenty to be learnt about children's exercise play. Its role in motor skill and economy of movement needs to be better substantiated. Its effects on strength and endurance are better evidenced, but may be mainly short-term; however, immediate benefits are still important and, for a young person coming into adolescence, having a history of being physically fit is going to be better than "starting from scratch." Finally, although in traditional societies children do help with subsistence tasks, they probably expend much less energy on this than do adults, and exercise play (either on its own, or combined with other tasks, Chapter 5) appears a useful way to get short-term and possibly longer-term fitness and motor skill benefits.

Physical fitness is not the only hypothesis advanced for the benefits of exercise play. Two other related hypotheses discussed by Pellegrini and Smith (1998a) were the fat reduction hypothesis and the thermoregulation hypothesis, related to the approach of Barber (1991) briefly described in Chapter 4. These suppose that exercise play uses up excess energy, prevents obesity, and/or regulates body temperature. This is consistent with some evidence, such as exercise play being more frequent on cold days (Smith & Hagan, 1980; Pellegrini et al., 1995) and less frequent in tropical climates (Cullumbine, 1950). However, these ideas do not obviously give any explanation for the age and gender differences observed, and the "surplus energy" foundations of such approaches are questionable.

Another, quite different, hypothesis is that exercise play encourages younger children to take breaks from being overloaded with cognitive tasks. This has been called the "cognitive immaturity hypothesis" and was put forward by Bjorklund and Green (1992). They argued that younger children have less mature cognitive capacities; they have more difficulty keeping extraneous information from entering short-term memory, which more quickly gets cluttered up, thus leaving less capacity for task-relevant activities. Hence, the benefits of concentrating on a cognitively demanding task decrease after a shorter time for younger than for older children. Younger children have a shorter attention span at tasks, which facilitates them taking bouts of exercise play, such as at school break times. This gives them a break from being overloaded on cognitive tasks or more focused school work. The "need" to exercise helps children "space out" these cognitive demands.

This hypothesis is consistent with the inverted U curve of age change, the results of deprivation studies, and also with some findings that exercise play in break time results in improved attention to school tasks (Pellegrini & Davis, 1993). However, school tasks are a relatively recent cultural invention, so while this may be a benefit of exercise play, it would be difficult to argue that it is a function in the sense of being selected for in our evolutionary history.

The greater male involvement in exercise play remains to be explained by any satisfactory functional explanation. In traditional societies, training in muscle strength could be seen as more important for males; in hunter-gather societies, hunting (usually done by males) would require more physical strength and efficient speed of movement, than gathering plants. Fighting (also much more of a male activity) would draw on similar aspects. Nevertheless, gathering activities (usually done by females) are often arduous and involve considerable travel, so endurance training would appear relevant for these. The gender difference in play fighting does appear to be greater than the gender difference in play chasing and exercise play generally, as might be expected on such an argument. As noted above, the gender difference does not seem consistent with the fat reduction or thermoregulation hypotheses; nor is it obviously consistent with the cognitive immaturity hypothesis, as this would seem to apply equally to boys and girls. However as Bjorklund and Brown (1998, p. 605) observed, "Future research concerning relations between physical play and cognitive development should examine the *types* of physical play engaged in by boys and girls." It may be possible to get further insights into all the above explanations by exploring gender differences in exercise play in a more differentiated fashion.

Rough-and-tumble play

Is play fighting just a "useless" activity, or is it really important in children's development? Does this differ for boys and girls? One hypothesis put forward, especially by those studying rough physical play between parents and young children, is that it helps children to understand (encode and decode) emotional expressions. Certainly, children need to understand the meaning of laughter and a "play face" to enjoy such rough physical play. Parke, Cassidy, Burks, Carson, and Boyum (1992) and Carson, Burks, and Parke (1993) found that the amount of time spent in vigorous play bouts with parents did correlate with the child's ability to understand emotional expressions such as happy, sad, angry, scared, and neutral. In addition, Pellegrini (1988) found that frequency of peer R&T correlated to ability to understand play signals. However, these correlational findings do not prove cause-and-effect; it might be that children who have more difficulty understanding emotional expressions (for whatever reason) also find it more uncomfortable engaging in vigorous or R&T play. This hypothesis fails to explain the gender difference in R&T, as understanding emotional expressions must be as important for girls as for boys (Pellegrini & Smith, 1998).

Girls tend to engage, relatively at least, in more play chasing. Although often girls only, some chasing games can be mixed-gender, typically with some girls inviting boys to chase them. Jarvis (2006) observed this in nursery school children. Pellegrini and Long (2003) have described it and episodes of boys chasing and teasing girls in early adolescence, where, they suggest, it is one way of initiating contact with the opposite sex (early "courtship" behaviors), again in a "safe" format as it can just be described as "play."

What about play fighting, which is much more common in boys (Jarvis, 2006)? As we saw in Chapter 4, because play fighting often looks like real fighting, Symons (1978) argued that for rhesus monkeys, play fighting served as relatively safe practice for real fighting skills. It is relatively safe due to features such as self-handicapping, choice of friends as play partners, and choice of safer spaces and surfaces for play fighting. Smith (1982) argued a similar case for play fighting in children, where the same features are found. The argument is consistent with age trends; real fighting becomes more important in adolescence, so before then play fighting provides safe practice for this. It is also consistent with gender differences. Physical fighting is more important for boys—girls can also be aggressive, but they tend to prefer verbal aggression, and relational aggression such as rumour-spreading (Bjorkqvist, Lagerspetz & Kaukiainen, 1992)—and both play fighting and real fighting are more frequent in boys. However, while this explanation appears strong for younger children, there has been an absence of confirmatory evidence from individual differences (are children who play-fight less, less good fighters?), or from enrichment or deprivation studies. This hypothesis has also been challenged in the animal play literature (Chapter 4), with alternative candidates such as enhancing emotional control being put forward.

Related to the fighting-skills hypothesis is the idea that R&T is (also) practice for hunting skills (i.e., physical aggression against prey animals, rather than conspecifics) (Boulton & Smith, 1992). Konner (1972, p. 299) observed that "most of the component behaviors in rough-and-tumble play—chasing, fleeing, laughing, jumping, play-noise and play-face . . . along with completed 'object beats' (striking with an object) can be seen in Zhun/twa children annoying large animals. . . . or trying to kill small ones," and argued (p. 301) that ". . . the basic primate pattern of rough and tumble play has become, in part, specialized in man to serve the acquisition of hunting behavior." Again this is consistent with sex differences (males primarily being the hunters in earlier human environments) and design features.

Pellegrini (2002) has proposed a developmental change in the function of playfighting, especially for boys. During childhood it may function as safe practice in fighting skills, and as an enjoyable activity that helps maintain friendships and develop skills of emotional control. In adolescence, however, it is hypothesized to function more to assess strength and to assert, display, or maintain social dominance. Dominance refers to being able to take precedence over another child, or beat them in a fight or conflict. A dominance hierarchy refers to children's recognition of an ordering with respect to dominance. Dominance relationships appear to become more important in adolescence, in both sexes, but as regards physical dominance more especially in boys' peer groups. On this argument, boys may use play fighting to test out others and try to improve their own status without actually fighting much (Pellegrini, 2002; Pellegrini & Smith, 1998a). Play fighting may help children understand better their own strength and that of others, establish their position in a dominance hierarchy, and display dominance to slightly weaker partners/opponents.

Symons (1978), studying rhesus monkeys (Chapters 3, 4), had explicitly attacked the idea that monkey play fighting could function to assert or maintain dominance, precisely because of the self-handicapping and reversals that often occur. A "dominant" youngster may actually allow him/herself to be "rolled over" into the inferior position by a younger or weaker partner. However, it is a common observation that play fighting becomes rougher with age, in monkeys and in children; and, as we saw above, in children, partner choice becomes influenced by strength ranking by 11 years (not before) (Humphreys & Smith, 1987). Pellegrini (1995b) found partner choice related to dominance status in adolescent boys. In early adolescence, it appears that some boys may "take advantage" of the play fighting convention to encourage another into an R&T bout, then inflict some actual hurt and/or display dominance while justifying this as "just being playing" (Neill, 1976)—this being the "cheating" kind of scenario mentioned earlier.

Pellegrini (2002) points out that gauging strength can still occur despite self-handicapping, and also that self-handicapping and similar features are less prominent in adolescence when "cheating" becomes more common. In addition, Pellegrini and Long (2003) found direct correlational evidence that boys who engage in play fighting at age 12 have higher dominance status, which in turn related to a measure of dating popularity. Having said this, it is also likely that using play fighting in this way is only one pathway to establish dominance. Using too much manipulation in play fights (too much "cheating") would give someone an untrustworthy reputation and likely lead to controversial if not rejected social status. It would be possible to try to manipulate this in turn; for example, after hurting someone in a "play fight" and thus displaying dominant status to others watching, someone could "apologize" for hurting, under the guise of it being only play (in effect, passing off "cheating" as an "honest mistake"). These kinds of Machiavellian procedures do of course characterize a lot of adult political life!

Gosso et al. (2005, p. 233) have challenged the functionality of R&T in humans. They wrote:

> Parakanã children, both boys and girls, do know what fighting means, but both play fighting and actual fighting are very rare indeed. . . . It is our view that play fighting, so important in so many mammals, may have lost nearly all of its relevance for humans. Its abundance in other mammals relates to male adult fighting for status, females, territory and food . . . Polygynic species exhibit more adult fighting, sexual dimorphism, and juvenile play fighting. Byers (1984) suggests that selection pressures for early rehearsal of adult competitive patterns probably did not appear until social groups and the potential for polygyny appeared. In our view, at some early point of human evolution, those benefits resulting from being a better fighter must have declined. Vertical hierarchy gave way to horizontal cooperation among males (and females). Access to females ceased to be the direct or indirect result of fights. A unique food-sharing pattern, devoid of priorities and disputes, made obsolete the advantages of being a good fighter.

However, even if there is little internal fighting in some hunter-gatherer or foraging communities, and excessive inter-personal aggression is not tolerated (Boehm, 1999), rates of aggression appear to be very variable in such groups, and fights with neighbouring groups can occur (Fry, 2005; Boehm, 1999). So far as the practice function of R&T is concerned, in my view this remains as a facultative adaptation. In so far as fighting and aggression are valued or not valued, children's R&T may be encouraged or discouraged (Fry, 1987). It probably functions to improve fighting skills in younger children. In adolescence, as suggested by Pellegrini on the basis of studies in Western adolescents, and by Fry on the basis of anthropological records, the distinction between R&T and actual fighting starts to blur, and male skill in such contests seems to predict dominance, or prestige in the peer group or community (and therefore probably reproductive success for males, in traditional societies). The possible losing of relevance of R&T that Gosso et al. refer to as happening at an "early point of human evolution" might however be made at the current technological phase in human evolution, since purely physical strength and force are now becoming more irrelevant to measures of adult success. In any event, despite some two decades of research now on R&T, there is still a lot to learn about its role, how it changes through childhood and adolescence, and especially the role of gender in R&T interactions.

Further Reading

For a series of studies on the nature and benefits of play in school yards, see A. D. Pellegrini (1995), *School Recess and Playground Behavior*. Albany, NY: State University of New York Press.

Chapter 7

Object Play

In this chapter we will look at children's play with objects. We will mainly focus on what Smilansky (1968) called "constructive play," although, as discussed in Chapter 2, the distinction between constructive play and fantasy play is not always clear. However, we will start with the sensorimotor play of babies, and a discussion of differences between exploration, play, and tool use.

Sensorimotor or Functional Play

Developmental stages

Babies are born with some reflexive abilities and behaviors, such as grasping and sucking. These are used early on, usually, for feeding from the mother's breast, but they can also be used for manipulating objects. Piaget (1936) described in some detail the stages of what he called sensorimotor development. He did this by carefully observing and documenting his own children's behavior. He delineated six substages through the first two years of life:

Reflex activity (approx. 0–1 months): reflexes such as sucking and grasping, spontaneous rhythmic activity (this would include rhythmic stereotypies, see Chapter 6, though Piaget did not use this term).

Primary circular reactions (approx. 1–4 months): Piaget here uses "circular" in the sense of "repeated"; he is referring to repeated reflexive behaviors or motor responses, generally centered on the baby's own body, such as thumb sucking.

Secondary circular reactions (approx. 4–10 months): again these are repeated actions, but they advance on the primary circular reactions in two ways. First, the baby may initiate new actions beyond the simple reflexes; and second, she starts acting on objects beyond her own body, for example repeatedly hitting a hanging toy. Piaget described this in his daughter Jacqueline, at 5 months:

> Jacqueline looks at a doll attached to a string which is stretched from the hood to the handle of the cradle. The doll is at approximately the same level as the child's feet. Jacqueline moves her feet and finally strikes the doll, whose movement she immediately notices . . . The activity of the feet grows increasingly regular whereas Jacqueline's eyes are fixed on the doll. Moreover, when I remove the doll Jacqueline occupies herself quite differently; when I replace it, after a moment, she immediately starts to move her legs again' (Piaget, 1936, p. 182).

In this example, what was a primary circular reaction, namely kicking the legs, becomes a secondary circular reaction as it is directed repeatedly at the doll.

Co-ordination of secondary circular reactions (approx. 10–12 months): here the infant, by now getting quite mobile, starts to coordinate different behaviors, such as grasping and sucking. This may be goal-related, such as hitting or pushing one object out of the way in order to grasp another. Here is another example from Piaget's daughter Jacqueline, rather early at 8 months, in which several behaviors are co-ordinated sequentially:

> Jacqueline grasps an unfamiliar cigarette case which I present to her. At first she examines it very attentively, turns it over, then holds it in both hands while making the sound *apff* (a kind of hiss which she usually makes in the presence of people). After that she rubs it against the wicker of her cradle then draws herself up while looking at it, then swings it above her and finally puts it into her mouth (Piaget, 1936, p. 284).

Tertiary circular reactions (approx. 12–18 months): here children's behaviors become more flexible and when the infant repeats actions, she may do so with variations which can lead to new results. Trial-and-error is used in exploring and experimenting with objects and the environment.

Internal representation (approx. 18–24 months): by this, Piaget meant that the child was by now not limited to acting directly on the world by physical actions, but was also able to have some mental representations of the world and things in the world (people, objects) within the brain. Besides manipulating objects directly in the physical world, he or she can also manipulate the mental representations of objects, thinking and planning. The child will also show full object and person permanence, that is, understanding that objects and people have continued existence and, if necessary, searching for them when out of sight. For example, if a child wants to reach for a toy, but there is another object between them and the toy, a younger child might just try to reach the toy directly; in doing so they might knock the object out of the way and succeed in reaching the desired toy, by "trial and error" rather than deliberate planning. But once mental representation is achieved, the child could plan such behavior, removing the intervening object and getting the toy easily. Here is another example from Jacqueline, now 20 months, who is trying to open a door while carrying two blades of grass at the same time:

> She stretches out her right hand towards the knob but sees that she cannot turn it without letting go of the grass. She puts the grass on the floor, opens the door, picks up the grass again and enters. But when she wants to leave the room things become complicated. She put the grass on the floor and grasps the door knob. But then she perceives that in pulling the door towards her she will simultaneously chase away the grass which she placed between the door and the threshold. She therefore picks it up in order to put it outside the door's zone of movement' (Piaget, 1936, pp. 376–7).

By this stage, toddlers have clearly developed problem-solving and tool-use skills. They can do a lot of complex manipulative activities with objects. In addition, the stage of internal representations brings the possibilities of *pretend play*, in which an object or action can stand in for or represent another: for example, a wooden block can represent a cake, or rotating hand movements represent turning a steering wheel. We will look further at the development of pretend play in Chapter 8.

Piaget's descriptions of infant sensorimotor development have stood the test of time fairly well, even though some of his theoretical assumptions, and his assertions about when aspects such as object permanence first appear, have been questioned. What is clear from his stages is that exploratory behaviors, playful behaviors, and goal-directed or tool-use behaviors all develop in these first two years. When an object is first encountered, behavior will be exploratory. What does this object feel like? Let's suck it and see (literally!). But when we get to the circular reactions, such behaviors are repeated, presumably because the infant finds such actions enjoyable—two criteria for playful behavior. As the infant moves from primary to secondary and then tertiary circular reactions, such repeated behaviors become more flexible and variable, such that some behaviors would definitely be described as playful: what

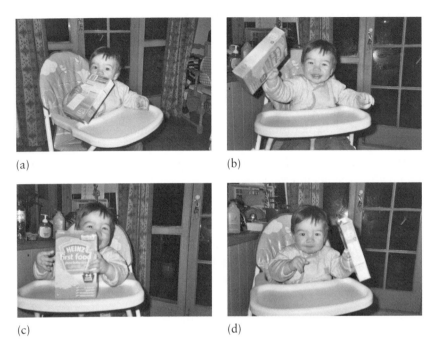

(a)   (b)

(c)   (d)

Figure 7.1 Pictures of a 10-month-old infant showing sensorimotor object play
(provided by the author)

Piaget calls sensorimotor play, such as banging objects together in various ways and laughing.

Any parent can see such behaviors in their young children. For example, I observed my son Edmund at 10 months, when given a small cereal pack with a plastic object that rattled inside. Edmund soon realized he could make a rattling noise, and proceeded to shake the box about, at first more gently and then more vigorously, also banging it on the surface of the high chair he was sitting in, waving it about with full arm extension, and also sucking it. He also looked at me a lot and was smiling and chuckling. I had no doubt that this "secondary circular reaction" was playful (see Figure 7.1).

These behavioral and cognitive advances also bring possibilities of more goal-directed activities, which could be called tool use rather than play. As an example, Connolly and Dalgleish (1989) described the development in toddlers of using spoons to feed themselves from a dish, a skill that parents will be pleased to encourage despite messy beginnings.

This is clearly goal-directed behavior, the goal being to get food into the mouth, ultimately an important survival skill. Having said that, toddlers may well introduce more playful elements into such routines (to the frustration of parents), banging the spoon, stirring porridge around the bowl, etc.

Power (2000, p. 107), following Yarrow, McQuiston, MacTurk, McCarthy, Klein, and Vietze (1983), describes "a category somewhere between 'pure' exploration and play, labeled functional exploration/ practice play"; also referred to as "mastery play," this is where infants explore the effects of different actions on various objects, practicing and refining their skills in doing this.

It seems that exploration, play, and tool use all develop in these first two years in rather interlinked ways. We can attempt to distinguish them, basically using criteria developed for older children where the distinctions are generally clearer. But beyond a certain point, we run the risk of entering into sterile semantic debates if we push these conceptual distinctions too far in the sensorimotor period.

Types of actions

Power (2000, p. 57) has collated the range of non-pretend object manipulative actions seen in infants and toddlers. These comprise:

- *Procuring*: picking up, holding, carrying, transferring, bilateral hold, two-handed hold.
- *Investigating*: poking/touching, mouthing/biting, scratching, pressing, rotating, bringing to eyes, instrumental sequential action.
- *Transforming*: tearing/breaking, twisting/untwisting/bending, wadding/ squeezing.
- *Relating*: rubbing, hitting/striking, dropping, touching together.
- *Other large-motor behaviors*: waving/shaking, pushing/pulling, throwing.

These behaviors show some developmental course in frequency. For example, according to the Uzgiris (1967) scales, mouthing is common at 2 months, visual inspection at 3 months, hitting on a surface at 4 months, shaking objects at 5 months, examining at 6 months, tearing, pulling, rubbing, and sliding at 7 months, and dropping and throwing at 8–9 months. Also, more objects are brought into behavior routines: Rosenblatt (1977) documented how infants in this first year mainly use one object at a time, but in their second year often use two or more objects in relation to reach other.

(a)   (b)

Figure 7.2 Pictures of a 2-year-old boy showing construction play (provided by the author)

As Power comments, put in this way, the range of object manipulation seen in human infants is quite similar to what is seen in other primates (see Chapter 4). There are some differences; primates do a lot of sniffing and licking of objects, for example. However, human children soon advance beyond the capabilities of primates in both constructive and pretend activities. For example, at the same time that my son Edmund was engaged in secondary circular reactions (above), which is something many primates could do, my son Rolland (25 months) was engaging in a whole range of object-related activities: stacking cubes (Figure 7.2), putting objects like toy cars in a line, putting similar objects together, solving simple jigsaw puzzles (i.e. placing the right pieces in the right form shapes), and doing simple pretend activities (pushing a toy train on a track making "choo" noises).

In constructive activities, toddlers start stacking and sorting objects (see Figure 7.2); they put cups of different sizes one inside another, can do jigsaw puzzles, start sorting objects by shape and colour, etc, in ways that soon exceed typical primates. Chimpanzees (especially semi-captive or trained chimpanzees) can indeed stack boxes (e.g. to stand on to reach bananas) and do simple sorting tasks (and in the wild they manipulate objects to make tools, for example wadding leaves to get drinking water, and preparing twigs to go termite fishing). But as children get older they soon exceed what the cleverest chimpanzee can do in this respect. So far as pretend activities go, objects and actions can assume "as if" meanings that soon develop into role play and complex sociodramatic play routines (Chapter 8). Again, some simple examples of pretend or symbolic play can be seen to great apes, but children soon go well beyond this.

Very broadly speaking, great apes do appear to achieve a kind of sensorimotor intelligence and internal representation (as shown by the achievements just mentioned, as well as simple sign language abilities, recognizing themselves in mirrors, and using tactical deception); but these real evolutionary continuities cannot hide the fact that by 3 or 4 years human children have advanced on all these fronts well beyond the cleverest ape. Herrmann, Call, Hernandez-Lloreda, Hare and Tomasello (2007) directly compared the abilities of 2.5-year-old children with those of chimpanzees and orang-utans on a battery of cognitive tests. The abilities of the young children and the apes were fairly comparable on physical cognitive skills, at this age. But the children were already markedly better at social cognitive skills. Much more than the apes, they would follow an adult's gaze, use pointing, and observe and imitate what adults did, making use of the social context of learning.

Social aspects of object play

This last finding points to important aspects of the social context of object play. Tomasello, Carpenter, Call, Behne and Moll (2005; and commentaries) argue that understanding and sharing intentions provides a crucial difference between humans and other species including the great apes. An integral part of this is shared attention to objects. One concept here is the "referential triangle." This refers to an adult, a child, and a toy which is the focus of shared attention; and the way the child takes account of the adult in this. From 9 to 12 months the infant starts to follow the adult's gaze to an object, and by 15 months direct the adult's gaze by pointing.

According to Tomasello and colleagues, shared attention and the referential triangle provide a means for the child to be aware of others (the adult) as an intentional agent and to interact with them, often in cooperative ways. The child may point to an object which is interesting. By contrast, chimpanzees do very little pointing and, if they do point, it is because they want something and have learnt this gesture can produce results. Great apes lack the motivation to share cooperatively, according to these authors (they see them as basically competitive, a view challenged by some primatologists) and thus do not have these early social cognition skills, which act as a lever up to more advanced human abilities and indeed what they call "cultural cognition."

If correct, this suggests that the social aspects of object exploration and play have a vital role in human development. It would also help explain why even great apes do not develop social pretend play, even though they may show some simple solitary pretend with objects (see Chapter 8).

A study of mother, father and older sibling play with second-born children, found bidirectional relationships between mother-created object play, and infant's sophistication at solitary object play, from 12 to 18 months (Teti, Bond, & Gibbs, 1988). Furthermore, the infant's level of play at 12 months did predict to some language mastery experiences at 18 months; although it did not predict infant cognitive level at the later age.

Beyond the Sensorimotor Period

Play and exploration

During sensorimotor development, the distinction between exploration and play is rather difficult to make. However, observations of infants suggests that by 18 months play accounts for more of the child's inter-actions with the environment than does exploration (Belsky & Most, 1981). By the preschool years, the distinction between exploration and play is clearer. In toddlers, exploration precedes play; children explore an object, or try out its properties, before they play with it. In Chapter 1 we briefly described a classic experiment by Hutt that illustrated this.

Hutt (1966) used a novel object to see what behavior it elicited in young children, and how this changed with repeated exposure. The main participants were 30 nursery-school children, aged 3–5 years. Each child had eight 10-minute sessions in a room in the nursery school. The first two sessions were for familiarization, and five toys were provided. For the ensuing six experimental sessions a novel toy was also available. This was a red metal box with a lever, whose movements could be registered on counters and could result in a buzzer sounding and a bell ringing (see Figure 7.3). The complexity of the novel object was varied by having four conditions: from "no sound or vision" (bell and buzzer switched off, counters covered up), through "vision only" and "sound only," to "both sound and vision" available. Hutt measured how much lever manipulation had taken place (from the counter readings) and the amount of time spent exploring the novel object (visually or tactually), from observations of the children.

The results showed that children looked at the object immediately on entering, and often approached it or asked the researcher what it was. They then examined the object visually and manually, holding and

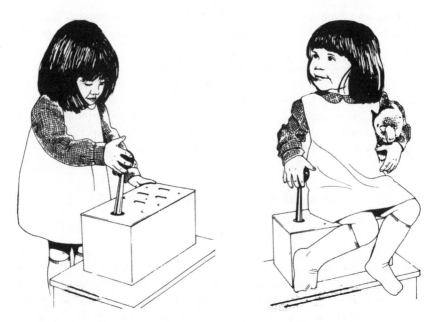

Figure 7.3 A girl exploring and then playing with a novel object
(from Hutt, 1966; shown as Box Figure 7.1.1, in Smith, Cowie, & Blades,
2003: 239)

manipulating the lever. For the "no sound or vision" and "vision only"
conditions, this exploration and manipulation declined rapidly over
sessions. However, for the "sound only" and "both sound and vision"
conditions, manipulation of the lever increased over the first five sessions. More detailed analysis of the observations showed that in these
conditions, although exploratory behavior declined, more playful or
game-like behaviors increased, for example running around the object
with a truck and ringing the bell each time, or using the object as a seat
and pretending it was a car. These observations led Hutt to suggest that
children typically proceed from specific exploration of the object to
more playful behavior. Exploration was characterized as relatively serious
and focused, essentially asking "what does this object do?" Play was
characterized as relaxed, and by a diversity of activities essentially asking
"what can I do with this object?"

This exploration/play distinction has been considered further by
Weisler and McCall (1976) and Wohlwill (1984). It has been argued
that the particular novel object used in this study probably makes the
distinction clearer than some situations might do.

Hutt (1970) stated that boys were much more exploratory than girls in this setting, but this sex difference has not been well replicated in other studies of exploratory behavior (McLoyd & Ratner, 1983).

Play with objects after the sensorimotor period

Object (or construction) play is common in the preschool years; Pellegrini and Bjorklund (2004) cite conservative estimates of 10–15% of children's time being spent on object play. As they point out, some studies suggest considerably higher rates of time spent with objects, maybe 30–35%, but such estimates usually do not differentiate object play, from exploration, and from tool use.

In traditional societies, as we saw in Chapter 5, play with objects is typically with surrounding materials, often involving pretend subsistence activities. But in modern societies, play with objects typically involves toys purpose-made for children's play, often based on mass media prototypes. Shops have a profusion not only of simple objects such as building blocks and bricks, balls, stacking cubes, jigsaws, toy trucks, dolls, teddies, toy animals, but also ranges of toys for pretend and fantasy activities, such as train sets, farm sets, castles, action figures, transformers, and figures and action objects based on either older but enduring or current TV series or films (e.g. Star Wars, Dr Who).

However in the preschool period, children of 2 to 4 years do not really need a huge range of specialized toys. The more traditional toys such as blocks, bricks, nesting cubes, and so forth provide a good range of possibilities for developing and displaying growing cognitive skills. Children are gradually developing skills of classification and seriation, and this is shown in some detailed studies of constructive play. In a classic study, Gesell (1940) examined stages in block construction play from 1 to 5 years of age. Initially, infants just grasp and suck individual blocks, but from 18–24 months they will start stacking or arranging them in simple ways. This becomes more sophisticated by 3 years, although it is still predominantly one-dimensional (and now more horizontal than vertical). By the time they are 4-years-old, children are building complicated two-dimensional structures such as enclosures, and by 5 years, three-dimensional structures, often named as part of some pretend play activity (as for example a castle, or a boat). Similarly, studies of children's play with nesting cups shows clear developmental progression (DeLoache, Sugarman, & Brown, 1985). Younger preschool children simply put one cup inside another, or stack one on another. Older preschool children develop a more hierarchically organized or planful way of proceeding; for example they may put one cup in another and then move both together into a third cup; or if a stack has a too large a cup at the top, they will take that off and insert it at the bottom of the tower to make a more stable assembly.

Gender differences in object play

There is not much evidence of gender differences in object play during the sensorimotor period (Belsky & Most, 1981; Power, 2000). There is also no pronounced sex difference in the overall frequency of object play between toddler boys and girls, but the nature and choice of toys does vary, especially after the sensorimotor period. A naturalistic study in the homes of 1 and 2-year-olds by Linda Daglish and myself (Smith & Daglish, 1977) found five significant sex differences in play even at these ages: boys played more with transportation toys and did more active play and forbidden play (such as playing with wall sockets, pulling curtains, climbing on furniture); girls did more play with dolls and with soft toys. These kinds of findings are echoed in other studies of 2-year-olds at home, and of 3 and 4-year-olds in nursery classes; boys tend to prefer transportation toys, blocks, and activities involving gross motor activity such as throwing or kicking balls, or rough-and-tumbling, while girls tend to prefer dolls and dressing-up or domestic play (Pellegrini & Smith, 2003). Many activities, however, do not show a sex preference at this age.

A more constrained experimental procedure was used by Sluss (2002) in a study of block play in 4-year-olds in the US. Altogether 24 same-sex pairs (12 boy pairs, 12 girl pairs) were observed in a laboratory playroom, with a set of blocks. After some 10–15 minutes to explore the new environment and the blocks, play was recorded for another 15 minutes. Sluss measured the level of play using Rubin's Play Observation Scale (POS; see Chapter 2). She found no significant differences between boys and girls on this measure. However, other differences were found. Boys made more spatially complex constructions with the blocks. Girls had more frequent and complex conversations during the block play.

Functions of Object Play

Theoretical perspectives

Two main hypotheses have been put forward for the function of object play in childhood. The first hypothesis is that object play helps children develop proficiency in skills relevant to subsistence activities. This shows continuity with the generally assumed functions of object play in animals, where, as we saw (Chapter 4), it is usually thought to provide practice or training for food extraction, prey catching, agonistic behavior, or tool use. The second hypothesis is that object play facilitates creative problem-solving. The emphasis here is on the flexible, unpredictable nature of play, and its role not so much in reproducing existing culture, but in taking it forward, and in the broader sense contributing to the evolutionary process (both genetically, and culturally; Pellegrini et al., 2007). These two hypotheses are not incompatible, of course. Indeed Bruner (1972) eloquently made the case for both of these functions of object play. We will look at both hypotheses in turn, and at what evidence there is to support each of them.

Object play, subsistence activities, and tool use

Bruner (1972) pointed out that the design features of object play make it a very suitable way of developing tool-using skills. Object play, while enjoyable in itself and intrinsically motivated, provides repeated practice in a range of relevant skills. We saw above, looking at developmental sequences, how children are acquiring skills such as fitting, stacking, and co-ordinating actions, and these are obviously going to be important if not essential aspects of later tool use. Indeed, they are hallmarks of stages of cognitive development in Piaget's and other theories. Short, repeated, but slightly varied "practice" bouts, such as play typically provides, are an excellent way of acquiring skills. On this argument, it is very difficult to see how children could *not* be learning such skills, in their object play (which is not to say that it is the only way to learn such skills, or essential for it).

In traditional societies, children would be acquiring the kinds of skills normative in adult society for food extraction, prey catching, agonistic behavior, or tool use. We saw in Chapter 5 how 3 to 6-year-old Parakanã Indian girls make little baskets out of palm leaves in their play, while their mothers use such baskets (better constructed!) to gather food. The little play baskets were too fragile to be used, but by seven or eight years the girls stop playing with baskets and begin to make real baskets to help their mother or for their own use. The boys make bows and arrows and play with them, but adult males use bows and arrows for hunting; and the adults may help older boys (7–11 years) make the transition from play to real hunting.

The gender differences in object play are consistent with this hypothesis. Pellegrini and Bjorklund (2004) developed the hypothesis that object play develops skills useful in subsistence activities, basing much of their argument on gender differences. In traditional societies, men generally hunt and women gather food. Different skills are required for each type of activity, and in their object play boys and girls can be seen as practicing these different skills. In modern societies, gender roles also vary, although considerable flexibility is recognized and some traditional aspects are under challenge. The differences seen in object play in children in contemporary societies could be accounted for by a combination of genetic, environmental, and self-socialization factors. Genetically, some gender differences (such as more use of objects in gross motor play by boys) probably have a quite deep evolutionary heritage and are causally influenced by hormonal and neural differences (Pellegrini & Smith, 1998a).

Certainly, children are also influenced by their environment; boys and girls are each provided with certain toys, often differentially; and they may be reinforced by both adults and peers in gender-appropriate toy choices and behaviors. Children also come to develop their own gender identity, and observe what males and females do in their culture. They then consciously choose to carry out gender-appropriate activities. These two processes serve to bring about gender differences in object play, which may vary in specifics from one culture to another, but which are likely to be adaptive for the roles found in that society.

While a relationship between object play and subsistence skill acquisition is consistent with the design features of object play and its gender differences, actual direct evidence for it is difficult to find. Some of the best evidence comes from Bock's (1995, 2002) work with multi-ethnic mixed-economy communities in the Okavango Delta, Botswana. Bock's (2002) most detailed analyses relate to "play pounding" of grain, an activity engaged in by young girls. They put some grain in a hollow in the ground or small container, and "pound" it with a stick; this is often in a pretend context. Parents may tolerate/encourage such play (more often in younger children), or they may require girls to take part in actual subsistence activities, such as actually pounding grain, sifting it, and so forth.

Pounding grain is a very important subsistence task in this culture, and is done only by women. It requires some combination of strength and skill. It takes a few years to acquire near-adult proficiency in this task. Bock's analyses show that the frequency with which girls engage in play pounding follows a characteristic inverted-U curve, peaking at around ages 5–6 years and falling off steeply at around ages 8–9 years, when a girl's productivity in actually pounding grain makes her useful for parents at this task (mothers then reallocate their time to mongongo nut processing, which is a more demanding skilled process).

Parents tolerate children playing, even though they could be doing other productive tasks (such as food gathering or looking after younger siblings); indeed, Bock argues that they may encourage children to play when the benefits of skill acquisition with future payoff outweigh the benefits of immediate productivity (this need not be a conscious decision based on such calculations; it could also or as well result from cultural practices and norms that have proved adaptive in the past). There is a developmental tradeoff between the child doing actual productive work (albeit at low efficiency), or engaging in play that is not productive in immediate terms but can improve skills for later use.

Bock's analyses support the hypothesis that the play pounding does indeed help develop later real pounding skills, and that these are indeed put to use as soon as it is productive to do so, in the sense that a reasonable level of skill has been reached and that further play brings "diminishing returns" in this respect. "Productive" here is most probably defined in terms of parental, maybe primarily maternal, interest. As Bock points out, there will be some conflict of interest between parents and children on time allocation to play or other activities. Indeed, if children can reliably expect parents to provision them, it would be to their own advantage to spend much more time playing (with later payoffs to themselves) rather than contributing earlier on to productive activities for the family.

Interestingly, while Bock's data are good evidence for a functional role for one kind of object play, they do not argue that play is essential or that it is the only way to acquire the relevant skills. Another skill for girls to acquire in these communities is sifting grain. This is not something they play at. It seems to be learned through instruction and by actually doing it (directly practicing in goal-directed ways).

Bock's data is among the best in terms of the detailed design features of play—not just what it looks like, but also when it happens in relation to the costs and benefits of engaging in non-play alternatives. There are also some correlational studies, in Western societies. For example, Johnson, Ershler, and Lawton (1982) observed 34 children aged 4 years in play and also gave them tests of cognition and intelligence. They found that constructive play (but not dramatic play) was positively and significantly correlated with intelligence scores. However, these and other correlational studies cannot rule out other factors or establish the direction of causality (perhaps more intelligent children can play better, rather than play necessarily developing intelligence).

The traditional approach to pinning down causal relationships comes from experiments. In experimental designs, we can attempt to use control groups and isolate certain variables as being important for certain outcomes. Such designs have been used in a number of studies with western children. These have typically been "supplementation" studies; children given extra play experiences are compared on outcome measures with those not given such extra experiences.

Most of these studies have been on creative problem-solving, related to the second hypothesis which we will examine next. A full critique of these experimental studies will be given then. A smaller group of studies have looked at symbolic play with objects in relation to the achievement of Piagetian conservation abilities, and will be reviewed in Chapter 8.

Object play, innovative problem-solving, and creativity

The second main hypothesis for the function of object play is that it enhances innovative problem-solving, and creativity. Bruner (1972) emphasized the flexible nature of play, and its likely role in creative problem solving—findings solutions in new situations. In part Bruner was probably influenced by the writings of Vygotsky ([1933] 1966), which were becoming quite widely spread amongst western developmental psychologists at this time. Bruner also took an evolutionary perspective, however; although less emphasized in the animal literature on object play, such a hypothesis can be argued there too (Pellegrini et al., 2007).

It has to be said that support for this position comes more obviously from studies in contemporary societies, than studies in traditional societies. The general picture from traditional societies is that children imitate and practice skills they see adults doing, and which they will need later as adolescents and adults (Chapter 5). At least in some traditional societies, especially those which Gaskins, Haight, and Lancy (2006) describe as "curtailing" play (rather than "cultivating" or "accepting" it), exploration of novel objects and unusual or creative forms of play are difficult to observe. An example described by Gaskins (1999) are the Yucatan Maya village children. Another example comes from rural Nepal, where Anderson and Mitchell (1984, p. 737) stated that "Much ... play, even among older children, was unvaried and repetitive. Little experimentation, exploration or diversification of the activity towards higher levels of mastery were observed."

There are clearly different cultural values put by adults in different societies, not only on children's play but on the importance of creativity and innovation in adult life. Compared to many traditional farming and pastoral communities, in which traditional practices tend to be highly valued, contemporary urban societies put high value on new ideas and creative thinking. The speed of technological change is seen as requiring flexible minds that can produce new products in a competitive, market-oriented environment. Educational systems in such societies also value flexible and innovative thinking, as opposed, for example, to rote-learning of established information, which is more typical of schooling in some traditional systems. Not surprisingly then, not only the theorizing but also the main evidence regarding the role of play in innovative problem-solving and creativity comes from modern technological societies.

As Bruner (1972) pointed out, some design features of object play, notably its unconstrained nature and freedom to try out new combinations and possibilities (without risk of "failure" as in goal-directed tasks), is consistent with the hypothesis. So, broadly, are the gender differences. We would not expect an overall gender difference in the importance of innovative problem-solving and creativity—it would be important for both sexes in the various tasks they do; hence, no overall difference in the amount of object play. However, the nature and type of object play would vary, as discussed before, with the nature of adult roles in each society.

An extensive study of Oxfordshire nursery schools was carried out by Sylva, Roy, and Painter (1980), working with Bruner. They looked at the design features or characteristics of different types of play, and were especially interested in what they called complex or challenging activities for nursery-school children. They described what they called "high-yield," "medium-yield," and "low-yield" activities, basically in terms of activities with some sort of goal and the means to achieve it. By this definition, constructive play activities such as building, drawing, and doing puzzles were "high-yield." "Medium-yield" activities were pretending, play with small-scale toys, manipulating sand or dough. "Low-yield" activities comprised informal and impromptu games, gross motor play and unstructured social playing, and "horsing around" (i.e. rough-and-tumble play).

The emphasis in Sylva and colleagues' study is on cognitive, rather than social, challenge or complexity. Some kinds of construction play clearly can present challenges, and some children may respond to this in what are for them innovative ways. However, their conclusions may not do justice to the social challenges in other kinds of play. Observations of sociodramatic play suggest there is considerable negotiation about social roles (see Chapter 8). Observations of rough-and-tumble show that co-ordination with a large number of partners is often involved, and suggest it may have social functions in terms of making friends, or practicing fighting or dominance skills (Chapter 6).

There are several correlational studies showing that children who engage in more innovative or creative play with objects subsequently score higher on some measure of creativity. One such study, by Hutt and Bhavnani (1972), used data from the novel toy experiment mentioned earlier (see Figure 7.3). The authors traced 48 children, who had been observed with the novel toy at around 4 years of age, when they were 8 years. From the earlier data they had recorded those children who, after investigating the toy, used it in many imaginative ways (15 of the 48). Four years later they gave the children some tests designed to measure creativity. The imaginative players scored significantly higher on these tests than did the other children, who at 4 years had not played so much with the novel object.

This is consistent with the idea that imaginative play fosters creativity —but no more than that. An alternative explanation would be that another factor (for example, shyness with adults) was responsible for the poor performance both with the novel object and later in the tests. Or, perhaps the playfulness of the imaginative children is just a by-product of their creativity, not a cause of it. These problems apply to other correlational studies, such as those of Liebermann (1977) who correlated teacher's ratings of children's playfulness with measures of divergent thinking. Correlations may be due to extraneous factors, and we cannot infer causal relations from them.

Experiments with Object Play and Creative Problem-Solving

A considerable body of experimental work has been done to test or support the hypothesis that children's object play can enhance innovative problem-solving or creativity. This is given detailed treatment here, as the development and subsequent critique of this work is paradigmatic of theory-driven research and attempts to draw on the advantages of experimental design and control, while its failures are due partly to the limitations of the experimental method, but largely to the prevailing "play ethos" referred to in Chapter 2.

The initial lure retrieval tasks

An early and possibly the most well-known study in this genre was reported by Sylva (1977), as part of her PhD thesis. Sylva was working with Bruner at the time, and explicitly sought to test his theories concerning play. She designed a lure-retrieval task, using sticks and G-clamps, for use with children aged 3, 4, and 5 years. The task was to retrieve a chalk from a box placed out of reach on a table where the child was sitting with a set of sticks and clamps in front of them. They were told that the task was to get the chalk from the box; that they could use any materials on the table; and that the only rules were that they could not get out of their chair. Using one stick as a reaching tool, a child could not, in fact, get the chalk from the box. The way to solve the task was to join 2 longer sticks together with a G-clamp, which produced a tool of sufficient length to solve the problem.

This is a tool-using task which requires some creative or innovative thinking on the part of the child, Sylva argued. The interesting question for her was whether prior play experience with the sticks and clamps would prove especially helpful. After spending one minute demonstrating how a clamp could be screwed on to a stick, Sylva tested children individually, putting 36 children each into one of five conditions. The conditions were (1) *play*: the child was allowed 10 minutes free play with the clamps, and sticks of different lengths; (2) *observe principle*: the child had 2 minutes watching the researcher clamp together two long sticks at their overlap (essentially, the principle for solving the problem, though of course they were not told this); (3) *observe components*: the child observed the researcher make constructions, yoked to what a child did in condition (1), again for 10 minutes; (4) *train components*: the child was instructed to make constructions, yoked to what a child did in condition (1), again for 10 minutes; and (5) *control*: there was no intervening condition in between the initial one-minute demonstration and being set the task.

The two yoked conditions deserve some comment. Sylva was interested not only in traditional group comparisons, but also in the process of what went on. From her perspective, the actual constructions made by the children in play would be vital in the extent to which they helped in later problem-solving. She therefore observed this. Her two yoked conditions then enabled her to give children in these two other groups comparable experience with the constructions the play children made, but in one case by observing rather than playing, and in the other case by instruction rather than playing. This procedure was used by her to compare the efficacy of observation, play, and instruction, independent of the actual constructions made in the conditions.

Following experience of one of these conditions, the child was given the task as above. Actually (as Sylva commented) the really creative solutions that stayed within the rules, were sitting in one's chair and tipping the table up towards you (if you were strong enough!), or gripping the chair with your hands and shuffling or jumping it around the table to get within reach of the box. Fortunately for Sylva's analyses, these were very rare responses; most children, like most adults, are not so very creative, and abide by the spirit as well as the letter of the rules.

When given the task, Sylva ascertained if there were any "spontaneous solvers" who needed no help. If after some time a child had not solved the task, the researcher could progressively give a series of hints, starting with suggesting using the materials and ending with presenting the child with an assembled tool. The number of hints needed, and also the time taken to solve the problem, were thus additional outcome measures.

In fact, there were no significant differences in solution time between children in the 5 conditions. However both conditions (1) and (2) had more spontaneous solvers than the other conditions. Children in condition (1) needed fewer hints than in (2), though more than in the other three conditions. Thus, some superiority for the play condition, (1), could be (and was) claimed.

This experiment was the first attempt to experimentally ascertain the value of play, which had been assumed without much critical questioning in textbooks up to that time. It was carefully planned, and ingenious in its yoking conditions. However, it and succeeding experiments had many shortcomings, which we will address after following the trail of succeeding studies.

The Sylva study had blazed a trail, but the actual findings of expected superiority for the "play" condition were not very substantial. Susan Dutton and I decided to do a follow-up study in which we sought to improve on the Sylva study in a few respects, and particularly to see how the play group fared compared to training on a truly innovative task, that is, one not shown directly in the training condition (Smith & Dutton, 1979). The "improvements" we made were to use sticks and small blocks with matching holes for the sticks to fit in, which while still relatively new to children were easier to manipulate than G-clamps; to allow a 2 minute exploratory period with these materials after the researcher had demonstrated how a stick could fit into a block; and to have a marble as the lure, which we thought more interesting than a piece of chalk. There were several sticks of different lengths provided, and several blocks. We had two tasks. In Task One, a child needed to join 2 long sticks with 1 block to reach the lure; in Task Two, the box was moved further away and they needed to make a tool from 3 long sticks and 2 blocks.

The children were 4 years old, and there were 36 in each condition (18 each in the 2 control conditions). The four conditions were (1) *play*: 8 minutes of free play with the materials; (2) *training*: 8 minutes in which the researcher makes 2-stick constructions of varying length and asks the child to imitate these and arrange them in length; (3) *control 1*: the child goes immediately to Tasks One and Two; (4) *control 2*: the child goes immediately to Task Two.

As can be seen, the training condition provides the "answer" to Task One. This is similar to Sylva's study, and we expected this training condition to do as well as the play condition if not better. But Task Two was innovative, going beyond the training; this was where, on Bruner's hypothesis, we thought that the superiority of play should be found. And, indeed, this was how the results turned out. Using the same measures as Sylva (number of spontaneous solvers, number of hints given, time taken to solution), we found no difference between conditions (1) and (2) although they mostly did better than condition (3). However on Task Two, the play condition (1) children did better than the training condition (2) children on all three measures (with control children generally doing worse than either).

We were very pleased with this finding. At that time I too was imbued with the "play ethos," and these results seemed confirmation that play could equal training on a direct problem-solving task (i.e. one that the training children had direct practice at), and exceed training on an innovative task, as the innovative problem-solving hypothesis had predicted. Soon after this, Vandenberg (1981) reported a similar two-task study with 4 through to 10-year-olds in the US. Vandenberg used notched sticks and pipe cleaners for materials and compared two conditions: (1) play (free play for 10 minutes); and (2) question-asking: the researcher asked the child questions about the physical attributes and lengths of the materials for 10 minutes. Here the results showed not much difference between the two conditions, but certainly the play children did as well as the question-asked children, in both tasks; and the middle age group of 6–7 year olds did need fewer hints in the play condition.

Critiques of the lure retrieval tasks

Cheyne (1982) provided a detailed critique of the early lure retrieval tasks, that set in motion further studies and indeed a re-evaluation of a considerable body of experimental work on children's play. In particular, he pointed out that the experimenters had not controlled for "experimenter effects." We know about this from the Clever Hans scenario; Clever Hans being the horse who could count by nodding his head the appropriate number of times (for example four times if asked "what is two plus two?"), but who was shown to be dependent on subtle, unconscious signals from his trainer (who for example might nod his own head slightly when Clever Hans had "finished"). As Cheyne pointed out, the researcher might give similar unconscious hints (smiling, nodding) as children moved towards making an appropriate tool; they might do this more in the play condition if they expected such children to do better. They might be more relaxed with the play children, or give hints more clearly. Such possibilities could be dealt with by having a researcher giving the tasks, who is blind to the prior treatment condition. There were also issues around scoring of responses which really should be done blind to treatment condition.

At the time I read Cheyne's critique, Tony Simon was starting with me as a doctoral student interested in play. It seemed an obvious step to redo the Smith and Dutton (1979) lure-retrieval task, but controlling for experimenter effects. I did not believe these experimenter effects would be so important, but clearly the issue had to be investigated. So we reran the Smith and Dutton task with more 4-year-olds, this time just comparing the *play* and *training* conditions (Simon & Smith, 1983). For half the children, the same researcher ran the conditions and then the task and scoring sessions; for the other half of the children, a second researcher took over the task and scoring sessions, blind to the prior play or training condition.

The results did not replicate Smith and Dutton (1979); no differences were found on any measure, either for Task One or Task Two, between the play and training conditions. We did not find any <u>direct</u> evidence for experimenter effects, as the "blind" manipulation had no impact on scores; but there might have been such effects in the earlier study, run by a different researcher. Nevertheless, initially skeptical of our new finding, we ran two further studies. Smith, Simon, and Emberton (1985) also manipulated the amount of researcher–child interaction; no difference between the play and training conditions were found. Simon and Smith (1985) used an alternative-materials control group (to see if the experimental materials had any effect, whether by play or training); this control group did as well as the play and training groups.

By now, it seemed that the superiority of play for innovative problem-solving was seriously under question. It seemed likely that in the strongest previous findings, the Smith and Dutton (1979) study, the researcher had unconsciously helped the play children in some way, quite possibly by giving unnecessary low-level hints to the training children (thus increasing their hint score and reducing the number of spontaneous solvers).

The associative fluency tasks

Another series of tasks, starting back with Dansky and Silverman (1973), had used short (10-minute) play or training conditions with everyday objects like beakers, paper clips, paper hankies, and clothes pegs, and then subsequently given an associative fluency test as a measure of creativity. In these tests a child is asked "How many uses can you think of for a [paper clip, screwdriver, etc]?" The scores are the number of standard uses (e.g. using a screwdriver to screw up a bolt) and the number of nonstandard uses (e.g. using a screwdriver to stab a burglar with). In this and subsequent studies (Dansky & Silverman, 1975; Li, 1978; Dansky, 1980), children in free play or make-believe play conditions did better than children in imitation, task, or control conditions on nonstandard uses (though not on standard uses).

This series of studies appeared to support the postulated link between object play and creativity, but were open to the same possible objections regarding experimenter effects. To check this out, Susan Whitney and I (Smith & Whitney, 1987) carried out a similar associative fluency task, but with appropriate controls for blind testing and scoring. No differences were found between play, training, and control conditions.

Conclusions regarding the experimental studies

The lure-retrieval and the associative fluency tasks, initially supportive of the link between object play and innovative problem-solving and/or creativity, were not found to be replicable once experimenter effects were controlled for. Several critical commentaries (Cheyne, 1982; Christie & Johnsen, 1985; Hutt, Tyler, Hutt, & Christopherson, 1989; Smith, 1988; Smith & Simon, 1984) focused on shortcomings of these, and a few other studies of a similar type (reviewed in detail in Smith & Simon, 1984). Amongst the difficulties raised were:

- Possible experimenter effects: in testing, and in scoring.
- Inadequate controls: for example for familiarity with the materials, or the experimenter. In particular, some control groups had less familiarity with the researcher, before the tests were given.

- Is the play condition playful? The issue here is that play is regarded as intrinsically motivated—do children actually play with the objects in the play conditions? And if they are "told" to play with them, is this free play?
- Inappropriateness of "yoking" procedures: the difficulty here is that a "yoked" experience is pushed through by the researcher, irrespective of the yoked child's inclinations or abilities.
- Inappropriateness of outcome measures: for example, are nonstandard uses such as using a screwdriver to stab a burglar, problem-solving in any real sense?

Smith and Simon (1984) argued that, beyond the issues of possible experimenter effects, these experimental studies suffered a lack of ecological validity. The short 8 or 10-minute sessions were not appropriate for the kind of learning that might realistically occur through play, that is, gradually through often repeated short bouts or episodes. They concluded that quite likely the benefits of play in real life occurred over longer time periods; this would preserve the functional hypothesis, while acknowledging still a lack of direct causal evidence.

A more naturalistic approach along these lines was attempted by Pellegrini and Gustafson (2005). The play of 35 children aged 3 to 5 years was observed in a US preschool over an entire school year. The children were then given a lure retrieval task, an associative fluency task, and a WPPSI Block design test to measure spatial intelligence. They found that children who had engaged in a lot of construction activities did better on the lure retrieval task (less time, fewer hints needed) and on the associative fluency task (more novel uses given). This is essentially a correlational study, but the findings held up even when spatial intelligence was accounted for, which would be one obvious factor to control. This suggests that practice in construction activities is indeed helpful for these new problem-solving tasks. The relevance for play is somewhat uncertain as they define construction as "building something that is end oriented (not play)" (p. 121)! Their overtly "play" category, which included pretending, did not yield positive corrrelations with problem-solving.

Summary

While it is plausible that object play helps develop object-related skills and also innovative or creative problem-solving, the evidence remains shaky. In particular, attempts to show the superiority of play to various training experiences in this respect have proved to be unstable and non-replicable. The lure-retrieval tasks were given particular attention, owing to their historical importance in showing the limitations of short-term experimental studies in providing such evidence. Most such studies have lacked adequate precautions against experimenter effects and, when these were instituted, the positive findings disappeared. Also, experimental studies so far have lacked ecological validity, and the correlational studies are unconvincing.

Much object play involves pretense. We will look at pretend and fantasy play in the next chapter. We will also see that corresponding issues have dogged experimental attempts to assess the functional importance of fantasy play.

Further Reading

Power (2000) gives detailed reviews of object exploration and play in animals and children, and two chapters in Pellegrini and Smith (2005) cover object play in great apes, and in children.

Chapter 8

Pretend Play: Description

Pretend or fantasy or play is a fascinating aspect of the behavior of children from around 2 to 6 years of age. It is fun to watch, and adults can have a part in encouraging it, although increasingly with age it is a peer group activity. Pretense and fantasy are generally taken to mean an "as if . . ." orientation: actions, objects, and verbalizations have non-literal meanings. A circular motion of hands represents turning a steering wheel; a wooden block represents a cake; a grunting noise represents a bear growling. Often such play involves distinct pretend roles such as mummy, fireman, doctor, monster. Examples of pretend play, including such role-playing, are given in Table 8.1, these being from transcripts made by the author while observing in a preschool playgroup (similar transcripts from the same playgroup are in Smith, 2005, Table 8.2).

More than other kinds of play, pretend play appears distinctively human. There are clear similarities in the kinds of rough-and-tumble play and sensorimotor object play seen in mammals, especially the non-human primates, and in human children. But in the case of pretend play matters are different. Because of its representational nature and its reliance on language, pretend play is seen as practically unique to humans. But, just as much as other kinds of play, there has been and continues to be debate concerning the value of pretend play in development and its role in the early childhood curriculum. In this and the next chapter we will look at these issues. We will start, however, with a discussion of the definitions of pretend or fantasy play, and whether (or to what extent) it can be seen in non-human species.

Definitions of Pretend or Fantasy Play

At least by the common criteria we use for assessing pretend play in human children (that is, non-literal meanings for actions, objects, and

Table 8.1 An Example of Sociodramatic Play Sequences Involving Several Girls and Boys

---

Emma is pulling a toy wooden pram, which Denise is sitting in. "Wait there!" says Emma, as she fetches a small cushion which she puts on Denise's legs, then another which she puts behind Denise's head. She spends some time arranging the cushions around Denise, then leaves her. Soon Emma is playing on the slide.

Meanwhile Miles, Anthony, and Jim have made pretend guns (bricks with a stick stuck in them). They run around making "pow" noises with these. Jim goes on the climbing-frame. "You're not a monster" shouts Miles to him from below. "This is, and it shoots people" replies Jim, making "pow" noises with his stick-gun. Then he gets down, adding "I'm looking for the real monster."

He sees Amanda. "I'm going to shoot at you monster," he shouts at her. Jim is joined by Anthony and they both hold stick-guns stretched out in front of them, pointing at her. "You be a monster," says Jim to Amanda. Amanda rather tentatively nods her head, and Jim "pows" at her.

Jim now turns to Emma, on the slide. "Emma, Mandy's talking to you, you be a monster," he says to her. Emma at first ignores him, but then Anthony goes "peep-peep" at her with his stick-gun, and Emma and Amanda together make "monster" hand gestures at him.

"Yikes, monsters!" yells Jim, "po-oow." Anthony goes "peep-peep" again. Emma and Amanda lie on the ground, as if dead. "Pow, dead, pow, pow," says Jim.

Louise comes and lies next to Emma and Amanda. Jim "pows" at her as well. He also says "you are a monster, pow!" to Lucy who is passing, but she is not interested.

Emma and Amanda get up, make monster noises, then lie down and roll on the ground. Jim starts "pows" again, but then pretends his stick-gun has broken. Miles comes up, takes his stick-gun, manipulates it a bit, and "mends" it.

Amanda continues some monster chasing with Anthony, Jim, and Miles.

However, Emma now has gone back to her pram. She calls out for Denise to come back and sit in it. Denise comes back and gets in the pram.

Miles has gone to a play house. It has a door (with a slit in it, and a window). "Come in the house, come in the house!" yells Miles, and Jim, Anthony, and Amanda join him. Miles, Jim, and Anthony go inside. Amanda steps up on a chair outside, and makes "monster" faces and hands at them through the window. "Yikes!" yells Jim, and the boys "pow" at her with their stick-guns. Amanda comes round and stands at the door. "Get out!" says Miles, closing the door. A session follows in which Amanda runs between the door and the window, going "rrr-rrr" at the boys inside.

Table 8.1 *(continued)*

Lucy joins Amanda. "I know you're a monster Mandy but I'm a monster" she says. They make monster noises outside the play house. "Ice-monster!" yells Anthony, three times. Emma now comes up (leaving Denise in the pram, which she now gets out of) and joins Amanda and Lucy. Lucy climbs in the play house through the window, and the three boys run off. Lucy chases them, then comes back and joins Amanda and Emma inside the play house.

Louise comes and tries to enter with the (now empty) pram. "No, this is our house Louise" Emma says. "This is our house and we're monsters." She pushes Louise out. Then she notices one of the playgroup staff watching her, and lets Louise in with the pram.

Lucy, Amanda, and Emma make monster noises, Emma peering through the door slit. Miles tries to open the door, but Emma goes "rrr-rrr" and he runs off. Miles sees Jason who is doing some paper glueing at a table. "Jason, there's some monsters in our house, Jason!" Jason ignores him. "There's some monsters in our house!". Jim hears him however, "monsters!" he yells, and he, Miles, and Jim run to the play house. They are joined by Gareth, who is wearing a toy police helmet.

Amanda chases Miles away. Miles falls on the floor, rolls over, and lies still. "He's dead!" calls Jim, looking at him. "Policeman!" Jim calls to Gareth; he points to Miles and turns him over. Anthony lies down next to Miles. "Hey, he's dead!" says Jim. Miles shifts his position. "He's dead again!" says Jim.

verbalizations), it would appear to be entirely lacking in most animal species. A possible candidate for pretense in other species would be play signals such as the play face, or play bow, which signal playful rather than aggressive intent in mammals such as monkeys, canids, felids, ursids (Bekoff & Allen, 1998; Fagen, 1981; see also Chapter 3); these might be argued to have an "as if" meaning. Indeed play fighting itself could be seen as non-literal in the sense that the apparently aggressive actions are not actually aggressive (Mitchell, 2007). However, the usual argument against taking such behaviors as pretense is that they are simply preprogrammed signals or actions, seen only in play, which indicate or substantiate playful intent by the actor (Gómez & Martín-Andrade, 2005; Smith, 1982). In other words, there is no awareness of pretense or intention to pretend or deceive. "The simulation is in the eye of the observer, not the player" (Mitchell, 2007, p. 64).

If we see awareness and intention as part of the definition of pretend, then we can view pretend play as part of a package of symbolic abilities, including also self-awareness, theory of mind, and language, which characterizes humans and of which we see only simple precursors even in the cognitively most advanced non-human species. Any exceptions to the absence of pretend play in animals, may be found with the great apes (Gómez & Martín-Andrade, 2005).

There are some accounts of what might count as pretend play in the great apes. An early, classic account is by Hayes (1951). The Hayeses reared a young chimpanzee, Viki, and attempted to teach her spoken language. They did not get very far with this objective—this was well before the breakthrough in teaching sign language to chimpanzees, which was much more successful. However, they did provide an account of how Viki, at 16 months of age, apparently had an imaginary pull toy. This was when she actually did drag real pull-toys behind her. In what was interpreted as pretend play, Hayes observed Viki walking along making tugging motions with one hand behind her. She also placed one hand above the other as if raising the imaginary toy. These actions were seen several times with some variations. At a similar anecdotal level, Morris (1962), in a book about chimpanzee art, recounts how, after a visit to a vet for an injection, a chimpanzee gave itself pretend injections, making the appropriate hand movements.

Other examples of play in enculturated chimpanzees (those reared by humans in a largely human environment) are reviewed by Gómez and Martín-Andrade (2005). They include Washoe, the first sign-language-taught chimpanzee, washing a doll in water in a bath-tub; and Austin, a chimpanzee trained to use lexigrams, who ate pretend food as if using an imaginary spoon from an imaginary plate and rolling it around his lips. Amongst bonobos, de Waal (1989) has described games of blind man's bluff, and Savage-Rumbaugh (1986) described how Kanzi, also taught on lexigrams like Austin, would hide and eat imaginary food.

In gorillas there are also possible examples of pretend play. Patterson (1980; Patterson & Linden, 1981; Matevia, Patterson, & Hillix, 2002) brought up a gorilla called Koko to learn sign language. Koko was reported to take part in a variety of pretend episodes. These included using signs, for example, kissing a doll and signing "good," and pretending to drink from an empty cup and signing "sip." She also made loud slurping sounds while "drinking" from an empty cup.

Documented cases of great ape pretend in the wild are rare, the cases cited above having been documented with human-reared great apes. However Gómez and Martín-Andrade (2005) do quote a few possible examples, including an 8-year-old male chimpanzee who carried around a log in various positions reminiscent of carrying a baby, and an 8-year-old female who broke off a stick and carried it similarly, following her mother who was indeed carrying a baby. Overall, Gómez and Martín-Andrade consider that such symbolic play (usually, "doll" or maternal play) is "not a characteristic pattern of wild chimpanzees, but a marginal, exceptional occurrence" (2005, p. 147).

All these accounts are of quite simple types of pretend play, which scarcely develop to role playing or any extended narrative sequences. However, they may be sufficiently numerous and consistent to suggest some simple abilities for pretense in the great apes. In this sense, they parallel corresponding evidence for simple abilities in theory of mind, language, and self-recognition (Smith, 1996). Mitchell (2007) also mentions possible pretend play in dolphins: after seeing a person exhaling cigarette smoke, a young dolphin suckled a mouthful of milk from her mother, returned to the window where she saw the person, and squirted out the water "as if" it were smoke.

There is some debate about whether such examples in great apes (or other very intelligent species, such as dolphins) actually merit being called pretend play. Lillard (1994, p. 214), writing about human children, has defined pretense as requiring 6 features: a *pretender*, a *reality*, and a *mental representation* that is *projected onto reality*, with *awareness* and *intention* on the part of that pretender. This can be regarded as a "tough" definition of pretense. It implies conscious intention, and an awareness of both the pretend reality and the actual reality, and thus some metarepresentational ability. This would rule out most or all non-human pretense.

However adopting this "tough" definition will also rule out much pretend play in infants (say, from 15 months to 2 years). As we will see shortly, this need not and probably does not satisfy such requirements (Jarrold, Carruthers, Smith, & Boucher, 1994; Lillard, 1993). Generally, both non-human (e.g. great ape) pretense and that of young infants are simple imitative actions done in a non-functional context ("feeding" or cuddling a "baby", for example). We do not know to what extent the pretender is "aware" of intentionally simulating reality. Really, we only become certain of this when slightly older children use language to explicit assign roles ("you be daddy") or negotiate or explain pretense ("it's not for real, we're only pretending").

Mitchell (2007) has provided an illuminating discussion of the meaning of pretense and its applicability to non-human species. He provides a definition of pretense as follows: "Pretending is intentionally allowing an idea, at least part of which an agent knows to be inaccurate about or unrelated to current reality (i.e. fictional), to guide and constrain the agent's behaviors (including mental states)" (pp. 53–54). Mitchell points out the considerable overlap between pretense and deception. Incidentally, his definition, like Lillard's, is of pretense, not of pretend play. We could take pretend play to be pretense that has the usual attributes associated with play (it is fun, done for its own sake, emphasizing means rather than ends).

Mitchell's (2007) definition of pretense does not require the same level of conscious awareness as Lillard's; Mitchell considers that "the pretender could enjoy creating part of something, but not the whole thing, and enjoy that, and it would be pretend. In some sense that involves 'awareness' of the pretend and actual realities, but not at a very deep level at all—the pretender could simply recognize incompleteness without concerning itself with 'realities' of one sort or another" (personal communication to the author, May 10, 2005). This allows Mitchell to consider human and non-human pretense on more equal terms, and he suggests some simpler precursors to full-blown pretense: what he calls "schematic play" and "functional symbolic play."

Mitchell describes "schematic play" as "enactment of schemas based on relatively canalized processes for perceptual-motor integration that is not based on associative learning or imitation of another's actions" (2007, p. 64). This could apply to play fighting and use of play signals, for example. Mitchell continues by discussing the idea of presymbolic play or functional symbolic play. He suggests that this involves imitation; plus some ability in visual-kinesthetic matching—the ability to recognize the spatial or bodily similarity between their visual experience of another and their own kinesthetic experience, and make some matching action to that observed. Procedures visually observed in others ("feeding a baby") may be imitated though one's own body actions, as in the maternal or "doll" play examples sometimes reported in great apes.

In a previous discussion of the ontogeny and phylogeny of theory of mind (Smith, 1996), I made use of Karmiloff-Smith's (1992) discussion of levels of representation, and this may also be useful in discussing the definition of pretense and pretend play. Karmiloff-Smith posited a representational redescription model, with several levels. Level I was implicit; the representation is available for use (whether "inborn" or through imitative or associative learning), but is not available to link with other representations in a flexible way. Level E1 means having representations explicit at the level of cross-system availability of procedural

components; "component parts [of a procedure] ... become accessible to potential intra-domain links" (1992, p. 20). Level E2 means
representations are explicit at the level of conscious access or awareness,
and level E3 means available at the level of verbal report. These two
last levels are not so clearly separated in Karmiloff-Smith's account as
are the others, and I will refer to them as E2/3.

Play fighting and the use of play signals in mammals can be considered as at the I level. It is an easily learnt repertoire of actions associated with certain cues and contexts. Developmental changes in the
roughness of play fighting are, in principle, explicable in terms of maturational and hormonal changes in the individual, and their response to
differing stimuli from their play fighting partners. However, this is no
longer the case when play fighting is intentionally used for other ends,
for example by a rhesus monkey mother to distract her infant from suckling (Breuggeman, 1978). This would seem to require some E1 ability.
So too would "cheating" in play fighting. Cheating in play fighting that
is done with awareness and conscious intent would of course be E2/3
level, but we have no clear evidence of this except from human children
who are at or near adolescence, where the evidence comes from observation (Neill, 1976) and also verbal self-report (Boulton, 1992b; Smith,
Smees, & Pellegrini, 2004; see Chapter 6).

Karmiloff-Smith's level I seems to correspond well to Mitchell's
schematic play level; and her level E1, where there is availability of
procedures across domains but as yet without conscious awareness or
verbal report (therefore, not yet fully symbolic pretend play), seems to
correspond well to Mitchell's presymbolic play or functional symbolic
play level. Karmiloff-Smith's level E2/E3 would correspond to full symbolic play, as in Lillard's definition.

Karmiloff-Smith argued that chimpanzees (and, *a fortiori*, other non-
human species) did not get beyond level I, or, if there is any further level
representation, "the higher-level codes into which representations are translated during redescription are very impoverished" (1992, p. 192). My own
view (see also Smith, 1996) is that this is too harsh on chimpanzees and
other great apes (see also Gómez & Martín-Andrade, 2005) and possibly other species such as dolphins (Mitchell, 2007). This is especially so
when we consider enculturated apes, who seem to show more joint attention and more deferred imitation, and who provide most of the examples of possible non-human pretend play. However, I see no compelling
reason to put chimpanzees or any other non-human species at the E2/3
level, or as showing fully symbolic pretend play. I think we would need
apes to be able to talk to us to convince us they were pretending (as

aware, intentional beings). It is debatable whether even Koko's use of signs in possible pretense rises to this level.

I also think that great apes would have needed language as social support to have evolved abilities to have this level of awareness (the greater representational level found in enculturated apes is a partial pointer to the importance of this).

Verbal self-report is important in knowing whether play with objects involve pretense. As we saw in Chapter 2, Smilansky (1968) distinguished construction play from symbolic or pretend play, and a 3 or 4-year-old child assembling bricks or Lego might be classed as engaged in construction play. However, if you ask that child "tell me what you are doing?" they may reply "making a spaceship" or "making a cage to put monsters in" (Takhvar & Smith, 1990). It is the verbal report that allows us to infer an awareness of intent to pursue a non-literal idea and to be confident of symbolic pretend play.

The Development of Pretend Play in Children

Pretend play in children begins during the second year of life, peaks during the late preschool years, and declines during the primary school years (Fein, 1981). In a home observational study, Haight and Miller (1993) found rates of pretend to be .06 minutes/hour for 12 to 14-month-old children, increasing to 3.3 minutes/hour at 24 months, and to 12.4 minutes/hour at 48 months, or about 20% of observation time. It has been found to account for over 15% of the total in school time budget (Field, 1994), and for 10–17% of preschoolers' and 33% of kindergartners' play behaviors; but Humphreys and Smith's (1984) observations found that it made up only 5% of 7-year-olds play time, and about 1% at 9 and 11 years (see Figure 6.3).

The beginnings of pretend or fantasy play in children can be seen from about 12 to 15 months of age. Piaget (1951) was one of the first psychologists to describe this in detail, again by recording the behavior of his children. He made the following observations of his daughter Jacqueline at the age of 15 months (the numbers refer to Jacqueline's age, in years, months and days):

every appearance of awareness of "make-believe" first appeared at 1;3(12) in the following circumstances. She saw a cloth whose fringed edges vaguely recalled those of her pillow; she seized it, held a fold of it in her right hand, sucked the thumb of the same hand and lay down on her side, laughing hard. She kept her eyes open, but blinked from time to time as if she were alluding to closed eyes. Finally, laughing more and more she cried "Nene" [Nono]. The same cloth started the same game on the following days. At 1;3(13) she treated the collar of her mother's coat in the same way. At 1;3(30) it was the tail of her rubber donkey which represented the pillow! And from 1;5 onwards she made her animals, a bear and a plush dog, also do "nono." (p. 69)

A lot of studies of pretend play around the 1970s were carried out by watching a child when he or she was put with some objects in a laboratory play room. This had the advantage of a standardized procedure in documenting age trends. Such work (e.g. Fenson, Kagan, Kearsley, & Zelazo, 1976) identified three developmental trends, also obvious from observational studies such as Piaget's. These were:

- *decentration*—a shift from self as agent to other as agent;
- *decontextualization*—moving away from using realistic objects in pretense, to less realistic or imaginary objects;
- *integration*—combining pretend acts to form sequences and narratives.

Characteristically, young children do pretend actions first with themselves, then with another object or person. In Jacqueline's case, this started with pretending to sleep on a cloth. More generally this process of incorporating others into pretend activities has been called *decentration*. The other objects or persons may be parents (e.g. the child tries to feed a parent with an empty cup) or stuffed animals or dolls. By around 24 months the child can get the doll itself to act as an agent, rather than have things done to it.

Early pretend play also depends heavily on realistic objects—actual cups, combs, spoons, etc., or very realistic substitutes. *Decontextualization* refers to the ability to use less realistic substitute objects—for example, a wooden block as a "cake" or a stick as a "gun". The more different the object from its referent, the more difficulty children have in using it in a pretend way; but adults can help the process, by modelling or prompting the pretend use. This was shown in a study by Fein (1975). She presented 2-year-olds with either realistic (plastic cup; detailed horse model) or less realistic (clam shell; vaguely horsey shape) objects. After modelling by an adult, 93% of 2-year-olds would imitate making a detailed horse model "drink" from a plastic cup; however, only 33% would imitate making a horsey shape "drink" from a clam shell. The less realistic objects made the pretense more difficult, especially as two substitutions were needed (the horsey shape, and the clam shell). If the horse alone or the cup alone were realistic, 79% and 61% of the children respectively could imitate successfully.

By 3 years of age this kind of decontextualized pretense occurs much more spontaneously in children's play. They also begin to incorporate imaginary objects or actions without any real or substitute object being present. While possible for 3 and 4-year-olds, this is easier still in middle childhood. A study by Overton and Jackson (1973) asked children of different ages to pretend to brush their teeth or comb their hair. They found that 3 and 4-year-olds mostly used a substitute body part, such as a finger, as the brush or comb; whereas most 6 to 8-year-olds (and indeed, adults) imagined the brush or comb in their hand.

Integration refers to combining a number of pretend acts, and perhaps actors, into some kind of narrative sequence. For example, a child might put a teddy to bed; wake it up, wash it, and feed it breakfast. Perhaps another teddy will be brought along to play with it.

Solitary and Social Pretend Play

The studies which illustrated the above aspects of pretend play during the 1970s and 1980s were mostly based on experiments or observations in constrained laboratory situations, where infants were provided with particular toys. Basically, these were observations of solitary play. But some limitations of this approach were highlighted in a report by Haight and Miller (1993), based on videofilms of children playing at home. This was a naturalistic longitudinal study, starting when the children were 12 months and continuing until they were 48 months. Although the sample size was small (9 children), the data obtained were detailed and revealing. While a minority of the pretend play they observed was solitary, about 75% of pretend play was social—first with mothers or parents, later with friends (peers). Even early pretend play was mostly social in character. Obviously, the laboratory studies do not give a full picture of what is actually happening in development—although all the three aspects summarized above do appear generalizable.

Howes and Matheson (1992) have described stages in the development of social pretense, based on both the observational and experimental literature. It appears that the mother (or older partner, perhaps a sibling) typically has a "scaffolding" role—supporting the play a lot at first by, for example, suggesting and demonstrating actions. For instance, the mother might "give teddy a bath" and then hand teddy to the infant. Thus a lot of early pretend play by the child is largely imitative; it tends to follow well-established "scripts" or story lines, such as "feeding the baby," or "nursing the patient." Realistic props help to sustain pretend play, but as children get to 3 or 4 years, they are less reliant on older partners and realistic props. They take a more active role in initiating pretend play; they adapt less realistic objects or even just imagine the object completely; and they show an awareness of play conventions and competently negotiate roles within play sequences.

The role of the mother or other adult in encouraging pretend play has been shown in many studies. Bornstein, Haynes, O'Reilly, and Painter (1996) looked at variations in naturalistic pretend play in 20-month-olds. Mother's symbolic play, as well as the child's language abilities, particularly predicted collaborative pretend play. Working with children from 27 to 41 months, Nielsen and Christie (2008) found that adult modelling of pretend play (using a doll's house and related props) increased pretend play by the children immediately afterwards, and that while some of this pretend was imitative, much was novel, suggesting a general facilitation of pretense.

In her work on siblings, Dunn (2004) has argued that an older brother or sister may contribute a lot to a child's pretend play experiences. She and her colleagues carried out studies in Cambridge, England, in which a second-born child was observed in interactions with their older sibling (usually 1.5 to 3 years older; so a 2-year-old younger sibling typically with a 4-year-old older sibling). She comments (p. 25) that mothers almost always focused on object-based pretense, using objects as props (on 97% of occasions, in fact). Mothers would make relevant comments and suggestions, as "interested spectators." In contrast, the older siblings would take part in complementary role playing with their younger brother or sister. They would closely mesh their play, using talk and nonverbal actions. Some 27% of their bouts did not involve objects at all.

Sociodramatic Play

From the age of 3 onwards, pretend play very commonly involves quite sophisticated social role-playing skills with peers. The term "sociodramatic play" was brought into prominence by Smilansky (1968). This refers to dramatic play, that is, play in which the child is clearly enacting a role, and to social play (dramatic play can be solitary, but this is relatively uncommon and would not count as sociodramatic). Smilansky used other criteria, such as a sustained narrative sequence lasting at least 10 minutes, but these further criteria were not widely used by others.

Smilansky was working in Israel, and often with children of immigrant communities from what she described as "culturally deprived" backgrounds. Using her criteria, these children generally showed little sociodramatic play, and what there was lacked the complexity seen in more advantaged groups. Smilansky also argued that sociodramatic play was very important in development, and this led her to develop "play training" schemes. She found that providing suggestive props (dressing up clothes, semi-realistic toys), and taking children on visits (e.g. to a zoo, a hospital) were helpful in facilitating sociodramatic play, but that these were much more effective if nursery staff themselves took a lead in initiating such play, suggesting themes and helping children sustain the narrative. In effect, nursery staff were providing the "scaffolding" to get complex sociodramatic play going, for children who (presumably) had lacked such scaffolding from parents previously. We know that there are cultural differences in attitudes to pretend play (Chapter 5), and these children had come from poorer peasant communities where perhaps such pretend play had not been especially valued.

Smilansky's work on play training has held up, in the sense that many studies since have found that children who show little complex play (whether pretend generally, or specifically sociodramatic) can indeed be encouraged to do more by play training, or play tutoring as it is sometimes called. Furthermore, it is likely that the children can then sustain more spontaneous play of their own subsequently. This technique has therefore been used in supplementation studies of pretend and sociodramatic play, which we will examine in Chapter 9 together with Smilansky's assertions about the importance of sociodramatic play.

Imaginary Companions

As pretend play becomes "decontextualized" (freer from lifelike props such as dolls), many children not only make use of imaginary actions or objects, but actually develop an imaginary companion (IC). Young children talk to their ICs and engage in pretend activities with them, and complex narrative sequences and histories may be involved. The proportion of children who have an IC varies from around 25% to 65% in different studies, and it is most frequent between 3 and 8 years; they are mostly abandoned by age 10 (Taylor, 1999).

Newson and Newson (1968) interviewed parents of 4-year-olds in Nottinghamshire, England, in the 1960s. Overall 28% of parents reported some imaginary companion phenomena. For example, a miner's wife said

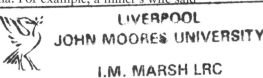

"Yes, she has Janet. It's a little girl. She came out with her—oh, more than a year ago. Everything's Janet—and yet she doesn't know anybody called Janet. But I mean—we can be watching television, and if my lad sits too close, its 'You're squashing her—get off!' And he *has* to get off, and all! I think we've all got used to Janet now!" (p. 185).

The Newsons found that ICs were more common in children in smaller families, reaching 41% in singletons. They were also more common in higher social class families. Many parents welcomed or were at least accepting of ICs, but some had worries. For example another miner's wife commented "I've said to him, you know, 'That's never happened, you're imagining things!' I've told him, I've said 'Now that's *wrong*—you've got a vivid imagination'" (p. 199).

Brooks and Knowles (1982) asked 100 parents of 3 to 5-year-olds in a lower-middle-class urban setting in the US for their views on imaginary companions (and other behaviors). Only 22% said they would encourage it, 42% were neutral, and 36% would discourage it. Views did depend on what the child might be doing with an IC. For example only 5% said they would discourage a child talking to an IC on the telephone; but 60% would discourage having to lay a place at dinner for the IC, and 62% would discourage the child from saying that they would only do something if the IC agrees. Clearly, some of the worries were practical ones, but some may be that IC and other fantasy activities are close to deceit and may lead to a confusion of fantasy and reality.

Leaving aside the practical issues of laying a table place for the IC, most evidence suggests that children with imaginary companions, while generally strong in pretend play orientation, are not confused about the status of their imaginary companions and are aware they are different from real friends. Taylor, Cartwright, and Carlson (1993) compared 12 children with ICs with 15 who did not have ICs, at 4 years of age. Those with ICs provided stable descriptions of them over a 7-month period; they were more likely to engage in fantasy play in a free-play session, but did not differ from those without ICs in their ability to distinguish fantasy and reality.

Majors (2007) carried out a detailed exploration of imaginary companions of five children aged 5 to 10 years, with them and their parents, in the UK. Four of the five children had several ICs—from three to six of them. Most ICs were human, a few were animal (a duck; a pony). One child, John, just had one IC but also created an elaborate imaginary world (sometimes called a "paracosm"). Majors found that the ICs were significant and important for the children, and she felt that they served several functions: these included being a pleasurable retreat or dependable companion, wish fulfillment, and entertainment. For example, one girl said she needed her ICs "when I can't get to sleep or when I'm lonely and times when I'm feeling sad or there's no one to play with or talk to." A boy who created a duck as an IC explained "I was swimming a width [in a swimming pool] and then I thought I would do another with my imaginary friend and I did and I needed it to be a swimming one so I chose a duck." This boy's swimming had since improved a lot and it is possible the imaginary duck helped him.

Relationships with ICs were generally very positive, but there could be negative elements; for example one boy had an IC called Tom who could be naughty and with whom the boy might fight. This boy commented that "it takes my anger out without actually hurting someone." Another interesting finding from this study was that while many ICs were public—known about by parents, siblings and friends—some were more private, especially amongst older children, who might feel more open to censure or teasing about it, if it were widely known.

Distinguishing Fantasy and Reality

When children have imaginary companions, and indeed when they are engaging in any pretend play, they do not usually confuse this with reality. Admittedly, this can happen sometimes. When an adult joins in with a 1 or 2-year-old's play, the child can be confused as to whether the adult is in "pretend" or "real" mode; for example, if a child knocks an empty cup over in play and mother says "you spilled your tea, better wipe it up," the child may actually pick up a cloth to wipe it. However, more usually, and especially by 3 or 4 years, the pretense–reality distinction is a stable one. Things would be difficult if it was not! Suppose a child pretends a wooden block is a cake, for a tea party; if they confused pretense and reality, they would actually try to eat the wooden block! This seldom happens. By 3 years children often signal the pretend mode in their play, for example, "Let's pretend to be families. You be daddy. . . ."

Direct interviews with 3-year-olds also confirm that they can generally distinguish real from imaginary situations, and understand the use of the words "real" and "pretend." Woolley and Wellman (1990) demonstrated that by 3 years children use terms like "real" and "pretend" in sensible ways in actual play: "you're not really dead, we're just playing." They also do so in experimental tasks; for example, if the researcher pretends to brush her teeth, and asks "Am I really and truly brushing my teeth or am I pretending to brush my teeth?", the great majority of 3 year olds answer correctly that this is pretense.

However, the possibility that children may sometimes confuse reality and pretense was raised by Harris, Brown, Whittall, Marriott, and Harmer (1991) in a series of experiments with children aged 3 to 6. For example, they showed children two boxes in a room and asked them to imagine that one had a friendly puppy (or rabbit) in it, and one had a scary monster in it. In fact the boxes were empty, and the children agreed they were just pretending about the animal or the monster. However, when a child was asked to put a finger or a stick through a hole into each box, they were noticeably more reluctant to approach the "monster" box and to put a finger (rather than a stick) into it. When questioned afterwards, they also admitted to some uncertainty about the reality status of the "monster" (something the authors called a "true fiction" error).

But, are we as adults always so sure about fiction and reality? Woolley (1997; followed by commentaries) reviews a number of studies in this domain, and emphasizes continuities from childhood to adulthood. There are many examples of what some would regard as superstitious behavior in adults (for example avoiding the number 13, which has no logical basis). Some adults believe in the reality of ghosts, UFOs, or Big Foot. Many adults also give some confusing messages to children, in talking about fictional entities such as Santa Claus or a tooth fairy as if these were real beings.

In a discussion of several studies of this kind, Bourchier and Davis (2002; followed by commentaries) proposed that, by 3 years, the distinction between reality and pretense is generally well understood, but that there can be exceptions. They then discussed a number of possible explanations as to when exceptions occur, of which they felt the most successful was what is termed the "availability hypothesis." This emphasizes mental availability in memory and the ease or availability of making judgments about real or pretend status. They concluded that confusions are likely when a reality check is difficult (for example, it is difficult to check the reality of the monster in the box without looking inside; whereas it is easy to check that a teapot is pouring imaginary tea, not real tea), and when there is a strong emotional component (such as fear), which makes a pretend entity such as a scary monster more salient (available for recall). The latter explanation was, however, not supported in a study by Carrick and Quas (2006). These authors found that the ability to discern fantasy and reality improved from 3 to 5 years, but for fantastic events this ability was actually better for frightening and angry images than for happy or neutral ones (although for real events, the reverse effect was found). They concluded that motivational processes were important, but that "children's fantasy–reality distinctions appeared to reflect their attempts to regulate their emotional reactions or their desires for positive events to occur and negative events not to occur" (p. 1286).

Gender Differences

There do not seem to be substantial differences in frequency of engaging in pretend play during the preschool period. Some studies find that girls engage in more frequent and more sophisticated pretend play than boys. Bornstein et al. (1999) found that mothers tended to engage in symbolic play more frequently with daughters than with sons, and these mother–daughter interactions predicted peer fantasy play. Nevertheless, in a review, Göncü, Patt, and Kouba (2002) concluded that findings are inconsistent and dependent on the play environment, toys available, and the kinds of activities measured. However there are sex differences in the themes of fantasy play. While girls' pretend play often involves domestic themes, boys' pretend play is often more physically vigorous, rough-and-tumble type activity, perhaps with super hero themes (Holland, 2003; Smith, 1977). Girls do seem to use their more mature language abilities in pretend play (Göncü et al., 2002). However the rough-and-tumble type fantasy play more typical of boys, generally involves more participants (Smith, 1977). Indications of gender differences can be seen in Table 8.1, where the boys do more rough-and-tumble type fantasy (although some girls join in), and the girls do more domestic fantasy. The sex role stereotypicality of the materials also influences boys' and girls' play. Boys' play with female-preferred toys, such as dolls, is less sophisticated then it is with male-preferred toys, such as blocks (Pellegrini & Perlmutter, 1989).

Pretend Play and Friendship

Children's pretense is more sustained and complex when they are playing with friends, compared to acquaintances (Howes, 1994). The mutuality and emotional commitment of friends may motivate children to sustain cooperative interaction (Hartup, 1996). A study comparing play in different sizes of preschool playgroup found that pretend play was more frequent in the small groups, even reaching to 50% of the time (Smith & Connolly, 1980); the smaller groups (of 10–12, compared to

20 or 30 children) led to some very close friendships, which very likely then supported such play.

The work of John Gottman and colleagues has examined the processes of developing and maintaining friendships in young children. Gottman (1983) observed pairs of children (aged 3 up to 9 years) playing in their homes; in one study the pairs were previously unacquainted, and Gottman observed them over 3 sessions. Often, children would establish a simple common-ground activity, such as colouring with crayons, that they could do side by side (a kind of "parallel play," see Chapter 2); they might "escalate" this by "information exchange" or "self-disclosure," perhaps commenting on the other's activity, or saying something about what they liked or wished to do. If successful, the pair would move on to introducing a joint activity. Often, such joint activity would involve pretend.

For example, Gottman (1983, pp. 56–57) describes interactions between D (in his own house) and J (visiting), both young 4-year-olds. After some information exchange, J says "pretend like those little roll cookies too, OK?" and D replies "and make, um, make a, um, pancake, too." Later D tries to introduce role play, and there is some negotiation:

> D: "I'm the mummy."
> J: "Who am I?"
> D: "Um, the baby."
> J: "Daddy."
> D: "Sister."
> J: "I wanna be the daddy."
> D: "You're the sister."
> J: "Daddy."
> D: "You're the big sister!"
> J: "Don't play house. I don't want to play house".

Despite D offering J progressively higher-status roles (but not equal to "mummy"!), this negotiation ended in failure, and what Gottman calls a de-escalation. For a while they returned to pretend meal preparation.

Gottman describes the social skill of friendship formation as managing levels of closeness ("amity") and conflict, by escalating, and when necessary de-escalating, levels of play. Colouring with crayons side by side has low risks and low benefits (in friendship terms). Simple pretend (e.g. pretending blocks are cookies) is a step up; and role play a step further. Thus, in Gottman's model, pretend play has a central role in the development of friendship.

Other Factors Affecting Pretend Play

Fantasy play is influenced by the play materials and the play companions available. Play themes generally follow those inherent in the materials available (Pellegrini & Perlmutter, 1989; Smith & Connolly, 1980). One controversial area here is the provision of toy guns, replica weapons, or combat figures for children's play. This has been referred to as "war play." It is often not approved of by teachers and is banned in many kindergartens. This specific issue is discussed further in Chapter 10.

Pretend play does seem to be affected by adverse circumstances (a theme we take up again in Chapter 10). It is less likely in malnourished children (Cullumbine, 1950), and in insecurely attached children. Securely attached children have been found to initiate more play interactions and the tenor of their interactions with their mother while playing is more positive than that of insecurely attached children (Roggman & Langlois, 1987; Bretherton, 1989).

Parental background and attitudes

There are a range of attitudes amongst parents to pretend play, and of course it can depend what form the pretense takes. The actor Peter Ustinov (1977, pp. 72, 74) has described how as a small boy "I was a motorcar, to the dismay of my parents. . . . I switched on in the morning, and only stopped being a car at night when I reversed into bed, and cut the ignition." On one occasion his continuing motor-car noises led his mother to shout at him to stop. But his grandfather intervened, reportedly saying "I know it is irritating . . . But don't think of it as the sound of an automobile, but rather as the sound of his imagination developing, and then you will see, it will become bearable."

In the Newson and Newson (1968) study mentioned above, some parents clearly valued pretend play. When asked if they would join in their child's imaginative play, an off-licence manager's wife replied: "He keeps saying, 'Mummy, will you come on this bus, it's sixpence at this end.' Course, you have to join in if you have the time. We do try to take an interest in that sort of thing, because we know that it's his mind at work all the while and he's learning all the while" (p. 173). Others did not join in such play, either because they thought it was less valuable, e.g. university lecturer's wife: "I'd say he does that more with other children, and therefore it's the more educative play that I indulge in"

(p. 178), or through lack of interest, e.g. labourer's wife: "I haven't got time for that sort of thing." Finally, a number were hostile to pretend play: "He'd make up [pretend] stories . . . It got so bad that I tried to stop it, because I didn't want him to go from an imaginary story to a downright lie—because there's not much difference between the two" (fitter's wife: p. 199).

Smilansky (1968) argued that the play of children from "culturally deprived" backgrounds was impoverished in terms of content, duration, and complexity. This led to a body of research suggesting that children from lower socioeconomic class backgrounds showed less fantasy play, due to less encouragement from parents. These studies were criticized by McLoyd (1982) for poor methodology. Some failed to define social class adequately, or confounded it with other variables such as race or school setting. The observations were mainly limited to nursery schools rather than other play environments such as streets or playgrounds. It is likely that global statements about social class effects on play are unwarranted; but there are related proximal influences such as the extent to which parents facilitate pretend play, and the availability and familiarity of materials available, which account for those differences that have been reported.

The way parents behave to children generally, may impact on social play. We saw above how Gottman (1983) described the role of play in friendship development. In a study with families of 4 to 6-year-olds, Kahen, Katz, and Gottman (1994) looked at possible links of this kind. They found that mothers and fathers who engaged in a lot of affective communication with their children had children who were better at establishing common ground with a play partner and getting into joint play. However, fathers who were emotionally volatile (often mixing positive and negative aspects of communication) had children who tended to stay at low levels of play engagement. Also, if parents were intrusive (interfering with children's actions), or used derisive humour with their child, their children were more often negative or conflictual in peer play.

A Universal Human Feature?

Fully developed pretend play, including role play and sociodramatic play, seems universal in human societies from anthropological accounts (Lancy, 1996). It is seen in hunter-gatherer societies (Konner, 1976; Eibl-Eibesfeldt, 1989), where pretend play occurs in mixed-age peer groups (e.g. children using sticks and pebbles to represent village huts and herding cows). Reviews of pretend play in non-Western societies by Schwartzmann (1978) and Slaughter and Dombrowski (1989) mention over 40 articles describing pretend play. There are certainly variations in the amount and type of such play, and it is influenced by the extent to which play is culturally cultivated, accepted, or curtailed (Chapter 5). It can appear "impoverished" in some societies (Smilansky, 1968; Gaskins, 1999); but it's presence appears ubiquitous.

In hunter-gatherer people such as the Kalahari San, Konner (1972) observed children using sticks and pebbles to represent village huts and herding cows. In the Hadza of Tanzania, children make dolls out of rags, and play at being predators (Blurton Jones, 1993). In a review Gosso, Otta, Morais, Ribeiro, and Bussab (2005) not only describe pretend and fantasy play amongst South American Indian communities such as the Parakanã (see also Chapter 5), but state that "children of all forager groups studied exhibit fantasy play" (p. 233). Such play is generally tolerated by adults rather than encouraged; and is generally imitative of adult roles in such societies.

Amongst settled agricultural communities, again pretend play is generally present; but some reports at least suggest it can be at low frequency. Gaskins (1999) observed children up to 5 years of age in a Mayan village community in the Yucatan, Mexico, and found that while pretend play happened, it was rare. Not only was it not encouraged by adults, but adults often placed early work demands on children. Even young children may be asked to help in looking after even younger siblings, running errands, scaring birds away from crops, preparing food, selling food, etc. Play in Kpelle children in Liberia has been described by Lancy (1996). Again, such play is imitative of adult roles. For example, make-believe play at being a blacksmith involves the kinds of social roles (blacksmith, apprentice, client) and behavioral routines (fetching tools, lighting fire, hammering) that, in more complex forms, are seen in the adult behavior.

Children with Autism

Children with some disabilities—including sensory disabilities, for example, hearing or visual impairments—may show some delay or difficulties in play (see Chapter 10). However, the syndrome that has attracted most research attention in relation to pretend play is autism. Many studies have shown that children with autism show less spontaneous pretend play than do control children matched for chronological or mental age.

In addition, what pretend play they do show tends to be repetitive and stereotyped (see e.g. Wing & Gould, 1979). This is sometimes taken as a core aspect of autism, and has been related to a metarepresentational deficiency (i.e. a difficulty in mentally constructing representations of representations; for example understanding that a block is a "cake" but just a "pretend cake") linking to their difficulties in theory of mind tasks (Baron-Cohen, 1989).

Jarrold, Boucher, and Smith (1993, 1996) suggested that while the deficit in spontaneous pretend play was a reliable finding, there was more evidence that children with autism could show pretend play when this was more specifically elicited or instructed by an adult. They compared children with autism to children with moderate learning difficulties, matched for receptive language abilities, in play with doll figures and junk objects. The children with autism did produce less spontaneous pretend play (as in previous studies), but, if instructed, as for example "make the [doll] eat a biscuit" or "show how the [doll] can be angry with someone," the children with autism did as well as the controls. In a later review, Jarrold (2003) raised the issue as to whether instructed pretend is really pretend (intentional representation) rather than just copying an action. However, not all such studies involved direct modeling by the experimenter.

Other possibilities raised to explain the difficulties children with autism have with pretend play are that these are generative (following from a lack of flexibility) rather than metarepresentational, or that they result from a lack of motivation or incentive (Jarrold, 2003; Kelly, 2006). A related suggestion is that children with autism feel inhibited in their pretend play (Kelly, 2006). This again is different from a metarepresentational account and, like lack of generativity, could be broadly classed as an "executive function deficit." Kelly (2006) carried out two studies comparing these accounts with the metarepresentational account, on the pretend play abilities of high-functioning autistic children (and in one study, Asperger's) in relation to typically developing controls. In general, although rather few differences were found in pretend play with these high-functioning autistic and Asperger's children, the role of inhibition in explaining such differences received some support.

Pretend Play as a Lifespan Activity?

Although pretend play declines in frequency after middle childhood, it can be argued that is does not disappear. Göncü and Perone (2005) consider that pretending forms a continuum from childhood to adult-hood. In adulthood, people pretend in dramatic improvisations, poetry, and dance—activities that enable development of representations of experiences with affective significance. Following the work of Vygotsky, adults, like children, are seen to move into an illusory world of pretending, trying to understand something they have not yet mastered in real life. Perhaps influenced by the "play ethos," these authors argue that pretend play is "as vital for Western adult functioning as it is for young children's development" (p. 145). We will examine the evidence for the functions of pretend play (in childhood) in the next chapter.

Further Reading

For pretense in animals as well as children, see R. W. Mitchell (Ed.) 2002. *Pretending and Imagination in Animals and Children*, Cambridge: Cambridge University Press. For social, pretend play see C. Howes 1992: *The Collaborative Construction of Pretend*, Albany, NY: SUNY Press; for make-believe play generally, D. and J. Singer 1991: *The House of Make-Believe: Children's Play and the Developing Imagination*, Cambridge, MA: Harvard University Press.

Chapter 9

Pretend Play: Theories and Functions

Many theorists have suggested that pretend play has important functions in development; for example for social and cognitive skills, narrative skills, imagination and creativity, and theory of mind. There are certainly good reasons to suppose that there are benefits to pretend play. Such reasons include the evolution of play and its species-specific nature in humans; its cross-cultural universality; the deficits in pretend play in autism and some other conditions; and the "design features" of pretend play. We will review these arguments, some of the main theories, and then the empirical evidence available.

Arguments for Benefits of Pretend or Fantasy Play

The evolution of pretend play

There is some evolutionary depth to the phenomenon of pretend play, as we saw in the beginning of Chapter 8. Nevertheless, the instances of pretend play in the great apes (and possibly a few other species such as dolphins) are relatively infrequent and quite simple. They do not take up any appreciable time or energy budget. There is no compelling argument for such play having a strong functional significance. Most likely, the episodes seen and described are by-products of the evolution of symbolic intelligence, going along with abilities to imitate, visual-kinesthetic matching, ability to recognize oneself in a mirror, proto-language abilities such as ape's signing, and abilities to engage in tactical deception.

On this line of reasoning, the motivation for children to engage in pretend play, and their facility in doing so, would have evolved during hominid evolution, during the approximately 4 million years since the australopithecines branched off from other ape-like species. Both Harris (2000) and Carruthers (2002) place this very recently in human evolution, with the advent of *homo sapiens* some 150,000 to 100,000 years ago. They cite what has been called the "sapient paradox" (Renfrew, 2007). This is a postulated gap between, on the one hand, the emergence of *homo sapiens* as a species and their rapid dispersal from Africa and, on the other, the obvious expression of many typically human behaviors that was delayed until the "creative explosion" of the Upper Paleolithic period about 40,000 years ago. This creativity was manifested in new stone-tool industries, cave art, body ornaments, burial practices, and a steady move towards engagement with the creative properties of stone, clay and metal from around 12,000 years ago. Harris (2000, p. x) sees this as evidence for "a new power of the imagination," the evolutionary emergence of which is related to the onto-genesis of pretend play in children. Carruthers (2002) suggests that during the "gap," a childhood disposition for pretend play was selected for over a period of perhaps 50–60,000 years. This selection would have been based on a pre-existing disposition to play (e.g. rough-and-tumble play).

Dating the emergence of pretend play so recently is interesting but very speculative. The existing evidence from the great apes suggests that the potential for pretend play may have been around at the time of the split, millions of years ago. If we assume that facility with pretend play would have depended on language ability, it is plausible that it evolved in parallel with the evolution of language. The timing of that is also a matter of great controversy, although advanced syntactical language may well date to the emergence of *homo sapiens* (MacWhinney, 2005).

Cross-cultural universality of pretend play

As we saw in Chapter 8, pretend play is more or less ubiquitous in human societies. It does vary in frequency, depending a great deal on time, opportunity, and the attitudes of adults; but it happens, and in favourable circumstances it happens a lot. Slaughter and Dombrowski (1989, p. 290) wrote that in the light of the anthropological evidence "children's social and pretend play appear to be biologically based, sustained as an evolutionary contribution to human psychological growth and development. Cultural factors regulate the amount and type of expression of these play forms."

Deficits in pretend play in autism and some other conditions

Pretend play is less frequent or absent in children with autism (Chapter 8); it is also less frequent and complex in children suffering emotional trauma (see Chapter 10). Harris (2000, 2007) takes this as an indication that the presence of pretend play is associated with positive functioning (rather than psychopathology) and thus may be associated with progressive aspects of development.

The "design features" of pretend play

Pretend play follows a rather predictable time course. It is fully characteristic of both genders. Harris (1994, p. 256) argued that "The stable timing of its onset in different cultures strongly suggests a neuropsychological timetable and a biological basis." This would tie in with the universality arguments to suggest that pretend play has benefits, especially during the preschool years and infant school years when it is most frequent. At these ages, it is clear that in pretend play, and especially in sociodramatic play, children are engaging in quite a lot of cognitive and social activities, compatible with it aiding various developmental competences in the preschool years.

Design features also provide a plausible argument that pretend and especially sociodramatic play give practice in narrative skills. Early pretend play has a simple story line ("feeding baby"), but soon becomes both more complex (i.e. a sequence of feeding, bathing baby, and putting to bed). In sociodramatic play, the narrative line being followed can be quite sustained and less dependent on routine scripts (i.e. more innovative elements such as putting out a fire, fighting monsters, travelling to a foreign country, are incorporated).

Theories Concerning the Function of Pretend Play

Amongst relatively recent theorists, Smilansky (1968) suggested that sociodramatic play was generally important for cognitive and language development, role-taking, and creativity. Her work on play tutoring (Chapter 8) led to a raft of studies in the 1970s and 1980s that examined pretend and sociodramatic play in relation to a wide range of cognitive and linguistic skills. These were critiqued (see below), but in my review at the time (Smith, 1982), I took the above general arguments for the benefits of pretend play to suggest that pretend makes play more complex and challenging than it would otherwise be and thus augments the general benefits it can bring. Alexander (1989) argued that social-intellectual play (or pretence) allows practice in "an expanding ability and tendency to elaborate and internalize social-intellectual-physical scenarios," using these to "anticipate and manipulate cause–effect relations in social cooperation and competition" (p. 480). This hypothesis remained undeveloped, but has some similarity to the more recent views of Mitchell and Harris.

Mitchell (2007) considers various aspects of pretend play—actions directed to self or others, use of substitute or imaginary objects (including whether miming is done by one's own body part or an imaginary substitute); and the traditional constructs of integration, decentration, and decontextualization. He regards integration as being the most indicative of developmental change in pretend as children get older. He suggests that "pretending about others was adaptive because of the utility of imaginative planning or apprenticing (learning by matching one's own actions to another's) or both" (Mitchell, 2007, p. 70). Lancy (1996, p. 89) argued that "make-believe play can provide opportunities for children to acquire adult work habits and to rehearse social scenes"; and this is a commonly held view in the anthropological literature.

Pretend play, imagination, and creativity

Harris (2000, 2007) has hypothesized the role of pretend play in the development of the imagination generally. He particularly cites how children use their imagination in a number of important cognitive processes. One is reasoning from unfamiliar premises. Suppose a child is told "All fishes live in trees. Tot is a fish. Does Tot live in the water?" A successful answer to this hypothetical question requires a child to suspend belief in the real world and enter into an imagined one. A second process Harris cites is judgments about obligation (for example, "you should wear an apron when you paint"). A correct judgment about an unfamiliar obligation (such as "you should wear a helmet when you paint") would require an ability to imagine a course of action not previously experienced in the real world. Harris also cites a third process, learning from testimony. Children can learn from what adults tell them ("testimony") concerning events, processes, or entities that are difficult for them to observe firsthand —perhaps about other countries, other people, mythical or religious entities. This too requires an ability to transcend experience that is directly encountered. Harris argues that imagination is necessary for all of these, and that pretend play is the crucible of the imagination in this respect.

Taking an evolutionary perspective (as noted above), Carruthers (2002) suggested that pretend play in childhood was selected for because it enhanced creativity in adulthood. He argued that creativity in adulthood would have payoffs directly, in terms, for example, of better tools and therefore better hunting and foraging success and of becoming more attractive to the opposite sex (by means of body ornaments, cave art, or other creative displays) and thereby increasing reproductive success. He thus argued that "the function of pretence should be to practice and enhance the kind of creativity which acquires so much significance in our adult lives."

His argument is in part based on the design features of pretend play. Creativity requires both the generation of a novel hypothesis or idea, and then the exploration of that idea by developing it and working out its consequences. In pretend play too there is first an initial supposition or imagined scenario, and then this is acted out or explored following familiar scripts and drawing inferences. (Although Carruthers does not make this additional point, *social* pretend play would be especially effective at developing a pretend supposition, because of the negotiations and sharing of meanings and knowledge that will take place).

Carruthers (2002) also critiques Harris' (2000) view that pretend play functions to provide practice in mental model building of the kind necessary for text and discourse comprehension, and understanding of testimony about the not-here-and-now. He asks why pretend play would be the best way to get such understanding—why do children have to suppose imaginary things, rather than just recollecting past events, or speculating about distant ones?

Pretend play, narratives, and early literacy

Sociodramatic play and imaginary companions have a story line and thus provide natural opportunities for developing narrative competence in children. Indeed, Nicolopoulou (2006, p. 249) argues that "we should approach children's play and narrative as closely intertwined, and often overlapping, forms of socially situated symbolic action." However she and others (Kavanaugh & Engel, 1998) argue that the integration of (pretend) play and of story-telling takes time. Sociodramatic play is seen as highlighting identification with and understanding of roles and developing rich and vivid characters, which are, however, of a generic type (doctor, monster, etc.), whereas children's initial story-telling shows more concern with constructing and elaborating coherent plots. Through the preschool years these abilities become more integrated.

This approach would be consistent with the theory of mind approach (next section), due to the emphasis on understanding multiple perspectives on roles and characters in pretend play. It also suggests that as play and story-telling become more integrated, they reciprocally assist in the development of narrative skills, including comprehension of stories, but also more widely the construction of possible and imaginary worlds (Bruner, 1986). Engel (2005) argues that the integration of play and story-telling skills allows children to engage in two types of narrative play, which she calls *what is* and *what if*. In *what is* play, children pretend the kinds of things they know of in their everyday world; in *what if*, they go beyond this into more fantastic realms beyond their direct experience. A child using a banana as a pretend telephone, to pretend to talk to their dad, would be an example of *what is* play; whereas if the banana was used as a magic rocket to go to the moon, this would be *what if* play. Engel (2005, p. 524) writes that "The worlds of *what if* and *what is* comprise particularly important spheres for the young child as they offer two different ways of exploring imagined experience. Both involve pretence, but one rests on plausible reconstructions of every day lived experience, while the other rests on exploring implausible and often magical events and explanations."

This contrast may be an important one, but in practice may be more blurred than Engel (2005) seems to imply. The examples of sociodramatic play in Table 8.1 show only very modest narrative skills, but appear to be a bit of a mixture of *what is* and *what if*. Early pretend is predominantly imitative, and it may be imitative of what children see adults doing at home, or (sometimes) at work, or what is read to them from a book, or what they see on a TV screen. Are the distinctions so large? Some adults do go to the moon. This argument has similarities to the discussion of distinguishing fiction and reality, considered in Chapter 8.

A related area is the argument that play, especially sociodramatic play, links to early literacy development (Christie & Roskos, 2006; Roskos & Christie, 2007). Narratives in play provide opportunities for enhancing pre-reading or literacy skills by structuring such play in various ways, for example by providing print materials, introducing message sending into the story line, etc. Christie and Roskos (2006) distinguish several relevant components of early literacy. One is oral language, and the evidence of sophisticated language use in sociodramatic play. Another is phonological awareness. The ability to talk about language is related specifically to children's phonemic awareness, or their awareness of the rule governing the sound system of English. An important component in learning to read involves children learning letter–sound correspondence (Pellegrini et al., 1995). This could be facilitated by the kind of rhyming and language games seen in toddlers. A third aspect is print awareness. Much sociodramatic play can facilitate this, for example "signing in" to a "doctor's surgery". General background knowledge and narrative integration are also seen as helpful in school readiness skills.

Narrative skills probably have a long history in human evolution, and it is quite conceivable that the play–narrative link is important in considering why pretend play evolved. However, the kinds of pretend and sociodramatic play seen in non-Western societies, and described in the anthropological literature, appear to be very predominantly *what is* play (see Chapter 5). The kinds of expanded or fantastical possibilities characteristic of *what if* play may be a relatively recent cultural development. Regarding possible links to early literacy skills too, we need to bear in mind that (unlike spoken language), literacy is a relatively recent human invention, dating back a few thousand years. It is not plausible that pretend play was selected for such skills in our evolutionary history, although this does not preclude that it can have such benefits in modern societies.

Pretend play and theory of mind

Since about 1995, a number of researchers have theorized that pretend play is causally related to acquiring a theory of mind. Possession of theory of mind is usually measured by the understanding that another person may hold a false belief, by means of tasks such as the unexpected transfer task and the unexpected object task (Mitchell, 1997). Since knowledge and beliefs are "representations" of reality, theory of mind involves a representation of a representation, a second-order or "metarepresentation." Adapting objects for pretend purposes (a wooden block might become a baby, for example) suggests some cognitive metarepresentational skills (an object is represented as something else, in the mind).

Leslie (1987) argued a very strong hypothesis in this respect: that pretend play is an indicator of metarepresentational abilities as early as 18 months, and is important in developing the ability for understanding that someone else may represent things differently (have different knowledge or beliefs) from yourself. According to him, the early age of onset of pretend play would suggest it has a leading role in these respects. However, Lillard (1993), and Jarrold et al. (1994) reviewed the evidence for Leslie's view, and each concluded that it is not supportive. Much early pretend play (up to 3 years of age) appears to be largely imitative, as is shown by Howes (1994; Howes, Unger, & Matheson, 1992). From their detailed descriptive analyses, there is little reason to suppose that social pretend play implies metarepresentational abilities on the part of the child until around 37–48 months. Similarly, Rakoczy, Tomasello, and Striano (2006) reported a considerable lag between what they call "earlier implicit understanding of pretence" and "a later more explicit understanding." Such a transition was assisted, in their study, by explicit training in using "pretend to" and "pretend that" language. The period when pretend play does show evidence for metarepresentation (3–4 years), is also the period when first-order theory of mind abilities emerge by most criteria, so there is no compelling age-related reason to postulate that pretend play has the leading role in theory of mind development that Leslie proposed.

Nevertheless, a more mainstream view has continued that at around 3 and 4 years "pretend play is perhaps our best candidate for a cooperative activity which furthers the eventual understanding of false belief" (Perner, Ruffman, & Leekam, 1994, p. 1236). The argument is consistent with an evolutionary perspective (both being abilities that are present at very simple levels in great apes, but much more evolved in humans) and with the simultaneous deficits of both pretend play and theory of mind in autism. The design features of pretend play also provide a plausible case. In social fantasy play, children typically talk about mental and cognitive states in the process of negotiating roles; for example, "doctors can't say that" (Pellegrini & Galda, 1993). De Lorimier, Doyle, and Tessier (1995) found children more intensely involved in negotiations in pretence than in non-pretence contexts. Howe, Petrakos, and Rinaldi (1998) found that at 5–6 years siblings who did a lot of pretend play were more likely to use internal state terms, especially in high-level negotiations about play. Brown, Donelan-McCall and Dunn (1996) observed interactions between 4-year-olds and their older siblings, a best friend, or their mother. Mental state terms were used a lot with siblings and best friends. Mental state term use co-occurred with pretend play.

Some support also comes from studies on attachment security, and having older siblings/playmates (Smith, 2005). Fonagy, Redfern, and Charman (1997) found that securely attached 3 to 6-year-old children scored better on a false belief task, even when chronological age, verbal mental age, and a measure of social maturity were controlled for. Meins (1997) found that sensitive mothers/caregivers who showed "mind-mindedness" and treated their children as "mental agents", taking into

account their comments, actions and perspective, had children who suc-
ceeded better on theory of mind at 4 years. Why might there be a link
between security of attachment, and ToM abilities? Pretend play is
enhanced by security of attachment and was advanced as one possible
causal link (together with others such as competence in peer group interaction, and quality of conversational exchange).

There is also considerable evidence that children with older siblings
pass theory of mind tests earlier; Ruffman, Perner, Naito, Parkin, and
Clements (1998) found a nearly linear effect, with each extra older
sibling (up to 3) being equivalent to about 6 months of age/experience.
Lewis, Freeman, Kyriakidou, Maridaki-Kassotaki and Berridge (1996)
extended this finding to the number of adults and of older children that
the child was in regular or frequent contact with, and argued for an
"apprenticeship" model of theory of mind development. The causal mechanisms proposed by these authors are several, but include cooperative
activity and role assignment and enactment in pretend play (as well as
others such as familiarity in interactions; talk about feelings, causality
and inner states; reasoning about moral issues; familiarity with deception; and management of conflict).

Summary

There are clearly a range of theories concerning benefits of pretend play,
with some supportive evidence, for example, from "design features." Before
looking at the sources of evidence for these, we need to consider how
to match up the evidence against different expectations. In earlier
publications, I (Smith, 2002, 2005) suggested three models for examining the relationship between pretend play (or indeed, play generally) and
developmental outcomes (see Figure 9.1).

Models of the Role of Pretend Play in Development

The three models vary in the degree of importance they attach to (pretend) play.

- Model [1] is that pretend play is a by-product of other aspect(s) of
  development, with no important developmental consequence(s) of it's
  own.

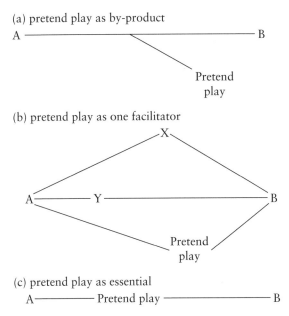

(a) pretend play as by-product

(b) pretend play as one facilitator

(c) pretend play as essential

Figure 9.1 Diagrammatic depiction of 3 models of how pretend play might function in development, as a child progresses from A to B

- Model [2] is that pretend play is a facilitator of developmental consequence(s); it can help bring about important developmental consequence(s) but it is not essential for this if other expected developmental pathways are present.
- Model [3] is that pretend play is necessary for important developmental consequence(s); in the absence of pretend play, these developmental consequences will not occur or will at least be significantly held back.

Model [3] is essentially that of the "play ethos" discussed in Chapter 2. Many play workers and theorists would assume this. Model [1] would be the opposite, seeing no intrinsic specific benefits to play (beyond an enjoyable way of spending time). Model [2] is a compromise; it sees benefits to play (compared to doing nothing), but also sees other non-play routes to these benefits (called "equifinality" in Chapter 2).

These are models of the function of play in individual development (rather than, say, of possible functional roles of pretend play in a societal context). They are obviously "broad-brush" models: in models [2] and [3] there could be further issues about threshold effects—whether certain amounts, frequencies, or types of pretend play are necessary or sufficient to have developmental consequences.

The models are meant to be applied to play as it is in contemporary children, but it is also possible that through the course of human bio-cultural evolution there have been shifts from one model to another. We could envisage some shift from model [3] to model [2] if recent cultural changes now provide more pathways to development than was the case in earlier times. For example, reverting for a moment to physical play, physical training might have been a strong or essential function of physical activity play in our hominid ancestors, but organized physical training exercises in schools and even kindergartens could now provide such benefits. Or, it is possible that model [1] shifted to model [2] or [3] if an existing ability was put to new uses. Indeed, the Harris and Carruthers arguments (above) about the selection for pretend play in *homo sapiens* would be such a case, if we assume that the prior ape-like abilities of simple pretence were "spin-offs" (model [1]).

My own overall view is that model [2] is the most supported in terms of the evidence—for pretend play, and indeed for most kinds of play. However, the evidence is certainly not conclusive. We will look next at the sources of evidence, particular examining cross-cultural comparisons, within-culture correlational studies, and experimental studies.

Evidence for the Functions of Pretend Play

Cross-cultural comparisons

An interesting cross-cultural comparison of play in four communities was reported by Morelli, Rogoff, and Angelillo (2003). They observed children aged around 2 to 3 years in the Efe of the Democratic Republic of the Congo, a traditionally hunter-gatherer (foraging) people though now also doing some farming work; a Mayan agricultural town in San Pedro, Guatemala where people worked either at home (weaving, trading, carpentry) or as labourers or farmers; and two middle-class European American communities (in Massachusetts, and Utah) where parents had a lot of formal schooling, and a majority were employed away from home.

The main differences found were between the Efe and San Pedro community children on the one hand, and the U.S. children on the other. Both the Efe and San Pedro children were seen some three to five times

more often in "emulation of work in play," imitative of adult work activities (for example playing store, pretending to cut firewood, making
tortillas out of dirt, pretending to shoot animals with a bow and arrow,
comforting a doll). Indeed, they had much more opportunity to observe
adult work activities, than children in the two U.S. communities. By contrast, the U.S. children were seen four to five times more often in play
with an adult. They were also seen sometimes in "scholastic play"
(literacy- or numeracy-related activity for fun, such as singing alphabet
songs, reading a story); and some ten times more often in conversations
with adults on child-related topics (e.g. "Did you have a nice time playing on the swings?").

In pre-modern societies there is likely to be some tension between skills
children may acquire through play (mainly through imitating adult subsistence activities), and contributions they might actually make directly
to subsistence. There is going to be a developmental trade-off between
skills gained through play and skills learnt and contributions to subsistence actually made through helping in the activity itself; in other
words, between "practising for the future" and "contributing now." As
children get older, the balance shifts. This was shown by Bock's (1995,
2005) work in the Okavango Delta, Botswana, referred to in detail in
Chapter 7. Bock examined object play (play pounding), but this is often
done in pretend contexts. Parents may tolerate/encourage such play or
require girls to take part in actual subsistence activities, such as actually pounding grain, sifting it, etc. From his data, the developmental
crossover for girls' play pounding is at 9–10 years.

This tension between play and work seems less in foraging societies,
but more pronounced in agricultural communities. Finally, in contemporary societies we have a situation where (apart from housework) adult
subsistence activities are both less visible to children and also much more
complex. Whereas a child play-pounding grain may actually develop some
useful skills for real pounding, it is unlikely that a child playing a doctor develops useful skills for being a real doctor to any similar extent.

However, in contemporary societies adults enter much more into children's play. They encourage certain kinds of play, including pretend play;
talk about play; and generally channel, structure, or co-opt play towards
more educational ends. These are examples of what MacDonald (1993)
calls parental investment. This can be seen in a positive light, as increasing the skills dividends that pretend and sociodramatic play might provide. But it is worth bearing in mind that parents' interests are not identical
with children's interests, and when parents attempt to channel children
into more "educational" forms of play; this may or may not be in the

child's own interests. Parents themselves may be manipulated by media, commercial, and manufacturing interests to purchase and "consume" toys, backed up by the prevalent "play ethos" (Smith, 1994; Sutton-Smith, 1986; and see Chapter 10).

So far, the evidence suggests a sensitivity of levels of pretend play to context and adult encouragement, and a balancing of energy and time costs of play against other priorities (e.g. conserving energy if malnourished). This seems very compatible with model [2]. Model [1] fails to predict the ubiquity of pretend play (even when disapproved of). Model [3] fails to explain why pretend play is so volatile in relation to other circumstances, without obvious impact on the kinds of predicted developmental outcomes.

Correlational studies of pretend play

A considerable number of correlational studies have been carried out, linking pretend and sociodramatic play to a range of outcomes. Many of these were reported in the 1970s and 1980s and linked pretend play to language skills, conservation abilities, creativity, and role-taking and perspective-taking abilities. These studies often produced some positive findings.

For example, Connolly and Doyle (1984) assessed the frequency of social fantasy play, and its complexity (based on pretend transformations) in 91 preschoolers aged 35 to 69 months. They correlated these with 8 measures of social competence. Of 16 correlations, 8 were significant: both frequency and complexity of social fantasy play correlated with teacher rating of peer social skill, peer-ranked popularity, affective role-taking, and an observational measure of social activity. They did not correlate with teacher-rated cooperation, cognitive role-taking, and observational measures of successful attention seeking and resource use, or of negative interactions. Although these correlations did not partial out age, subsequent regression analyses confirmed that the significant findings remained when age was taken account of.

Notably in this study the correlations were stronger for social than for cognitive variables. In fact, several studies have failed to find correlations between pretend or dramatic play and cognitive variables. The Johnson et al. (1982) study on 4-year-olds (Chapter 7) found no relation between dramatic play, and scores on verbal intelligence, nonverbal intelligence, or Piagetian conservation tasks. Johnson (1978) observed 42 children aged 4 years with their mothers; imaginative (pretend) behavior by mothers was, as expected, correlated with imaginative behavior by the children. However, these were not found to correlate with two measures of divergent thinking ability. Peisach and Hardeman (1986) examined pretend play in 65 children aged 4 to 7 years, in relation to a range of measures of logical thinking. Across the whole sample, "there were very few significant correlations, and the values were low" (p. 241). Cole and LaVoie (1985) assessed play in 78 children aged 23 to 6 years, in play dyads; they also measured emotional role-taking, spatial egocentrism, and verbal intelligence. Controlling for age, correlations with sociodramatic play were actually negative with role-taking, and non-significant for the other two variables.

More recently, many studies have correlated pretend play to theory of mind abilities. Harris (2000) reviewed four such studies, and concluded that "we have persuasive evidence that role play . . . is a correlate . . . of later success in false belief tasks" (p. 45). Let's look at one example of the studies he cites. Taylor and Carlson (1997) studied 152 children aged 3–4 yrs. They measured pretend and fantasy play (including level of pretend play, impersonation, imaginary companions) and derived a Principal Fantasy Component. They correlated scores on this with performance on theory of mind tasks. They controlled for verbal intelligence. They found no relationship for 3-year-olds, but a significant relationship for 4-year-olds ($r=.27$, or .20 when controlled for verbal intelligence) and a modest correlation for the whole sample of $r=.16$, $p<.04$—significant, although accounting for only 2.6% of the variance. Taylor and Carlson concluded "our intuition is that extensive fantasy experiences help children develop an understanding of mind," (p. 452), and that "the results of this study provide strong evidence that there is a relation between theory of mind and pretend play development in 4-year-old children" (p. 451), while admitting that inferences about causality are not warranted.

This example is typical of quite a large number of studies, and the conclusion quoted is a fair one, if we read "relation" simply to mean "correlation." But let's review some of the limitations of correlational studies. One is very well-known: a positive (or indeed negative) correlation found, could be due to one or more "third factors." For example, verbal intelligence could both help children in complex pretend play and separately help their performance on theory of mind tasks. Thus, Taylor and Carlson did well to control for this. Similarly, chronological age, or developmental status measured in other ways, or experiences such as having older siblings, or having a lot of adult conversations, might be "third factors" in this domain. Taylor and Carlson separated their two main age groups, which is in some ways better than just partialling out age from the correlations. This showed that the correlation was absent at 3 years and present at 4 years. Nevertheless, any study is limited in the number of aspects it can partial out or control for and, of course, a crucial one may be omitted. Most correlational studies simply control for either age, or verbal intelligence (a few do neither, and thus their results are of little value).

Correlational studies can be strengthened by introducing a longitudinal component—obtaining the correlations at two (or more) points in time from the same children, and then examining the cross-lagged correlations. In another study cited by Harris (2000), Astington and Jenkins (1999) did this for language skills and theory of mind. Controlling for age and earlier abilities, earlier language ability predicted later theory of mind, but earlier theory of mind did not predict later language ability, which suggests that skill in language development might be an underlying factor that explains theory of mind skills.

Another set of issues about correlational studies are what measures are actually correlated. For example, there are many possible measures of pretend play: frequency, complexity, use of role play or impersonation, transformations, diversity of themes—and so on. In fact, Taylor and Carlson had nine measures of pretend play, in addition to their overall measure. Most such studies have fewer measures. If you have a lot of measures, you get more useful information, but there can be a danger then of "cherry-picking" the perhaps one or two significant findings, without applying appropriate (e.g. Bonferroni) corrections for multiple statistical tests.

But, however many measures you have, you may be missing out on the aspect of play that is important—for example, maybe it is language use in pretend play that is important, not just overall amount of time spent in it. And the measures need to be age-appropriate. Indeed, Taylor and Carlson (1997, p. 451) invoked this kind of argument: "we are not certain why this relation between fantasy and theory of mind was not found for the 3-year-olds. Perhaps our methods for assessing individual differences in fantasy were not as appropriate for younger children as for the older ones."

Harris (2000) specifically suggested that role play would be an important correlate, rather than simple measures of the amount of pretend or fantasy play. This is because Harris argues for a simulation process in pretending; a child imagines him- or herself in an imaginary situation and acts appropriately. He then suggests that such a simulation process could also be used to predict (imagine oneself in) another person's mental state. Harris contrasts this approach (which he advocates) with a more representational view of pretending; this latter would suppose that pretend play is metarepresentational, and thus will facilitate an understanding of mental representation. The former (simulation) approach predicts that role play will be specifically important for mental state interpretation, whereas the latter (representational) approach would predict that any kind of pretend play will be helpful.

Since Harris (2000) wrote his book, more correlational studies on pretend play and theory of mind have appeared. In order to attempt a systematic analysis, I collated nine studies that presented such data (Smith, 2005, 2007). Together with an additional study, the results are summarized in Table 9.1. This shows correlations obtained between theory of mind abilities (e.g. false belief tasks, deception tasks) and various pretend play measures. In all cases except one (as indicated) these correlations are controlled or partialled for age, or a general age-related measure (e.g. picture vocabulary score, mean length of utterance).

I related this pattern of correlations, to what might be expected from the three models described earlier; see Table 9.2. Clearly model [1], the "by-product" model, would predict that pretend play would correlate with theory of mind (or indeed other measures) only by virtue of age or general developmental status. Once these were controlled for or partialled out, correlations would be around zero. Model [2], the "equifinality" model, would predict that correlations would generally be positive, but not especially large, as pretend play would just be one of a number of facilitators; correlations might also vary a lot across studies, since the various opportunities for other (non-pretend) routes to theory of mind outcomes might vary in different samples (for example, by numbers of older siblings, amount of language stimulation in the home, etc.). Finally, model [3], the "play ethos" model, must surely predict consistently strong positive correlations. If pretend play is essential for theory of mind, or at least the major player in this development—if this is it's primary functional significance—then we would predict a broad range of substantial correlations (by substantial, I would suggest around .7 or more, that is, explaining at least half of the variance in theory of mind differences).

Table 9.1 shows that the overall pattern of correlations was very patchy. Firstly, out of over 50 correlations reported, only one is negative; the pattern of positive correlations does seem to contradict expectations from model [1]. (A proviso here is that some correlations, indicated as *ns* in Table 9.1, were simply given as non-significant with no actual value reported.) But, about two-thirds of the correlations are not statistically

Table 9.1 Correlations Between Measures of Pretend Play and Theory of Mind in 3 to 5-year-old Children in 10 Different Studies

Play measure	Correlations	Study
Amount of fantasy/ pretend play, or general fantasy/ pretense	.16	Astington & Jenkins, 1995
	ns, .26	Youngblade & Dunn, 1995
	.16* (3 yrs: ns; 4 yrs: .27*)	Taylor & Carlson, 1997
	.09	Nielsen & Dissanayake, 2000
Diversity of themes	ns, ns	Youngblade & Dunn, 1995
	.27	Lillard, 1999
Imaginative play predisposition	.07	Taylor & Carlson, 1997
	.06, .46**	Schwebel, Rosen, & Singer, 1999 [1st study]
Favourite play activity	.11	Taylor & Carlson, 1997
Solitary pretend play	.12, .27	Schwebel et al., 1999 [1st study]
	.17, −.22, .07	Schwebel et al., 1999 [2nd study]
Joint pretend play	.14, .36*	Schwebel et al., 1999 [1st study]
	.18, .03, .36**	Schwebel et al., 1999 [2nd study]
	.25*	Dunn & Cutting, 1999
Joint proposals	.49**	Astington & Jenkins, 1995
Explicit role assignment	ns, ns	Youngblade & Dunn, 1995
	.37**	Astington & Jenkins, 1995
	.35*	Nielsen & Dissanayake, 2000
Role enactment, role play	.31*, ns	Youngblade & Dunn, 1995
	.24	Nielsen & Dissanayake, 2000
Imaginary companion	.20*, ns	Taylor & Carlson, 1997
Impersonation	.21**, .17*	Taylor & Carlson, 1997
	.15	Lillard, 1999
Pretend actions, object substitution, transformations	.26**, .13	Taylor & Carlson, 1997
	.01	Lillard, 1999
	.17, .03, .29*	Schwebel et al., 1999 [1st study]
	.35*	Nielsen & Dissanayake, 2000
Body part as object pantomime	ns	Suddendorf, Fletcher-Flinn, & Johnston, 1999
	.09	Nielsen & Dissanayake, 2000
Imaginary object pantomime	.25**	Suddendorf et al., 1999
	.35**	Nielsen & Dissanayake, 2000
Identify pretense	.26, .16, .08	Rosen, Schwebel, & Singer, 1997 [no controls]
Brain pretend questions	.14	Lillard, 1999
Attribution of animacy	.23	Nielsen & Dissanayake, 2000
Moe task	ns	Lillard, 1999

Table 9.2 Predictions Regarding Correlational and Experimental Evidence for Each Model of the Function of Pretend Play in Development

	Correlational evidence (correlations of pretend play measures with other developmental skills).	*Experimental evidence* (comparing developmental outcomes for groups with enhanced or deprived pretend play experiences and control groups).
MODEL 1 (no important function)	Any correlations would be around zero, once age or general IQ or language ability is partialled out.	No differences expected between groups if other experiences are equated.
MODEL 2 (one of many routes)	Correlations would be positive, but very variable in size depending on other circumstances.	Any differences favouring pretend play groups would be very dependent on what the control group experiences are.
MODEL 3 (essential for development)	Correlations would be consistently positive and of appreciable magnitude.	Consistent differences favouring enhanced pretend play groups (or disadvantaging deprived play groups).

significant; and no single correlation reached the r=0.50 level (the largest is .49, explaining one-quarter of the variance, but most are much lower in size). I concluded that these findings were consistent with pretend play being one kind of experience useful for theory of mind skills (model [2]), but not consistent with it being a very important or essential factor (model [3]). Looking at the different measures of pretend, it does seem that just the amount of pretense or pretend play is not a major correlate with theory of mind. Verbal indicators such as making joint proposals, or explicit role assignment, have higher correlations, but not consistently in the latter case (as Harris might predict).

Not included in Table 9.1 are studies that only examined understanding of pretence. For example, Mitchell and Neal (2005) reported correlations of .56 and .49 between false belief scores, and measures of understanding the nature of pretending actions. These cognitive measures seemingly produce higher correlations than the behavioral measures in Table 9.1, although language ability was not controlled for and might plausibly contribute to both sets of measures.

Experimental Studies

Controlled experimental studies have been seen as the best approach to testing causal hypotheses. Although longitudinal correlational studies can potentially provide stronger evidence for causal links than conventional (single time point) correlational studies, they are still open to the "third factor" objection. But if participants are randomly assigned to experimental and control groups, and the experimental group receives (say) an enhanced pretend play experience, then any beneficial outcomes should be due to this difference between the experiences of the two groups; "third factors" are controlled for so long as the experimental and control groups are genuinely randomly assigned and (better still) are shown to be equivalent on such measures (e.g. age, verbal intelligence).

However, experimental studies also have problems, and a more critical evaluation of this body of work appeared by the 1980s, as was documented in Chapter 7. Some main problems identified there (selective interpretation of results; possibility of experimental bias; and use of inappropriate control groups) unfortunately apply just as strongly to the studies looking at pretend and sociodramatic play.

A considerable number of experimental studies on pretend and sociodramatic play have been carried out since the 1970s. We will look at three types: first, some studies carried out on individual pretend play, in relation to cognitive abilities—these were short-term experimental studies, with durations of some 10–15 minutes, of the kind reviewed in detail in Chapter 7; second, longer play-tutoring studies inspired by the work of Smilansky (1969); third, a small number of more recent studies on pretend and theory of mind.

Short-term studies of individual pretend play

A series of studies by Dansky and colleagues suggested that pretend or make-believe play helps associative fluency (a measure of creativity), as measured by unusual uses of familiar objects. This was argued for play generally, but most specifically for make-believe play (e.g. Dansky, 1980). As discussed in Chapter 7, these studies had shortcomings and could not be replicated when blind testing and scoring was implemented (Whitney & Smith, 1985).

Another series of studies was reported by Golomb and colleagues (Golomb & Cornelius, 1977; Golomb & Bonen, 1981; Golomb, Gowing, & Friedman, 1982). They suggested that the transformations that occur in pretence (for example, a chair is transformed into a space rocket, then later back to a chair again) would assist in understanding the kinds of transformations that occur (in size and shape, etc.) in the standard Piagetian conservation tasks. Working with 4 or 5-year-olds, they compared pretend play conditions (involving reversible transformations) over a small number of sessions with control conditions (constructive play or conservation training). Two studies found that pretense play training was especially effective in bringing about understanding of conservation (the Golomb and Bonen study, with late conservers, found that pretend play training was equally effective as additional conservation training).

These studies too did not take systematic precautions to exclude experimenter effects; the same person trained the children and tested them. Subsequent studies of this kind, by Guthrie and Hudson (1979) and Hutt et al. (1989), have failed to replicate the results obtained.

Longer-term play tutoring studies

Another spur for experimental work was the research of Smilansky (1968), who had observed that immigrant children in Israeli preschools did not show much sociodramatic play and that they were also behind in language and cognitive skills. She argued forcefully that sociodramatic play was essential for normal development in preschool children, and that, if a child was deficient in it, intervention should be carried out to encourage and enhance it. Smilansky, and others, found that it is quite possible to get children to do more and better sociodramatic play by having preschool teachers and staff model such play, encourage it, take children on visits (e.g. to hospitals, zoos), and provide suitable props and equipment—what was called "play tutoring."

A number of intervention studies through the 1970s and 1980s used play tutoring to test Smilansky's hypothesis about the importance of sociodramatic play. Equivalent groups of children (e.g. classes from the same school) either experienced play training, or acted as a control group to allow for effects of age and general preschool experience. Differences between pre- and post-test performance on various developmental tasks were compared; if the play-tutored children improved more, this was felt to be strong evidence that sociodramatic play really was important. Studies of this kind all reported positive results—it seemed, whatever outcome tests the researchers used, play-tutored children improved more!

In these studies, the interventions typically lasted some months, often a school term, and were embedded in the normal preschool or kindergarten setup. Thus, they avoided the artificiality of the short-term studies; but other difficulties (equivalence of control groups, testing and scoring bias, selective presentation of results) still were common. Of these, the issue of control group equivalence was probably the most important. Most studies did not employ control group(s) that only differed on the measure (e.g. pretend-play experience) that inferences were being made about. For example, a pretend-play-enhanced group was compared with a control group which not only had no pretence enhancement, but also less verbal stimulation or adult involvement generally. Thus it was not clear whether improvements in the experimental group were due to pretend play or verbal stimulation.

Further experiments were run to control for these difficulties, with better control groups and with blind scoring. Generally, the specific benefits of play tutoring were not then found. When control groups were equated for verbal stimulation ("skills tutoring"), then both play and control groups improved with time and age (Christie & Johnsen, 1985; Hutt, Tyler, Hutt, & Christopherson, 1989; Smith, Dalgleish, & Herzmark, 1981; Smith & Syddall, 1978). For example, in Smith et al. (1981), we compared play tutoring with skills tutoring; both conditions had similar adult involvement and verbal stimulation (this was checked by systematic observations), and differed only in the pretend nature of this. Comparing two pairs of preschool classes, over a term and with a later follow-up, we found that these two tutoring conditions had very similar impact on a range of measures of cognitive, socio-cognitive, and linguistic development. The only differential impact of play tutoring was on social participation, perhaps because the play tutoring, more than the skills tutoring, encouraged more social interaction between the children themselves.

In general it seems that the general adult stimulation is important, rather than specifically the pretend play. Indeed Hutt et al. (1989, p. 116) commented: "We would seriously question the importance placed upon fantasy play as an aid to cognitive development." In my view, these findings are again consistent with pretend or sociodramatic play being one way to gain skills, but no more so necessarily than other ways of actively engaging with the social and physical environment.

Subsequent to this critical debate in the 1980s, some experimental studies have been made of pretend play in relation to narrative competence and theory of mind. These generally do not refer to the critical studies of earlier work we have just reviewed.

A recent study of pretense and narrative competence

A study by Baumer, Ferholt, and Lecusay (2005) reports the effects of playworld educational practice on the development of narrative competence in 5 to 7-year-olds. The playworld practice was developed in Sweden and Finland by Lindqvist and Hakkarainen; it involves adults working with children to encourage pretend play, dramatic performance of a text from children's literature, and visual art production. The Baumer et al. study attempted an evaluation of this approach, in a public school in Southern California. They used the C. S. Lewis text *The Lion, the Witch, and the Wardrobe* as the foundation for the study. In one class (experimental), the teacher led 14 sessions in which portions of the text were enacted, followed by guided discussion. In another class (control) the teacher led 14 sessions without pretense or dramatization, reading the book followed by guided discussion and picture drawing or story writing.

The children were pre- and post-tested on four measures of narrative competence, using sequencing and discussion of five pictures. On all four measures, the experimental class improved more than the control class, statistically significant on two (length of utterances and narrative coherence).

How does this study measure up against previous concerns? The two conditions were reasonably well matched; both groups had a pre-treatment period of getting acquainted with the book, where it was ascertained that the two teachers were handling the reading activity in a similar manner. The experimental condition does appear to be generally more exciting and active, however. It seems that the testing was done blind to condition, although this is not stated explicitly: graduate students not involved in the project did the testing. So far as presentation of results is concerned, a claim for significance is made for one variable, narrative comprehension, which does not involve a proper comparison of the two groups. However, the main limitation, acknowledged by the authors, is the small sample (20 and 18 children in the two classes).

More recent studies on pretend and theory of mind

Dias and Harris (1988, 1990) reported two studies of the effects of make-believe play on deductive reasoning. They produced experimental evidence that setting current reality aside and imagining a fictive alternative may be important in understanding false beliefs, and thus in theory of

mind development. However, their studies suffered some of the limitations of the earlier studies of the 1970s–80s. In the 1988 study, there was no blind testing (though scoring was done blind). In the 1990 study, there was neither blind testing nor, apparently, blind scoring. Also in all studies, a "let's pretend" instruction was actually present in all conditions. Leevers and Harris (1999) reported further studies within this paradigm, leading them to reinterpret the earlier work. They now argued that it was not the fantasy or pretend component, but simply any instruction that prompts an analytic, logical approach to the premises, which helped at these syllogistic tasks.

A direct training study on pretend play and theory of mind by Dockett (1998, and personal communication), in an Australian preschool center, compared two groups of children who attended morning and afternoon sessions. All children were pre- and post-tested on measures of shared pretence and on theory of mind ability. One group of children received play training for 4 weeks, focusing on sociodramatic play around a pizza shop theme. There was a visit to a pizza restaurant where the chef demonstrated how pizzas were made, followed by designing a pizza area in the preschool and centering a lot of play and activities around this. Teachers took opportunities to extend such play. The control group experienced the normal curriculum.

The play training group significantly increased in frequency and complexity of group pretence relative to the control group. They also improved significantly more on the theory of mind tests, both at post-test and at follow-up 3 weeks later. Dockett argued that the social negotiations and verbal communications in the shared pretence had helped develop the theory of mind skills of the intervention group children. This study provides the best evidence yet for a causal link from pretend play to theory of mind. However the sample was small (15 and 18 children, respectively), and the two groups were not closely matched; also the testing was not done blind to condition. Replication of this finding with better controls is necessary to establish the generalizability and validity of the finding.

Summary

We have seen that the patchy correlational evidence for benefits of pretend play (including, but not limited to, theory of mind), appears most consistent with an equifinality model (Model 2, Table 9.2). So far, I believe this is also true of the experimental evidence. The work from the 1970s and 1980s showed that the outcomes of pretend or sociodramatic play training were very dependent on the nature of the control group experiences. When control groups are given reasonably equivalent stimulation, they tend to improve just as much as the play training groups. Exceptions to this may be explained by non-equivalent aspects of the groups. For example, in Smith et al. (1981) the play-tutored groups did improve more on social participation, perhaps because the skills-tutored groups were less encouraged to engage in pupil–pupil (rather than pupil–adult) interaction. In the Baumer et al. (2005) study, the two conditions may not have been equated for excitement and engagement.

Having said this, I would add two provisos. The first is that pretend play experiences and pretend play training may naturally bring about a range of experiences that are relatively difficult to duplicate by other forms of experience or training. For example, sociodramatic play is by definition social; acting out stories in dramatic play is social, and likely to be exciting and engaging. Thus, the possible non-equivalence of play and control groups, as noted above, for example, may be rather intrinsic to play rather than, ultimately, something to easily "control" for. Second, there remains a dearth of well-designed experimental studies of respectable sample size. A few promising recent studies (Baumer et al.; Dockett) were on very small samples. In addition, studies must institute blind testing; they also need to try and equate non-play experiences of the control group(s) (e.g. verbal stimulation), and give a good description of the various conditions.

Finally, even if model 2 is correct, this emphatically is *not* an argument for devaluing pretend play and its educational role. It clearly is one pathway to many beneficial outcomes, through the experiences it generates. It is also fun. An enjoyable activity with educationally beneficial outcomes is a natural opportunity for teachers, and parents. But, unlike model 3, it should not lead us to over-emphasize and idealize play. If an otherwise happy and healthy child chooses not to do a lot of pretend play, or if in a certain society pretend play is not heavily valued, we have little basis on which to be concerned, or censorious.

Further Reading

P. L. Harris (2000), *The Work of the Imagination*, Oxford: Blackwell, takes forward his ideas on pretence, role play, and imagination more generally. K. Roskos and J. Christie (eds), (2007), *Play and Literacy: Research from Multiple Perspectives* (2nd edition). Hillsdale, N.J.: Lawrence Erlbaum, is a useful collection around pretend play, narratives and early literacy.

Chapter 10

Some Practical Issues Concerning Play

In preceding chapters we have looked at the types of play in non-human animals and then, quite extensively, in human children. We've seen the variety of types of play; and examined the evidence for whether such play is important in the developmental process. Much of this research may seem somewhat academic—which it is!—but play research also has important practical implications. In this chapter we will look at some of these: the role of parents in encouraging and structuring children's play; the role of play in the early childhood curriculum and play training; attitudes to war play; the arguments for (and against) recess breaks; the role of play in helping children under stress, or with illness or disability; and the use of play therapy. In all of these areas, play research has some important input; though none is without controversy and debate.

The Role of Parents in Encouraging and Structuring Children's Play

Quintessentially, children's play is seen as something children do with each other (or sometimes alone). But, in fact, adults are often involved in children's play. Parents may engage in physical activity play with infants (Chapter 6), peek-a-boo or social contingency games, and can do a lot of scaffolding of early pretend play (Chapter 8). As we saw in Chapters 5 and 8, such parental (or adult) involvement in play is something especially characteristic of modern Western societies, and of more educated or higher SES groups in such societies. Lancy (2007) has highlighted contrasting perspectives on mother–infant play, and from an anthropological perspective makes the point that the Western encouragement of mother–child play is far from universal.

But is this involvement to be welcomed? Does it bring benefits to the children who are played with in this way?

Let's first look at the evidence from non-human play, especially primates. There, the great majority of play is between peers (Chapter 3). But, adult–infant play does occur, certainly in monkeys and apes. When it does, it is usually mother–infant, or adult male with an infant it might well be a father to. For example, adults may play-fight (showing restraint, of course!) with infants. This takes up some time and energy for the adult, which in behavioral terms is a "cost," so we should expect a corresponding "benefit." This might be in terms of strengthening the social relationship, or in helping the infant develop the kinds of skills that such play might facilitate. This would be called "parental investment." The parent is investing time and energy in activities that will benefit the infant.

There is another possible explanation for adult-infant play, however. Breuggeman (1978), in watching rhesus macaque play, noted that mothers might use play as a distractor. For example, an infant might persist in trying to suckle, more than the mother wants to tolerate (weaning conflict), so the mother might tickle or play-fight with the infant in order to stop this. Or, if two infants are squabbling, an adult might play-fight with one of them as a distraction. Here, play is being used manipulatively—that is to say, the play is for the benefit of the adult and not obviously for the benefit of the infant (who might want to continue suckling or fighting). Similar uses of play have been described by van Lawick-Goodall (1968), in chimpanzees.

In humans, cultural factors become of major importance, but we can still trace these two strands of argument. On the one hand, play is part of the process of cultural transmission from one generation to the next (Chapter 5), and to varying extents in different cultures, parents may see themselves, often quite consciously, as helping their children by playing with them. Of course, it is generally fun as well! But the play ethos, journals and books for parents, and many organizations, definitely encourage it. Parents who do not naturally value play are encouraged to do so. The considerable investment that some parents put into structuring play with their children, and buying many toys for them, suggests they see this as valuable for children's development. MacDonald (1993, pp. 128–129) argued exactly this: "the movement to encourage higher levels of parent–child play among lower-class families . . . is . . . an attempt to modify parenting practices toward a high involvement, high investment parenting style which is ideally suited to life in an advanced post-industrial society."

There may indeed be some benefits to children from enhancing their play; but we should not (in my view) overvalue it, or "idealize" it (Sutton-Smith & Kelly-Byrne, 1984). From the viewpoint I have advanced, and which I believe the evidence supports, play is just one way to learn various skills or acquire various experiences. Play is generally fun; but not all play is fun, and not all play is approved of by parents (see later section on war play). And, let's not forget the second strand of argument: there can be manipulation involved in play, and in the encouragement of play. Parents may manipulate children, a theme coming through in some of the anthropological literature, where play is seen as a way of getting children out of an adult's way and keeping them occupied. And another level of manipulation comes in, with "culturally cultivated" play (Chapter 5). There is obviously an industry for play, and especially for toys to play with—in many cases, a profligate use of resources to produce toys that have transient interest for the child. Simple materials —blocks, cardboard boxes, paper, crayons, and similar staples—can keep children occupied for hours, without much need for the panoply of sophisticated and media-driven toys that many well-off parents in developed societies typically provide.

The Role of Play in the Early Childhood Curriculum: Play Training

Similar analyses can be brought to bear on the role of teachers and nursery staff in nursery and infant schools. However, here there has been more diversity of positions in modern industrial societies. One comes from some advocates of the "play ethos" who see play as pre-eminently "the child's way of learning" and argue that free play is most beneficial for children well into infant school. Thus, neither structuring of play, nor direct instruction methods are seen as appropriate. Another perspective comes from the play training work promulgated by Smilansky (1968) and extols the virtues of nursery staff encouraging and structuring pretend and sociodramatic play, especially in "disadvantaged" children, by means of play tutoring, because of the educational benefits this would bring. This was taken up quite widely by advocates of structuring play in the early years at school (Manning & Sharp, 1977). A third, and generally more recent, perspective, notably in the USA (see Zigler & Bishop-Josef, 2004) and the UK (see Hall, 2005), is an emphasis on direct instruction and a neglect of play opportunities, in order to improve cognitive and literacy skills in young children, including those from disadvantaged backgrounds.

The idealization of free play has some point if one is concerned about the manipulation of play by adults and wants children's play to be "natural" and unconstrained. It may well facilitate children's opportunities for social learning, and for physical exercise (see discussion of recess breaks, below), though the postulated educational (cognitive) benefits of free play with objects are probably exaggerated (Chapter 7). Adult structuring of play may well boost play in some children who do not do much, and may well turn it to more conventionally educational ends; but the more adult structuring there is, the more we get away from true play, and the more scope there is for manipulating activities in the interests of adults. Adults may encourage sedentary and pretend play with toys, rather than active physical or rough-and-tumble play. They may encourage "toy consumption" (Sutton-Smith, 1986). Is this good for the child? There is no simple answer to this, but we should bear in mind that children do also enjoy and probably get benefits from the kinds of play that adults do *not* prefer.

Finally, direct instruction can be an efficient way of learning—but only if it holds a child's attention and they feel motivated. Play may often be a less efficient way of learning, but it does have the advantage of the child enjoying it. Again, we have no easy single answer. The play training studies, by and large, suggest some equivalence of outcomes between play opportunities, structured play, and instruction. Given the uncertainties, and the varied needs of differing children, many researchers, myself included, argue against extreme positions and for a "blended program" that combines all these types of experiences, in the early years (Christie & Roskos, 2006).

Attitudes to War Play

Although children's play tends to be seen positively by adults, play fighting is not always approved of by teachers, and even more controversial is play with war toys. The term "war play" has been applied to games with toy guns, weapons, and combat figures, as well as pretend fighting or warfare. This kind of play has elicited concern from some writers; unlike most pretend play this is *discouraged* by many adults and is banned in many kindergartens. A "zero tolerance" approach has been taken by many education authorities and early education establishments in the UK, USA, and other countries (Holland, 2003).

There appear to be periodic waves of concern about the use of war toys by children. Andreas (1969) has documented how, in the 1960s (the period of the Vietnam war in the USA), advertisements for war toys in magazines like *Toys and Novelties* and *Sears Christmas Book* nearly tripled over the period 1961–64/5. Following protests by parents and educators, this level of advertising fell back by 1967.

A new wave of concern can be dated to the 1980s. Carlsson-Paige and Levin (1987), in *The War Play Dilemma*, contrasted a developmental view—that play including war play is a primary vehicle for children to express themselves—with a socio-political view that children learn militaristic political concepts and values through war play. They followed this up with a more practical handbook, *Who's Calling the Shots* (Carlsson-Paige & Levin, 1990). They argued that war toys and combat figures encourage stereotyped, good-versus-evil aggressive scripts in play, which impoverish the child's imagination and encourage actual aggression. They recognized the difficulties in banning such play entirely; for example, if replica guns are banned, children may make them from Lego or just use their fingers! However, they did advocate adults intervening to shape such play toward more constructive and less aggressive ends.

Not all writers agreed with such concerns. For example Sutton-Smith (1988) argued that for children, war play is clearly pretend and just reflects an aspect of real life like other pretend play does. He quoted one boy who said when his father asked him not to use toy guns: "But Dad, I don't want to shoot anybody, I just want to play."

A study carried out on parent's attitudes in Italy and the UK (Costabile, Genta, Zucchini, Smith, & Harker, 1992) found that views of parents were very varied, but could be split into three broad camps. Firstly, some followed a developmental view that war play is a natural kind of play, clearly pretend, and that it may even help children come to terms with an adult world in which much violence occurs:

> "A natural part of a child's development, just as they act out cooking etc. War/fighting is featured in so many things it would be difficult and unnatural to exclude it from a child's life."
> "It is just imaginative play that all children need. It helps to get rid of frustration which has built up in them."
> "Harmless, like adults reading war books, watching war films. It is a fact of life that conflict exists and a child learns all things through play."

A quite opposite view echoed the concerns of writers such as Carlsson-Paige and Levin:

> "I do not like it. In fact children who do war play become less sensible and less obedient."

"I do not buy any toys in this field as I feel it makes children very aggressive."

"I say it is very noisy and does she really want to kill people because that is what happens when people are shot. As soon as she puts the toy down I remove it."

Finally, a third group adopted an intermediate view. They allowed such play, but often within limits:

"I'm bothered if it's excessively noisy and violent, but otherwise can accept it as part of a child's acting out internal tensions and external experiences."

"If the play involves other children who are overzealous in their play I put a stop to it. If it is just fun with a friend I do not mind."

"Unsure. We don't encourage it, but don't discourage it, either."

Many parents commented that this was a difficult issue, and a majority (three-quarters) did support some ban on war play in nurseries or play groups, even if it was allowed at home. In recent years, many nursery and infant schools in a number of countries have put restrictions on such toys and activities.

Do war toys have long-term effects on individuals, or produce a climate of acceptance of violence? The issue is somewhat analogous to the debate on violence in the media and its effects on children; this has been characterized by a great deal of research of an often inconclusive nature, which is open to varying interpretations, and allows no consensus to be reached (Gunter & McAlean, 1997). There is not a large research base specifically about war toys on which to make informed judgments about whether the concerns are justified. A study by Watson and Peng (1992) reported that for 3 to 5-year-old boys (not girls) there was an association between a history of toy gun play and levels of real aggression, but this correlational study might simply mean that temperamentally aggressive children like playing with toy guns.

Dunn and Hughes (2001) studied 40 "hard-to-manage" and 40 control children in London, filming them playing alone in a room with a friend when they were 4 years old. The "hard-to-manage" children showed more violent fantasy; and the extent of violent fantasy (across both groups) was related to poorer language and play skills, more antisocial behavior , and also to less empathic understanding two years later at age 6. The longitudinal nature of this study does give stronger evidence for causality, and does suggest concerns specifically for the effects of such play on these rather disturbed children.

There has been some shift amongst writers and practitioners, away from the more extreme versions of banning war toys (not actually advocated by Carlsson-Paige and Levin, who advised redirecting the play). In the UK, Holland (2003) has documented her shift from an original position of banning war toys to a recognition that, for boys especially, rough-and-tumble type fantasy activities are a common and enjoyable activity which it can be counter-productive to ban. This work is cited in guidance from the Department for Children, Schools and Families (2007): *Confident, Capable and Creative: Supporting Boys' Achievements*. This states (p. 16) that "Images and ideas gleaned from the media are common starting points in boys' play and may involve characters with special powers or weapons. Adults can find this type of play particularly challenging and have a natural instinct to stop it. This is not necessary as long as practitioners help the boys to understand and respect the rights of other children and to take responsibility for the resources and environment." This was highlighted in the press: "Let boys play with toy guns, ministers advise nursery staff" (*The Guardian*, December 29, 2007).

In fact the guidance in the DCSF document is balanced, with its final sentence on rights and responsibility for others and the environment. We clearly need to consider the interests of children themselves, their parents and families, and the wider society, as well as being aware of the pressures on toy manufacturers to sell their products (Smith, 1994).

As a rule children may choose toys and play in a way that satisfies their needs, and this should be allowed. Totally banning any kind of war toys or war play is likely to be unnecessary (it is pretend, not real), unjustified (there is little or no evidence for negative effects for most children), unethical (we may want a more peaceful world, but the world is not peaceful, and it is debatable that we should use children as pawns in trying to change this), and counter-productive (children who want to do so will find ways around the ban, and it may even make such "forbidden" toys more attractive).

Having said this, some concern about certain forms of this play seem to legitimately remain. One concern might be when such play becomes disrespectful of particular groups, for example, minority groups. As an extreme example, "a miniature Nazi concentration camp complete with crematoriums for turning tiny figures of Jews into soap" (cited in Andreas, 1969) would be beyond acceptability for most people. A second concern is that (as in the Dunn and Hughes, 2001 study) some already disturbed or violently aggressive children may have these tendencies amplified or exacerbated by war toys and violent fantasy. Such a child using very violent play may, even if satisfying their own needs, be disruptive of others, and failing to develop more constructive or prosocial activities.

As in many areas of life, there may not be a very clear answer to the "war play dilemma.". My own view is that we should not be too concerned about the ordinary range of such play, in most children. However, we should be concerned if such play becomes very violent or obsessive—and look for reasons for this (not just in the toys themselves). Any toys that stereotype minority groups in any negative way should not be allowed. Also, some restrictions on very realistic war toys (guns, bombs) might well be reasonable in nursery and infant schools, provided that this does not go to the extent of banning rough-and-tumble type fantasy activities that many boys especially enjoy.

The Arguments For (and Against) Recess Breaks

Another policy area involving play, is the provision of break time or play time (recess breaks in the USA) in schools. These typically occur mid-morning, at lunch break, and mid-afternoon, for periods ranging from 10 or 15 minutes up to an hour. The length and timing of playground breaks does not appear to be based on any sound evidence regarding their benefits or otherwise for children, but rather on tradition, convenience, and assorted opinions.

There has been pressure to reduce playground breaks, on both sides of the Atlantic (Pellegrini, 1995a). In a survey of schools in the UK, Blatchford and Baines (2008) found that (following earlier reductions in the 1990s) there have been further reductions in the length of lunchtime breaks, and the afternoon break has been virtually abolished for children aged 7 years and above; a majority of pupils in their survey thought that lunch time breaks were not long enough. These changes have been rationalized by a desire to maximize classroom teaching time and avoid disruption to lessons. In addition, opponents of recess have cited the likelihood of antisocial behavior and bullying occurring in playground breaks. These arguments against recess are weak. Let's consider them one-by-one.

Recess time diminishes time spent learning

This is true, on a very limited, narrow definition of "learning." Of course, recess time is not normally spent on standard curriculum activities. But even if we take that view of learning, the cross-cultural evidence suggests no negative effects of recess breaks. Stevenson and Lee (1990) compared educational achievement in American, Japanese, and Taiwanese schools. The children in Japanese and Taiwanese schools generally achieved better; in these schools there were also frequent short breaks between lessons (usually 10 minutes every hour). Of course, many other factors may contribute to the differences in achievement observed, but the efficacy of breaks would be consistent with much psychological literature on the benefits of spaced practice rather than massed practice on learning (Dempster, 1988).

Moreover, taking a broader definition of learning, children are undoubtedly learning a lot during recess breaks, primarily in the area of social relationships. Blatchford, Baines, and Pellegrini (2003) documented what happened in recess breaks, in 7 to 8-year-old English children (cf. also Figure 6.1). They found that peer interaction dominated recess; using Parten's (1932) categories (see Chapter 2), 80% of time was spent in social play. Although separation between boys' and girls' activities was common, this was not inevitable. There was little ethnic separation in the playground, and this decreased with time.

The sorts of things children are learning were well documented by Sluckin (1981). For example they are learning how to get into games. They need to learn to ask the right person:

> Jane: "Can I play?"
> Helen: "It's not my game, it's Tracey's."
> Jane (to Tracey): "Can I play?"
> Tracey: "Yes."

or to use what assets they have:

> Malcolm (to Damad): "You're not playing."
> Damad produces a sweet.
> Malcolm: "It's my game, I'll let you play."

They are learning how to manage and repair relationships:

> Pete: "Once I tried to be friends with Jamie and he pushed me over into a big puddle, and I got up and started chasing him, and we shook on it to make sure that we're friends."

Learning in the playground is not limited to social skills. For example counting games (as in choosing who is "it") will involve cognitive skills.

In fact, what is being practiced are social-cognitive skills: Sluckin found that often children skilfully manipulate a situation to avoid being "it," or ensure that a chosen person is "it." They can do this by choosing the starting point for counting in the circle, or repeating the rhyme an extra time or so until it ends up on the desired person.

Recess disrupts lesson times

There is very little firm evidence on this, and what there is discussed in Pellegrini (1995a); see also Chapter 6. What do we do have fairly good evidence for, is that young children become more fidgety as time goes on, when confined indoors. A longer confinement means they engage in more physically active play later in recess, for a period of perhaps some 20–30 minutes. This is true for preschool children (Smith & Hagan, 1980; Figure 6.1), and for 5–9 year olds (Pellegrini, 1995a; Pellegrini et al., 1995), especially for boys in the older age group. Pellegrini (1995a) found that boys fidgeting and being off-task increased with a longer wait before recess, probably indicating a need for a recess break; after recess, he found that children who engaged in a lot of physically active play were less attentive in class, but that children who engaged in less vigorous but social activity were more attentive. He concluded that recess was definitely conducive to learning for some children; for others, the greater fidgeting in some boys might have happened anyway. But this was based on just one study of 23 children. As Pellegrini commented (1995a, p. 84), "Future research in this area is badly needed." It is extraordinary how little research attention such an important policy area has received.

Recess leads to anti-social behaviour and bullying

It is true that an appreciable proportion of the bullying that does happen in school, happens in the playground. In a large survey in England, Whitney and Smith (1993) found that, so far as primary schools were concerned, the majority of bullying was reported in the playground. However, this is not surprising, since the playground provides the most opportunities for lightly supervised peer social interactions and, of course, these are not always positive. But fighting and bullying make up only a small proportion of what goes on. The Blatchford et al. (2003) study found only 0.7% of their observations of 7–8 year olds in playgrounds recorded aggression, 0.4% distress/crying, and 0.6% teasing/taunting. What also is important in these considerations is how such negative behaviors are managed. An interesting playground environment, and good playground supervision, can greatly reduce the incidence of bullying (Smith & Sharp, 1994). Negative interactions are part of life and cannot be avoided, but pupils can learn how to manage disagreements, both with adult help or through peer support (Cowie & Smith, in press), and this is an important learning process.

The main arguments against recess are thus, in my view, not strong ones. Ranged against them are several positive arguments for recess.

Opportunities for social-cognitive learning

As demonstrated above, many social interaction skills can be learnt in recess. This includes managing negative interactions, given appropriate support. Although social interaction does occur elsewhere in school, and . outside school, well-organized and well-supervised recess probably provides an excellent and relatively safe venue for such learning. These social relationship skills are vitally important, as concern about social and emotional learning at school has come to recognize.

Improved concentration at lessons

This is unproven as yet, but is predicted by the "cognitive immaturity hypothesis" proposed by Bjorklund and Green (1992) and indirectly supported by the cross-cultural evidence from Stevenson and Lee (1990). This predicts stronger effects for younger children, and there was some supportive evidence from Pellegrini (1995a). It needs further investigation.

Opportunities for physical exercise

This is the most obvious benefit of recess breaks. Children use recess to be more physically active, either in exercise play or (in older children) in organized games. Beighle, Morgan, Le Masurier, and Pangrazi (2006) assessed 9-year-old children's physical activity levels using pedometers, in a school in the southwest USA. They found that boys spent 78% of their school recess time in physical activity, and girls 63% (probably much of this was exercise play, although this was unspecified). By contrast, after school (and before bedtime), the respective figures were 23% and 20% of time spent in physical activity. Furthermore, although there appear to be short-term deprivation rebound effects within the school setting, Dale, Corbin, and Dale (2000) found that 9-year-old children who experienced two school days with little physical activity (recess was spent indoors at a computer terminal), did not compensate by increasing their levels of physical activity after school. It seems that the school playground is a favoured venue for getting the benefits of physical activity.

Benefits of exercise play were discussed in Chapter 6. While there are still unsettled issues, it was concluded that it appears a useful way to get short-term and possibly longer-term fitness and motor skill benefits. Given current concerns about levels of obesity in children in developed countries, this is emerging as an especially powerful argument for recess.

The design of playgrounds is important. Verstraete, Cardon, De Clercq, and de Bourdeaudhuij (2006), in a study in Belgian elementary schools, found that moderate to vigorous physical activity (MPVA: measured in this study by accelerometers worn by the children) took up about 50% of playground time in 10-year-olds, but this was significantly increased by providing suitable items of equipment (jump ropes, balls, hoops, rings, racquets, paddles, etc.) and adult encouragement. Ridgers, Stratton, Fairclough, and Twisk (2007) examined the effects of implementing playground redesign (multicoloured zoning and physical structures to encourage certain activities) in 27 English primary schools. Some increases in MPVA and VPA (vigorous physical activity) were found in assessments 6 weeks later, compared to control schools; and there were more marked for younger children. Salmon, Booth, Phongsavan, Murphy, and Timperio (2007) reviewed evidence for the effectiveness of interventions to promote physical activity in children and adolescents. They found that many studies had methodological flaws, but that many interventions had an impact. Those delivered through the school and combining activity (recess) breaks, physical education and family strategies were more effective than just family-based interventions.

The Role of Play in Helping Children under Stress, or with Illness or Disability

Children with disabilities and developmental disorders may not play at the same levels as normally developing children. Some children have sensory disorders, such as impaired sight or hearing. Others have cognitive disabilities and/or physical disabilities, often tied to conditions such as Down's syndrome, cerebral palsy, or spina bifida. In general, opportunities for play are not at the same level in such children.

In many cases, play seems to develop along the same sequence as in normally developing children, but at a slower rate (Hellendoorn, 1994). For example, in Down's syndrome children, pretend play develops, but more slowly and in pace with their mental age. For this reason, Down's syndrome children are often used as age-matched controls for examining pretend play in children with autism, where there may be a specific deficit. In a study with children with learning difficulties (LD), Nabuzoka and Smith (1999) found that LD children were able to distinguish play fighting and real fighting (cf. Chapter 6), but were less accurate and used fewer cues; nevertheless, the acquisition of meaning of particular cues was thought to be the same as for non-LD children, just delayed.

Children with impaired sight or hearing have specific difficulties which may lead to developmental delays (Diamond, 2002). It is all the more important for such children that their well-functioning sensory modalities are fully stimulated. Blind or sight-impaired children can benefit from toys and play materials that combine auditory and kinesthetic (touch) stimulation, and from suitably devised play apparatus along these lines. Deaf or hearing-impaired children can benefit from toys and apparatus that are visually as well as kinesthetically stimulating. Children with other kinds of disabilities (e.g. muscular disorders or learning impairments) will also benefit from toys and playthings that are adapted to their capabilities and are within their range of use while slightly "stretching" their current level of ability.

At one level, intervention simply involves providing appropriate toys, perhaps borrowed from a toy library, and, in the case of physically impaired children (for example with cerebral palsy or spina bifida), ensuring that they have adequate positioning support equipment to facilitate play opportunities (O'Brien, Boatwright, Chaplin, Geckler, Gosnell, Holcombe, & Parrish, 1998). At another level, adults can intervene more directly to encourage or train certain types of play activities. How this is done obviously varies with the type of disability, as well as with the educational philosophy of the trainer.

Nakken, Vlaskamp, and van Wijck (1994) described play interventions with multiply handicapped children. For example, Tom was a boy who was blind, deaf, and with profound physical and mental disabilities. At this level, intervention involved providing suitable play things (a rattle, tactile materials), and encouraging basic sensorimotor type activities with these. Working with children with less extensive but still substantial disabilities (cerebral palsy, Down's syndrome), de Moor, van Waesberghe, and Oud (1994) described an instruction program involving the teacher pointing, demonstrating, giving physical guidance, questioning/instructing, highlighting, and naming/verbalizing play actions by the child. Hellendoorn (1994) described imaginative play training sessions with severely retarded children. Children with autism, or Asperger's syndrome, are generally not very interested in pretend play and avoid much social contact. However, one form of social contact they do often enjoy are gentler forms of rough-and-tumble play, perhaps initiated by an adult. Also, they can be encouraged into some pretend play, via the use of suitable props (realistic toys for pretend) and modeling by adults, to make the pretending easier for them (Preissler, 2006).

Such kinds of play training usually result in benefits for spontaneous play and concentration at activities subsequently (e.g. Hellendoorn, 1994), but not always; de Moor et al. (1994) found no effects of their instruction program (compared to no-treatment control) when applied to children with cerebral palsy or Down's syndrome. The evaluation of these training programs does encounter the kinds of difficulties discussed in Chapter 9 with respect to normally developing children. Zion and Jenvey (unpublished ms., Monash University) reviewed play intervention programs for children with intellectual disabilities. These may attempt to improve play skills, but also cognitive and communication skills. These authors concluded that the outcomes of interventions are influenced by many factors, and that the play itself is far from being the only determinant of any learning that takes place. They also warn that an over-emphasis on using play as a means of instruction will detract from the spontaneous and voluntary nature of normal play. They recommend that play is used as a context for observing and facilitating intervention, rather than being the tool of intervention.

The use of play therapy

Besides being challenging and imaginative, play can also be reassuring. A child who is feeling upset or lonely can find some solace in playing with familiar toys and materials. A child in hospital is in a strange environment, as well as probably having some illness. Provision of play rooms and facilities is an important aspect of a children's ward, giving some opportunities for the enjoyment of play as in the child's normal home life. In addition, play may express the child's emotional preoccupations, be a diagnostic of their developmental state, and—more debatably—act in a cathartic way to help work through anxieties, fears and traumas.

A child who is emotionally upset or who has experienced some trauma, may express this in their play. The upset might be caused by parents arguing, or the illness or death of someone in the family, or by some natural disaster. For example, Saylor, Swenson, and Powell (1992) described observations by 200 parents of their preschoolers play following the experience of Hurricane Hugo. This hurricane struck South Carolina in September 1989, with winds up to 175 mph and a tidal surge of up to 23 feet, and caused widespread destruction. Parents described re-enactments of this later, in their children's play. For example (of a 2-year-old boy and 3-year-old girl): "our children used to (still do at times) play what they call 'Hurricane.' They pretend the hurricane is coming . . . they have a new version where they are doing repairs—one is the workman, one is the homeowner who cannot live in the house and moves away while the work is being done . . . they also verbalize the noises, trees falling, wind, rain, etc" (p. 145).

It is widely thought that such play can help children work through some of the anxieties by acting out the themes "at one remove" in pretend play. Play therapists use such play to help understand children's anxieties; and most therapists also believe that it can help the child work towards resolution of them.

There are a variety of methods of play therapy (as of therapy generally). O'Connor and Braverman (1997) is a source for details of the following types: child-centered; psychoanalytic; cognitive-behavioral; Jungian; filial; developmental; gestalt; family theraplay; ecosystemic; Ericksonian; Adlerian; dynamic family play therapy; and strategic family play therapy. These obviously have different principles and procedures. The origins of play therapy lie in psychoanalysis, and the work of Anna Freud, Margaret Lowenfeld, Melanie Kline, Donald Winnicott, and others. Their approaches emphasize an active interpretation of the child's play by the therapist. The humanistic tradition of Carl Rogers and the work of Virginia Axline (1947) helped bring about a more child-centered approach in which the therapist is reflective of the child's feelings.

Clark (2007) argues that child-direction is a crucial aspect of play, and that the play therapist must respect this. Despite differences in emphasis, most play therapists now follow a child-centered approach to a considerable extent. In the play sessions, the child is presented with a range of play materials and is allowed freedom of expression with these, within certain limits or boundaries. The adult therapist does not impose interpretations on the child directly, but provides a safe, warm, and accepting environment in which the child can express their feelings, anxieties, and preoccupations through play. The therapist typically empathizes with the child and reflects their feelings back, helping them to develop self-understanding, and gradually come to terms with the issues concerning them. Procedures may be used such as Winnicott's "squiggle game," in which the therapist draws a squiggle on a sheet of paper and invites the child to add to it; successive improvisations on the drawing, and comments by the therapist, allow a scaffolding of therapeutic play in which the therapist has a role but does not dominate the interaction (Clark, 2007). A review of such play therapy procedures is given by Porter, Hernandez-Reif, and Jessee (2009).

Two common processes thought to be at work in play therapy, are catharsis, and abreaction (Clark, 2007). In catharsis, unexpressed, unconscious, or hidden emotions are released, reducing anxiety and tension. Thus, it is thought that allowing the child to represent their fears and enact them through play, will in itself help resolve them. In abreaction, the repressed emotional disturbance is brought to consciousness, and there is then an opportunity to develop ways of coping with or reducing the impact of these feelings.

The role of the play therapist may well be important, as it appears unlikely that children's spontaneous pretend play will function effectively to resolve emotional difficulties; although working with ill children in hospital, Clark (2007) asserts that children may use play as a kind of self-therapy. Bretherton (1989) argued that pretend play helps the child explore and master emotional difficulties, including more mundane ones such as fear of the dark, as well as coping with family conflicts. As an attachment theorist, however, she noted that this process was most plausible for "securely-attached" children, who typically show more elaborate, socially flexible play, with more benign resolution of pretend conflicts. By contrast, "insecure-avoidant" children have more aggressive and fewer nurturant themes and may become obsessive in their play.

Similarly, Gordon (1993) reported that children who have experienced emotional trauma (compared to non-traumatized children) show more non-resolution of negative affective experience through pretend activity, more non-coordination and disorganization of play objects and activities, more perseveration of activity and repetition of single schemes, and generally a global inhibition of pretend play. Thus, these children do less play, and it is relatively disorganized and negative in quality. These findings suggest that spontaneous pretend play may be diagnostic of a child's disturbed emotional condition, but they are hardly strong evidence that pretend play functions in itself to help emotional mastery. In a review of pretend play and emotion learning in traumatized mothers and children, Haight, Black, Ostler and Sheridan (2006, p. 211) concluded that "at the very time when children may benefit most from pretend play, they are less inclined to reengage in it."

Yet another example comes from a study of 3 to 5-year-old children experiencing the birth of a sibling (Kramer & Schaefer-Hernan, 1994). Children who did not interact very positively with siblings showed no change in overall rate of fantasy play, from 3 months before to 6 months after the birth of the sibling. Children who did interact positively, showed an inverted U curve: fantasy play declined to its lowest shortly after the birth of the sibling, then rose again. As the authors put it, "better adaptation to becoming a sibling was significantly associated with a temporary suppression in fantasy engagement during the most stressful period of the transition" (1994, p. 757). This disruption was specific to fantasy play, not play in general. The children who did interact positively, did show more transition-relevant themes in their fantasy play; and there was in increase (for most children) in conversations about babies and siblings. The authors concluded that "the ability to engage in coordinated fantasy play with another child may serve as a 'barometer' of their general level of adaptation to a critical life transition", but also that "there is actually very little empirical evidence that children regularly enact fantasy themes in accordance with their current concerns, and furthermore, that such enactments are beneficial for adaptation" (1994, p. 764).

Such research challenges any simple cathartic function of fantasy play. It seems that many play therapists too are moving away from a simple cathartic viewpoint—that obsessive repetition of negative play acts is in itself sufficient—towards using the play therapy setting to help the child think through issues more deeply. As Alvarez and Phillips (1998) put it, "Naturally, the older functions of play still apply: traumatized or abused children may need to spend session after session in the process of digesting, reflecting upon, and generally coming to terms with disturbing experiences. But they may need also to spend just as much, if not more, time trying out other ideas—those connected with a safe, nonabusive world" (p. 101). Thus, the therapist both provides a safe environment in which the child knows that they can express their fears, anger and negative emotions (within certain boundaries), but also encourages the child to develop a sense of agency and control. "One child horribly abused made an amazing discovery: that she could 'make a mark' on plasticine. This seemed to signal the discovery that there was some portion of her world where her initiatives could be received" (Alvarez & Phillips, 1998, p. 101).

Evaluations of play therapy

Evaluations of play therapy generally report positive outcomes, but not necessarily more so than child psychotherapy that does not use play methods (Casey & Berman, 1985). Landreth and Sweeney (1997) cited six studies in which the outcomes of child-centered play therapy were compared with outcomes for controls. The children receiving the play therapy showed more improvement on outcomes such as self-concept, externalizing behaviors, and empathy. These gains were achieved in up to 30 sessions over periods of some weeks. Bratton, Ray, Rhine, and Jones (2005) carried out a systematic meta-analysis of 93 controlled outcomes studies, published between 1953 and 2000. All had pre- and post-tests and some kind of control group. The average age of children was 7 years, and the mean number of sessions was 16. They reported an overall effect size of 0.8, which is quite large. Effect sizes were greater for humanistic (child-centered) than non-humanistic treatments. Interestingly, they were also greater for filial therapy, where a parent is trained to use basic child therapy procedures.

However, many studies have small samples, not surprisingly; and many may suffer from the kinds of drawbacks discussed for experimental studies of play generally, in Chapter 7. Bratton et al. (2005) commented that their conclusions were "hindered by a lack of specificity in many of the studies" (p. 385). No information was provided in this review on precautions against experimenter effects; these might be appreciable, given the strong belief many adherents might have concerning the efficacy of play therapy. The adequacy of control groups can also be questioned. As Bratton et al. (2005) stated, "because most play therapy research uses the design of play therapy versus absence of intervention, researchers are unable to declare play therapy as the most effective method of treatment", compared to for example "traditional behavioral plans, cognitive techniques, or school guidance curricula" (p. 386).

Selectivity in reporting results may feature. For example, Rae, Worchel, Upchurch, Sanner, and Daniel (1989) described the impact of a therapeutic play intervention with children hospitalized for acute illness. The abstract highlights a positive result: children in the therapeutic play condition (compared to diversionary play, verbal support, and no treatment) showed a significant reduction in self-reported hospital fears. However, there were no differences on at least ten other measures, and a negative finding (an increase in somatic complaints in the therapeutic play group) on one measure. Overall, this suggests some selective interpretation of results in the abstract, and an inconclusive set of findings overall.

In a more recent study, Ray, Schottelkorb, and Tsai (2007) reported outcomes of play therapy with children aged 5 to 11 years showing symptoms of ADHD (attention problems and hyperactivity). Thirty-one children received 16 weekly sessions of play therapy in specially equipped playrooms. Twenty-nine children were given 16 weekly sessions of reading mentoring. Children were randomly assigned to these two treatment groups. Assessment was by teacher ratings. Children in both treatment groups improved equally on two assessments of ADHD symptoms. However, the play therapy children improved more on teacher-rated temperament and behavior, and specifically on emotional lability and anxiety/withdrawal. This study has many good features, but the reading control does seem less exciting than the therapy condition, with only the latter having a special play room. Although teachers were not told of a child's treatment condition, their lack of awareness was apparently not systematically checked.

Although findings are promising, there is a need for more and rigorous evaluation of different types of play therapy and of what exactly produces beneficial outcomes. From what we know of the decreases in fantasy play with stress, the most likely conclusion is that fantasy play itself acts as a "barometer" of stress, and/or diagnosis of particular emotional difficulties. However, the resolution of such difficulties probably depends much more on the therapist's work with the child, the climate of acceptance in a safe but boundaried environment, and the sensitive help given to the child in discussing their issues and developing their coping strategies. "To be helpful to children, pretend play during times of extreme stress or trauma appears to require the support, structure, and guidance provided by a trusted adult" (Haight et al., 2006, p. 211).

Further Reading

J. Hellendoorn, R. van der Kooij, and B. Sutton-Smith (eds) (1994), *Play and Intervention*, Albany, NY: SUNY Press, considers issues of play therapy, and play for children with special needs. J. H. Goldstein (1994), *Toys, Play and Child Development*, Cambridge: Cambridge University Press, considers a range of educational and policy issues in relation to research on play. P. Blatchford (1998), *Social Life in School*, London: Falmer, provides good background on pupil's experiences of breaktime and recess, and A. D. Pellegrini (2005), *Recess: Its Role in Education and Development*, Lawrence Erlbaum, brings research findings to bear on the issues. K. J. O'Connor, & L. M. Braverman (Eds) (1997), *Play Therapy: Theory and Practice*, New York: Wiley, provides an overview of approaches to play therapy.

Chapter 11

Concluding Comments: Play and the Middle Way

Play: Ignored or Idealized?

We have seen how play is a major part of the activities and time budget of young mammals, and of children. It is enjoyable: it seems to be great fun for those taking part, and youngsters actively seek out play opportunities and play partners. And there is evidence that play, while not "essential for development," does have important and beneficial functions.

But consideration of play often seems to fall between two opposite poles—it is either ignored or idealized. This is actually quite a paradoxical state of affairs, and suggests some ambivalence on the part of adults to the phenomenon of play.

Play as ignored

Play is an important aspect of the behavioural repertoire of many animal species, including most if not all mammals; and at least for physical activity play and rough-and-tumble play, there are likely to be important insights and continuities for those studying human play. We have seen how modern evolutionary theory can inform theorizing about the costs and benefits of play. So, how much does play feature in relevant texts? It is completely absent in two well-known texts of evolutionary psychology:

D. M. Buss (1999), *Evolutionary Psychology: The New Science of the Mind*, Needham Heights, MA: Allyn and Bacon. David Buss is a social psychologist and he covers a range of topics with a lot of emphasis on human behaviour over about 400 pages. There are 15 pages of index: under "P" we have "Plants, toxins in" and "Pleiotropic theory of senescence," but no entry for "Play" in between these.

L. Barrett, R. Dunbar and J. Lycett (2002), *Human Evolutionary Psychology*, Basingstoke and New York: Palgrave. These authors are psychologists with backgrounds in biology and primatology. There are some 380 pages of text. There are 4.5 pages of densely printed subject index, each page in four columns: under "P" we have "Placenta" and then "Pleistocene," but no entry for "Play" in between these.

These are both excellent texts in many respects, but they ignore play. Of course, not all evolutionary psychology books ignore play, and a note-worthy exception is D. F. Bjorklund & A. D. Pellegrini (2002), *The Origins of Human Nature: Evolutionary Developmental Psychology*, Washington, DC, APA. Both these authors are interested in child development and in play, and they give play excellent coverage. But in mainstream evolutionary psychology texts it often gets short shrift.

How about psychology texts? Play does ordinarily get a mention here, but typically it is one or two pages amongst many hundreds of pages. For example, H. Gleitman, A. J. Fridlund and D. Reisberg (1999), *Psychology*, 5th ed., New York: Norton, has no entries for "Play," although there is one single page reference for "Play therapy" in 18 pages of references and 849 pages of text. Even in lifespan development texts, play is not usually treated very extensively. For example H. Bee (1998), *Lifespan Development*, 2nd ed., New York: Addison-Wesley, has "Play: preschoolers" (two entries) and "Play: sex-role stereotypes," one entry, in 10 pages of references and 620 pages of text. J. W. Santrock (2002), *A Topical Approach to Lifespan Development*, McGraw-Hill, does have 10 entries under play, but it only takes up 4 pages out of 579 pages of text.

Textbooks devoted to child development obviously have more coverage, but nevertheless it is typically limited to single figure index entries and a single figure number of pages—usually, a section of a couple of pages in the peer relations chapter, and maybe one or two shorter sections elsewhere. My own co-authored text, P. K. Smith, H. Cowie & M. Blades (2003), *Understanding Children's Development*, 4th ed., Oxford, Blackwell, is certainly unusual in this respect, with a dedicated chapter on play.

Play as idealized

The rise of the play ethos was documented in Chapter 2. Many writers on play, and practitioners and researchers in early education and in playwork, subscribe (to varying extents) to this view, that play is vital for development and a main and essential way of learning in young children. It contrasts sharply with the lack of attention given to play by many writers outside these areas (as in textbooks, above), and the lack of priority often given to play in wider society.

Perhaps this is the explanation of the play ethos. More needs to be done to research its origins, but certainly in recent years it has been used to defend the role of play curricula in early education, and opportunities for play both at school and outside school (e.g., Zigler & Bishop, 2005). In many western countries, children's play has a low priority in terms of government spending, children may lack decent play areas on residential estates, school recess times are being shortened or removed, and there is pressure for testing, achievement, and instruction–based curricula even in the early school years. The area where plenty of money flows is children's toys (Kline, 1995, 1997; Sutton-Smith, 1986, 1997). Toys are big industry. But toys are not synonymous with play. Many play ethos advocates bewail the lack of opportunities for spontaneous play, which requires time and space and freedom but not necessarily a great deal in the way of manufactured toys. Of course, some toys are helpful in stimulating play, but toys, like many other products, are clearly overconsumed in much of Western society.

I suspect that the play ethos has arisen, and is maintained in some sectors, as a reaction against an overly materialistic and achievement-oriented ethos dominating many western societies (and indeed most modern societies). When children's freedom to play is threatened by concerns about league tables of school achievement, or the financial costs of play areas, defenders of play may resort to saying how essential play is. If play is the child's work (Table 2.1), then it should be given the same status as work is for adults!

I am sceptical of the play ethos in its strong form, but I sympathize with many of the aims of defending children's rights to play. I do believe that there is a middle way we can take, both in our theorizing about play and in our practice in society.

Play: a middle way?

The play ethos overstates the case for play. The evidence has been carefully reviewed in the previous chapters. Neither the evolutionary evidence, the anthropological evidence, nor the psychological evidence provides a compelling case that play is "essential." But, there are two very good reasons for ensuring that children's play continues to be supported and encouraged.

The first is simple, and obvious from the definition of play: play is fun, and enjoyable. It is also usually harmless. (It is not always harmless, because of the risks in play, such as falls, and potentially antisocial kinds of play, as in violent war play). Generally speaking, an enjoyable and largely harmless activity is something to be treasured and celebrated. In adult life, we do not question the resources and media attention given to sport (admittedly, also commercialized). Children too deserve to have their enjoyment. This is sometimes recognized by politicians. At the time of writing, in the UK, the Children's Plan announced in December 2007 undertakes to develop a national play strategy and to invest in upgrading children's play areas, amongst other initiatives welcomed by play workers (National Children's Bureau, 2008).

The second reason emerges from the research we have reviewed. Play may not be essential, but there is little doubt it is useful. Again, the evolutionary, anthropological, and psychological evidence come together to confirm this. Play is one way in which children get a lot of experience about the world—the physical world and the social world. Inevitably, they learn things through doing this. Indeed, in a broad sense play may have evolved as a general purpose learning mechanism—for physical coordination and muscular strength, learning about making and using objects, finding out about peers and how they think and behave.

Although the experimental studies of play—when viewed critically —do not prove that play is essential, or in most cases even superior to certain other possible experiences, nevertheless play comes out well on the overall balance sheet. Typically, children experiencing play do as well as children experiencing some kind of non-playful instruction. Of course, a lot depends on the age of children, what outcomes are being measured, and so on, but play is clearly one way for children to learn lots of things. For young children it is a natural, enjoyable way, and often as effective as more structured activities. In my view, and those of others (e.g., Roskos & Christie, 2007) this suggests some kind of blended approach to the early child curriculum, with a variety of experiences including both free play and structured play.

Unanswered questions

It is now over a hundred years since Karl Groos wrote his two influential books on play (Chapter 1). Since then we have seen waves of research in various play-related areas, with ebbs and flows of research interest. There are societies dedicated to the study of play, notably *The*

Association for the Study of Play (TASP: www.csuchico.edu/kine/tasp/). The *International Toy Research Association* (ITRA: www.toyresearch.org/) encourages toy and plaything research in order to broaden and spread knowledge about toys and promote the development of good toys for children. The *International Play Association: Promoting the Child's Right to Play* (www.ipaworld.org/home.html), promotes the importance of play in child development, provides a vehicle for inter-disciplinary exchange and action, and brings a child perspective to policy development throughout the world.

Undoubtedly, we now know a lot more about play from a variety of perspectives. I have argued for a "middle way" above, rejecting both the idealization of the play ethos, but also the ignoring or devaluing of play in many other sectors of society. However, not everyone will agree with me! Taking the three models described in Chapter 9 (and Figure 9.1), it would still be possible to argue for each of these, at least in certain play domains. Also, these models are too simple. Within the bounds of the equifinality, "many routes" model, it is still conceivable that play is "the leading source of development in the preschool years," as Vygotsky argued; it is possible that "play is quintessentially capable of activating the very best that the cortex is capable of," as Panksepp (in Gallagher, 2008, p. 28) has stated. This is a "primus inter pares" argument, different from idealizing play as "essential." We need to work toward more differentiated models for different kinds of play, at different ages, and with various developmental outcomes in mind.

We need more studies, well designed and controlled, but ecologically sensitive—a difficult balance to strike in the case of play. Many possible areas of future research seem called for, in the light of what has been reviewed in this book. For example, much more sound research is needed on the impact of recess breaks of varying length and times, and tests of the cognitive immaturity hypothesis in relation to physical activity play. We need to know more about how rough-and-tumble play changes as children get into adolescence and its function appears to change. Hypotheses about the role of object play in problem-solving and creativity remain to be properly tested by ecologically valid studies. And the particular role of pretend play, probably uniquely selected for in human evolution, still remains a bit of a mystery. Its possible role in theory of mind is intriguing, but may turn out to be just one more idea amongst many that have been proposed. We have learned much about play; but there remain plenty of challenges for play researchers in the future.

References

Alexander, R. D. (1989). Evolution of the human psyche. In P. Mellars & C. Stringer (Eds.), *The human revolution* (pp. 455–513). Edinburgh: Edinburgh University Press.

Alvarez, A., & Phillips, A. (1998). The importance of play: A child psychotherapist's view. *Child Psychology & Psychiatry Review*, 3, 99–103.

Anderson, R., & Mitchell, E. M. (1984). Children's health and play in rural Nepal. *Social Science Medicine*, 19, 735–740.

Andreas, C. (1969). War toys and the peace movement. *Journal of Social Issues*, 25, 83–99.

Arnold, W., & Trillmich, F. (1985). Time budget in Galapagos fur seal pups: The influence of the mother's presence and absence on pup activity and play. *Behaviour*, 92, 302–321.

Arrington, R. E. (1943). Time sampling in studies of social behaviour: A critical review of techniques and results with research suggestions. *Psychological Bulletin*, 40, 81–124.

Astington, J. W., & Jenkins, J. M. (1995). Theory of mind development and social understanding. *Cognition & Emotion*, 9, 151–165.

Astington, J. W., & Jenkins, J. M. (1999). A longitudinal study of the relationship between language and theory of mind development. *Developmental Psychology*, 35, 1311–1320.

Axline, V. (1947). *Play therapy*. New York: Ballantine.

Baldwin, J. M. (1896). A new factor in evolution. *American Naturalist*, 30, 441–451; 536–553.

Baldwin, J. D., & Baldwin, J. I. (1974). Exploration and social play in squirrel monkeys (*Saimiri*). *American Zoologist*, 14, 303–315.

Baldwin, J. D., & Baldwin, J. I. (1976). Effects of ecology on social play: A laboratory simulation. *Ethology*, 40, 1–14.

Barber, N. (1991). Play and energy regulation in mammals. *Quarterly Review of Biology*, 66, 129–147.

Baron-Cohen, S. (1989). The autistic child's theory of mind: A case of specific developmental delay. *Journal of Child Psychology and Psychiatry*, 30, 285–297.

Barrett, P., & Bateson, P. (1978). The development of play in cats. *Behaviour*, 66, 106–120.

Bateson, P. P. G. (2005). Play and its role in the development of great apes and humans. In A. D. Pellegrini & P. K. Smith (Eds.), *The nature of play: Great apes and humans* (pp. 13–26). New York: Guilford.

Bateson, P. P. G., Martin, P., & Young, M. (1981). Effects of interrupting cat mothers' lactation with bromocriptine on the subsequent play of their kittens. *Physiology & Behavior*, 27, 841–845.

Baumer, S., Ferholt, B., & Lecusay, R. (2005). Promotiomg narrative competence through adult-child joint pretense: Lessons from the Scandinavian educational practice of playworld. *Cognitive Development*, 20, 576–590.

Beighle, A., Morgan, C. F., Le Masurier, G., & Pangrazi, R. P. (2006). Children's physical activity during recess and outside of school. *Journal of School Health*, 76, 516–520.

Bekoff, M., & Allen, C. (1998). Intentional communication and social play: How and why animals negotiate and agree to play. In M. Bekoff & J. A. Byers (Eds.), *Animal play: Evolutionary, comparative, and ecological perspectives* (pp. 97–114). Cambridge: Cambridge University Press.

Bekoff, M., & Byers, J. A. (Eds.). (1998). *Animal play: Evolutionary, comparative, and ecological perspectives*. Cambridge: Cambridge University Press.

Belsky, J., & Most, R. K. (1981). From exploration to play: A cross-sectional study of infant free play behaviour. *Developmental Psychology*, 17, 630–639.

Beraldo, K. E. A. (1993). Gênero de brincadeiras na percepção de crianças de 5 a 10 anos [Perception of play gender among 5 to 10-year-old children]. Unpublished master's thesis, Instituto de Psicologia, Universidade de São Paulo, Brazil.

Berenbaum, S. A., & Snyder, E. (1995). Early hormonal influences on childhood sex-typed activity and playmate preferences: Implications for the development of sexual orientation. *Developmental Psychology*, 31, 31–42.

Berger, J. (1980). Ecology, structure and functions of social play in bighorn sheep. *Journal of Zoology (London)*, 192, 531–542.

Biben, M. (1986). Individual- and sex-related strategies of wrestling play in captive squirrel monkeys. *Ethology*, 71, 229–241.

Biben, M., & Symmes, D. (1986). Play vocalisations of squirrel monkeys. *Folia Primatologica*, 46, 173–182.

Bichara, I. D. (2002). Crescer como índio às margens do Velho Chico: um desafio para crianças Xocó [Growing up as an Indian around Velho Chico a challenge for Xocó children]. In E. R. Lordelo, A. M. A. Carvalho, & S. H. Koller (Eds.), *Infância brasileira e contextos de desenvolvimento* (pp. 137–163), São Paulo: Casa do Psicólogo/Salvador: Editora da Universidade Federal da Bahia.

Bichara, I. D. (2003). Nas águas do Velho Chico [In Velho Chico's water]. In A. M. A. Carvalho, C. M. C. Magalhães, F. A. R. Pontes, & I. D. Bichara (Eds.), *Brincadeira é cultura: viajando pelo Brasil que brinca* (Vol. I) (pp. 89–107). São Paulo: Casa do Psicólogo.

Bjorklund, D. F., & Brown, R. D. (1998). Physical play and cognitive development: Integrating activity, cognition, and education. *Child Development, 69*, 604–606.

Bjorklund, D. F., & Green, B. (1992). The adaptive nature of cognitive immaturity. *American Psychologist, 47*, 46–54.

Bjorklund, D. F., & Pellegrini, A. D. (2000). Child development and evolutionary psychology. *Child Development, 71*, 1687–1708.

Bjorklund, D. F., & Pellegrini, A. D. (2002). *The origins of human nature: Evolutionary developmental psychology.* Washington, DC: American Psychological Association.

Bjorkqvist, K., Lagerspetz, K. M. J., & Kaukiainen, A. (1992). Do girls manipulate and boys fight? Developmental trends in regard to direct and indirect aggression. *Aggressive Behavior, 18*, 117–127.

Blatchford, P. (1998). *Social life in school.* London: Falmer Press.

Blatchford, P., & Baines, E. (2008). *A follow up national survey of breaktimes in primary and secondary schools.* Final Report to the Nuffield Foundation.

Blatchford, P., Baines, E., & Pellegrini, A. (2003). The social context of school playground games: Sex and ethnic differences, and changes over time after entry to middle school, *British Journal of Developmental Psychology, 21*, 481–505.

Bloch, M. N. (1989). Young boys' and girls' play at home and in the community: a cultural-ecological framework. In M. N. Bloch & A. D. Pellegrini (Eds.), *The ecological context of children's play.* New Jersey: Ablex Publishing Co.

Blurton Jones, N. G. (1967). An ethological study of some aspects of social behaviour of children in nursery school. In D. Morris (Ed.), *Primate ethology* (pp. 347–368). London: Weidenfeld & Nicolson.

Blurton Jones, N. G. (Ed.). (1972). *Ethological studies of child behaviour.* Cambridge: Cambridge University Press.

Blurton Jones, N. G. (1993). The lives of hunter-gatherer children: Effects of parental behavior and parental reproductive strategy. In M. E. Pereira & L. A. Fairbanks (Eds.), *Juvenile primates: Life history, development, and behavior* (pp. 309–325). New York: Oxford University Press.

Bock, J. (1995). *The determinants of variation in children's activities in a southern African community.* Unpublished doctoral dissertation, Department of Anthropology, University of New Mexico, USA.

Bock, J. (2002). Learning, life history, and productivity: Children's lives in the Okavango Delta, Botswana. *Human Nature, 13*, 161–197.

Bock, J. (2005). What makes a competent adult forager? In B. Hewlett & M. Lamb (Eds.), *Hunter-gatherer childhoods* (pp. 109–128). Hawthorne, NY: Aldine de Gruyter.

Bock, J. & Johnson, S. E. (2003). Subsistence ecology and play among the Okavango Delta peoples of Botswana. *Human Nature, 15*, 63–81.

Boehm, C. (1999). *Hierarchy in the forest: The evolution of egalitarian behavior.* Cambridge, MA: Harvard University Press.

Bogin, B. (1999). Evolutionary perspective on human growth. *Annual Review of Anthropology*, *28*, 109–153.

Bornstein, M. H., Haynes, O. M., O'Reilly, A. W., & Painter, K. M. (1996). Solitary and collaborative pretense play in early childhood: Sources of individual variation in the development of representational competence. *Child Development*, *67*, 2910–2929.

Bornstein, M. H., Haynes, M., Pascual, L., Painter, K. M., & Galperin, C. (1999). Play in two societies: Pervasiveness of process, specificity of structure. *Child Development*, *70*, 317–331.

Boulton, M. J. (1991). A comparison of structural and contextual features of middle school children's playful and aggressive fighting. *Ethology and Sociobiology*, *12*, 119–145.

Boulton, M. J. (1992a). Rough physical play in adolescence: Does it serve a dominance function? *Early Education and Development*, *3*, 312–333.

Boulton, M. J. (1992b). Participation in playground activities in middle school. *Educational Research*, *34*, 167–182.

Boulton, M. J., & Smith, P. K. (1992). The social nature of playfighting and play-chasing: Mechanisms and strategies underlying co-operation and comprimise. In J. H. Barkow, L. Cosmides, & J. Tooby (Eds.), *The adapted mind* (pp. 429–444). New York: Oxford University Press.

Bourchier, A., & Davis, A. (2002). Children's understanding of the pretense-reality distinction: A review of current theory and evidence. *Developmental Science*, *5*, 397–426.

Bratton, S., Ray, D., Rhine, T., & Jones, L. (2003). The efficacy of play therapy with children: A meta-analytic review of treatment outcomes. *Professional Psychology: Research and Practice*, *36*, 376–390.

Bretherton, I. (1989). Pretense: The form and function of make-believe play. *Developmental Review*, *9*, 383–401.

Breuggeman, J. A. (1978). The function of adult play in free-ranging Macaca mulatto. In E. O. Smith (Ed.), *Social play in primates* (pp. 169–191). New York: Academic Press.

Brooks, M., & Knowles, D. (1982). Parent's views of children's imaginary companions. *Child Welfare*, *61*, 25–333.

Brown, J. R., Donelan-McCall, N., & Dunn, J. (1996). Why talk about mental states? The significance of children's conversation with friends, siblings and mothers. *Child Development*, *67*, 836–849.

Bruner, J. S. (1972). The nature and uses of immaturity. *American Psychologist*, *27*, 687–708.

Bruner, J. S. (1986). *Actual minds, possible worlds*. Cambridge, MA: Harvard University Press.

Bruner, J., & Sherwood, V. (1976). Peekaboo and the learning of rule structures. In J. S. Bruner, A. Jolly, & K. Sylva (Eds.), *Play: Its role in development and evolution* (pp. 603–608). New York: Basic Books.

Burghardt, G. (2005). *The genesis of animal play: Testing the limits.* Cambridge, MA: MIT Press.

Byers, J. A. (1977). Terrain preferences in the play behavior of Siberian ibex kids *(Capra ibex sibirica). Zeitschrift für Tierpsychologie, 45,* 199–209.

Byers, J. A. (1984). Play in ungulates. In P. K. Smith (Ed.), *Play in animals and humans* (pp. 43–65). Oxford: Basil Blackwell.

Byers, J. A. (1998a). Biological effects of locomotor play: Getting into shape, or something more specific? In M. Bekoff & J. A. Byers (Eds.), *Animal play: Evolutionary, comparative, and ecological perspectives* (pp. 205–220). Cambridge: Cambridge University Press.

Byers, J. A. (1998b). The biology of human play. *Child Development, 69,* 599–600.

Byers, J. A., & Walker, C. (1995). Refining the motor training hypothesis for the evolution of play. *American Naturalist, 146,* 25–40.

Carlsson-Paige, N., & Levin, D. E. (1987). *The war play dilemma.* New York & London: Teachers College, Columbia University.

Carlsson-Paige, N., & Levin, D. E. (1990). *Who's calling the shots.* Philadelphia, PA: New Society Publishers.

Caro, T. M. (1979). Relations between kitten behaviour and adult predation. *Zeitschrift für Tierpsychologie, 51,* 158–168.

Caro, T. M. (1980). Effects of the mother, object play and adult experience on predation in cats. *Behavioural and Neural Biology, 29,* 29–51.

Carrick, C., & Quas, J. A. (2006). Effects of discrete emotions on young children's ability to discern fantasy and reality. *Developmental Psychology, 42,* 1278–1288.

Carruthers, P. (2002). Human creativity: Its cognitive basis, its evolution, and its connection with childhood pretence. *British Journal of the Philosophy of Science, 53,* 225–249.

Carson, J., Burks, V., & Parke, R. D. (1993). Parent–child physical play: Determinants and consequences. In K. MacDonald (Ed.), *Parent–child play* (pp. 197–220). New York: State University of New York Press.

Carvalho, A. M. A., & Beraldo, K. (1989). Interação criança–criança: ressurgimento de uma área de pesquisa e suas perspectivas [Child–child interaction: resurgence of a research and its perspective]. *Caderno de Pesquisa, 71,* 55–61.

Carvalho, A. M. A., & Rubiano, M. R. B. (2004). Vínculo e compartilhamento na brincadeira de crianças [Bond and sharing in child play]. In M. C. Rossetti-Ferreira, K. S. Amorim, A. P. S. Silva & A. M. A. Carvalho (Eds.), *Rede de significações e o estudo do desenvolvimento humano* (pp. 171–187). Porto Alegre: Artmed.

Carvalho, A. M. A., Smith, P. K., Hunter, T., & Costabile, A. (1990). Playground activities for boys and girls: some developmental and cultural trends in children's perceptions of gender differences. *Play and Culture, 3,* 343–347.

Carvalho, A. M. A., Beraldo, K., Santos, F., & Ortega, R. (1993). Brincadeiras de menino, brincadeiras de menina [Boys' play, girls' play]. *Psicologia: Ciência e Profissão, 13,* 30–33.

Casey, R. J., & Berman, J. S. (1985). The outcome of psychotherapy with children. *Psychological Bulletin, 98*, 388–400.

Chaves, A. M. (2000). Os significados das crianças indígenas brasileiras [Significance of Brazilian Indian childhood] (séculos XVI e XVII). *Revista Brasileira de Crescimento e Desenvolvimento Humano, 10*, 1–26.

Cheyne, J. A. (1982). Object play and problem solving: methodological problems and conceptual promie. In D. J. Pepler & K. H. Rubin (Eds.), *The play of children: Current theory and research* (pp. 79–96). Basel: S. Karger.

Christie, J. F., & Johnsen, E. P. (1985). Questioning the results of play training research. *Educational Psychology, 20*, 7–11.

Christie, J. F., & Roskos, K. A. (2006). Standards, science, and the role of play in early literacy education. In D. Singer, R. Golinkoff & K. Hirsh-Pasek (Eds.), *Play=Learning*. Oxford, U.K.: Oxford University Press, pp. 57–73.

Clark, C. D. (2007). Therapeutic advantages of play. In A. Göncü & S. Gaskins (Eds.), *Play and development: Evolutionary, sociocultural and functional perspectives* (pp. 275–293). Hillsdale, NJ: Lawrence Erlbaum.

Clastres, P. (2003). *A sociedade contra o Estado: Pesquisa de antropologia política* [Society against the State: Political anthropology's research]. São Paulo, Cosac & Naify.

Cohn, C. (2002). A experiência da infância e o aprendizado entre os Xikrin [Xikrin's childhood experience and learning]. In A. L. Silva, A. V. L. S. Macedo, & A. Nunes (Eds.), *Crianças Indígenas: Ensaios antropológicos* (pp. 117–149). São Paulo: Global.

Cole, D., & LaVoie, J. C. (1985). Fantasy play and related cognitive development in 2- to 6-year-olds. *Developmental Psychology, 21*, 233–240.

Collaer, J. L., & Hines, M. (1995). Human behavioural sex differences: A role for gonadal hormones during early development. *Psychological Bulletin, 118*, 55–107.

Connolly, J. A., & Doyle, A-B. (1984). Relation of social fantasy play to social competence in preschoolers. *Developmental Psychology, 20*, 797–806.

Connolly, K., & Dalgleish, M. (1989). The emergence of a tool-using skill in infancy. *Developmental Psychology, 23*, 894–912.

Costabile, A., Smith, P. K., Matheson, L., Aston, J., Hunter, T., & Boulton, M. (1991). Cross-national comparison of how children distinguish playful and serious fighting. *Developmental Psychology, 27*, 881–887.

Costabile, A., Genta, M. L., Zucchini, E., Smith, P. K., & Harker, R. (1992). Attitudes of parents toward war play in young children. *Early Education and Development, 3*, 356–369.

Cowie, H., & Smith, P. K. (in press). Peer support as a means of improving school safety and reducing bullying and violence. In B. Doll, W. Pfohl, & J. Yoon (Eds.), *Handbook of youth prevention science*. New York: Routledge.

Cullumbine, H. (1950). Heat production and energy requirements of tropical people. *Journal of Applied Physiology, 2*, 201–210.

Dale, D., Corbin, C. B., & Dale, K. S. (2000). Restricting opportunities to be active during school time: Do children compensate by increasing physical activity levels after school? *Research Quarterly for Exercise and Sport, 71*, 240–248.

Dansky, J. L. (1980). Make-believe: A mediator of the relationship between play and associative fluency. *Child Development, 51*, 576–579.

Dansky, J., & Silverman, I. (1975). Play: a general facilitator of associative fluency. *Developmental Psychology, 11*, 104.

Darwin, C. (1859). *The origin of species by means of natural selection.* London: Murray.

Darwin, C. (1871). *The descent of man and selection in relation to sex.* London: Murray.

Dawkins, R. (1989). *The selfish gene* (2nd ed.). Oxford: Oxford University Press.

DeLoache, J. S., Sugarman, S., & Brown, A. L. (1985). The development of error correction strategies in young children's manipulative play. *Child Development, 56*, 928–939.

de Lorimier, S., Doyle, A-B., & Tessier, O. (1995). Social coordination during pretend play: Comparisons with nonpretend play and effects on expressive content. *Merrill-Palmer Quarterly, 41*, 497–516.

De Moor, J. M. H., van Waesberghe, B. T. M., & Oud, H. H. L. (1994). Effectiveness of play training with handicapped toddlers. In J. Hellendoorn, R. van der Kooij, & B. Sutton-Smith, (Eds.), *Play and intervention* (pp. 145–155). Albany: State University of New York Press.

Dempster, F. (1988). The spacing effect. *American Psychologist, 43*, 627–634.

Department for Children, Schools and Families (2007): *Confident, capable and creative: Supporting boys' achievements.* 00682–2007BKT–EN.

Department of Education and Science (1967). *Children and their primary schools.* London: HMSO.

Department of the Environment (1973). *Children at play: Design Bulletin 27.* London: HMSO.

DeVore, I., & Konner, M. J. (1970). Infancy in hunter-gatherer life: An ethological perspective. In N. F. White (Ed.), *Ethology and psychiatry* (pp. 113–141). Toronto: University of Toronto Press.

de Waal, F. B. M. (1989). *Peacemaking among primates.* Cambridge, MA: Harvard University Press.

Diamond, K. (2002). The development of social competence in childen with disabilities In P. K. Smith & C. H. Hart (Eds.), *Blackwell handbook of childhood social development* (pp. 571–587). Oxford: Blackwell.

Dias, M., & Harris, P. L. (1988). The effect of make-believe play on deductive reasoning. *British Journal of Developmental Psychology, 6*, 207–221.

Dias, M., & Harris, P. L. (1990). The influence of the imagination on reasoning by young children. *British Journal of Developmental Psychology, 8*, 305–318.

DiPietro, J. A. (1981). Rough-and-tumble play: A function of gender. *Developmental Psychology, 17*, 50–58.

Dockett, S. (1998). Constructing understandings through play in the early years. *International Journal of Early Years Education*, 6, 105–116.

Draper, P., & Cashdan, E. (1988). Technological change and child behavior among the !Kung. *Ethnology*, 27, 339–365.

Dunn, J. (2004). *Children's friendships: The beginnings of intimacy*. Malden, MA and Oxford: Blackwell.

Dunn, J., & Cutting, A. L. (1999). Understanding others, and individual differences in friendship interactions in young children. *Social Development*, 8, 201–219.

Dunn, J., & Hughes, C. (2001). "I got some swords and you're dead!": Violent fantasy, antisocial behavior, friendship, and moral sensibility in young children. *Child Development*, 72, 491–505.

Eaton, W. C., & Enns, L. (1986). Sex differences in human motor activity level. *Psychological Bulletin*, 100, 19–28.

Eaton, W. C., & Yu, A. (1989). Are sex differences in child motor activity level a function of sex differences in maturational status? *Child Development*, 60, 1005–1011.

Edwards, C. P. (2000). Children's play in cross-cultural perspective: A new look at the six cultures study. *Cross-Cultural Research*, 34, 318–338.

Eibl-Eibesfeldt, I. (1989). *Human ethology*. New York: Aldine de Gruyter.

Encarta World English Dictionary (1999). London: Bloomsbury Publishing.

Engel, S. (2005). The narrative worlds of *what is* and *what if*. *Cognitive Development*, 20, 514–525.

Erwin, P. (1993). *Friendship and peer relations in children*. New York: John Wiley & Sons.

Fagen, R. M. (1974). Selective and evolutionary aspects of animal play. *American Naturalist*, 108, 850–585.

Fagen, R. M. (1977). Selection of optimal age-dependent schedules of play behavior. *American Naturalist*, 111, 395–414.

Fagen, R. (1981). *Animal play behavior*. New York: Oxford University Press.

Fagot, B. (1974). Sex differences in toddlers' behaviour and parental reaction. *Developmental Psychology*, 10, 554–558.

Farver, J. M., Kim, Y. K., & Lee-Shin, Y. (2000). Within cultural differences: examining individual differences in Korean American and European American preschoolers' social pretend play. *Journal of Cross-Cultural Psychology*, 31, 583–602.

Fein, G. G. (1975). A transformational analysis of pretending. *Developmental Psychology*, 11, 291–296.

Fein, G. G. (1981). Pretend play in childhood: an integrative review. *Child Development*, 52, 1095–1118.

Fenson, L., Kagan, J., Kearsley, R. B., & Zelazo, P. (1972). The developmental progression of manipulative play in the first two years. *Child Development*, 47, 232–235.

Field, T. M. (1994). Infant day care facilitates later social behavior and school performance. In H. Goelman & E. V. Jacobs (Eds.), *Children's play in child care settings* (pp. 69–84). Albany: State University of New York Press.

Florio, J. (1598). *A Worlde of Wordes*. London.

Fonagy, P. Redfern, S., & Charman, T. (1997). The relationship between belief–desire reasoning and a projective measure of attachment security (SAT). *British Journal of Developmental Psychology, 15*, 51–61.

Fry, D. P. (1987). Differences between play fighting and serious fights among Zapotec children. *Ethology and Sociobiology, 8*, 285–306.

Fry, D. P. (2005). Rough-and-tumble social play in children and adolescents. In A. D. Pellegrini & P. K. Smith (Eds.), *The nature of play: Great apes and humans* (pp. 54–85). New York: Guilford Publications.

Gallagher, S. (2008). How to undress the affective mind: An interview with Jaak Panksepp. *Journal of Consciousness Studies, 15*, 1–31.

Gardner, D. E. M. (1942). *Testing results in the infant school*. London: Methuen.

Gaskins, S. (1996). How Mayan parental theories come into play. In S. Harkness & C. Super (Eds.), *Parent's cultural belief systems* (pp. 345–363). New York: Guilford.

Gaskins, S. (1999). Children's lives in a Mayan village: A case of culturally constructed roles and activities. In A. Göncü (Ed.) *Children's engagement in the world: Sociocultural perspectives* (pp. 25–61). New York: Cambridge University Press.

Gaskins, S. (2000). Children's daily activities in a Mayan village: A culturally grounded description. *Cross-Cultural Research, 34*, 375–389.

Gaskins, S., Haight, W., & Lancy, D. F. (2007). The cultural construction of play. In A. Göncü & S. Gaskins (Eds.), *Play and development: Evolutionary, sociocultural and functional perspectives* (pp. 179–202). Hillsdale, NJ: Lawrence Erlbaum.

Gentry, R. L. (1974). The development of social behavior through play in the Steller sea lion. *American Zoologist, 14*, 391–403.

Gesell, A. (1940). *The first five years of life: A guide to the study of the preschool child*. New York: Harper & Brothers.

Goldstein, J. (1995). Aggressive toy play. In A. D. Pellegrini (Ed.), *The future of play theory* (pp. 127–147). New York: State University of New York Press.

Golinkoff, R. M., Hirsh-Pasek, K., & Singer, D. G. (2006). Why Play = Learning: A challenge for parents and educators. In D. Singer, R. Golinkoff, & K. Hirsh-Pasek (Eds.), *Play=Learning* (pp. 3–12). Oxford: Oxford University Press.

Golomb, C., & Bonen, S. (1981). Playing games of make-believe: The effectiveness of symbolic play training with children who failed to benefit from early conservation training. *Genetic Psychology Monographs, 104*, 137–159.

Golomb, C., & Cornelius, C. B. (1977). Symbolic play and its cognitive significance. *Developmental Psychology, 13*, 246–252.

Golomb, C., Gowing, E. D. G., & Friedman, L. (1982). Play and cognition: Studies of pretense play and conservation of quantity. *Journal of Experimental Child Psychology*, *33*, 257–279.

Gómez, J. C., & Martín-Andrade, B. (2005). Fantasy play in apes. In A. D. Pellegrini & P. K. Smith (Eds.), *The nature of play: Great apes and humans* (pp. 139–172). New York: Guilford.

Göncü, A., Mistry, J., & Mosier, C. (2000). Cultural variations in the play of toddlers. *International Journal of Behavioral Development*, *24*, 321–329.

Göncü, A., Patt, M. B., & Kouba, E. (2002). Understanding young children's pretend play in context. In P. K. Smith & C. H. Hart (Eds.), *Blackwell handbook of childhood social development* (pp. 418–437). Oxford: Blackwell.

Göncü, A., & Perone, A. (2005). Pretend play as a life-span activity. *Topoi*, *24*, 137–147.

Gordon, D. E. (1993). The inhibition of pretend play and its implications for development. *Human Development*, *36*, 215–234.

Gosso, Y. (2005). *Pexe oxemoarai: brincadeiras infantis entre os índios Parakanã* [Pexe oxemoarai: Children's play in the Parakanã Indians]. Unpublished doctoral thesis, Instituto de Psicologia, Universidade de São Paulo, Brazil.

Gosso, Y., Morais, M. L. S., & Otta, E. (2006). Pivôs utilizados nas brincadeiras de faz-de-conta de crianças brasileiras de cinco grupos culturais [Pivots used in make-believe play by Brazilian children from five different cultural groups]. *Estudos de Psicologia*, *11*, 17–24.

Gosso, Y., Morais, M. L. S., & Otta, E. (2007). Pretend play of Brazilian children. *Journal of Cross-Cultural Psychology*, *38*, 539–558.

Gosso, Y., & Otta, E. (2003). Em uma aldeia Parakanã [At a Parakanã village]. In A. M. A. Carvalho, C. M. C. Magalhães, F. A. R. Pontes, & I. D. Bichara (Eds.), *Brincadeira é cultura: viajando pelo Brasil que brinca* (Vol. 1, pp. 33–76). São Paulo: Casa do Psicólogo.

Gosso, Y., Otta, E., Morais, M. L. S., Ribeiro, F. J. L., & Bussab, V. S. R. (2005). Play in hunter-gatherer society. In A. D. Pellegrini & P. K. Smith (Eds.), *The nature of play: Great apes and humans* (pp. 213–253). New York: Guilford.

Gottman, J. M. (1983). *How children become friends*. Monographs of the Society for Research in Child Development, 48 (no 3; serial no 201).

Gould, S. J., & Lewontin, R. C. (1979). The spandrels of San Marco and the Panglossian paradigm: A critique of the adaptationist programme. *Proceedings of the Royal Society of London. Series B. Biological Sciences*, *205*, 581–598.

Gregor, T. (1982). *Mehinaku: o drama da vida diária em uma aldeia do Alto Xingu* [Mehinaku: daily life drama of Xingu's village]. São Paulo: Nacional.

Groos, K. (1898). *The play of animals*. New York: Appleton.

Groos, K. (1901). *The play of man*. London: Heinemann.

Gruber, H. E. (1974). *Darwin on man: A psychological study of scientific creativity*. London: Wildwood House.

Gunter, B., & McAlean, J. (1997). *Children and television* (2nd ed.). London: Routledge.

Guthrie, K., & Hudson, L. M. (1979). Training conservation through symbolic play: A second look. *Child Development, 50,* 1269–1271.

Haight, W., Black, J., Ostler, T., & Sheridan, K. (2006). Pretend play and emotion learning in traumatized mothers and children. In D. Singer, R. Golinkoff, & K. Hirsh-Pasek (Eds.), *Play=Learning* (pp. 209–230). Oxford: Oxford University Press.

Haight, W. L., & Miller, P. J. (1993). *Pretending at home: Early development in a socioculteral context.* Albany: State Univeristy of New York Press.

Haight, W. L., Wang, X., Fung, H. H., Williams, K., & Mintz, J. (1999). Universal, developmental, and variable aspects of young children's play: a cross-cultural comparison of pretending at home. *Child Development, 70,* 1477–1488.

Hall, G. S. (1908). *Adolescence.* New York, Appleton.

Hall, N. (2005). Play, literacy, and situated learning. In J. Moyles (Ed.), *The excellence of play* (2nd ed., pp. 86–97). Maidenhead: Open University Press.

Hamilton, W. D. (1964). The genetical evolution of social behaviour. *Journal of Theoretical Biology, 7,* 1–52.

Hanawalt, B. (1993). *Growing up in medieval London.* New York & Oxford: Oxford University Press.

Harcourt, R. (1991a). Survivorship costs of play in the South American fur seal. *Animal Behaviour, 42,* 509–511.

Harcourt, R. (1991b). The development of play in the South American fur seal. *Ethology, 88,* 191–202.

Harlow, H. F., McGaugh, J. L., & Thompson, R. F. (1978). *Psicologia.* São Paulo: Brasiliense.

Harris, J. R. (1995). Where is the child's environment? A group socialization theory of development. *Psychological Review, 102,* 458–489.

Harris, P. L. (1994). Understanding pretense. In C. Lewis & P. Mitchell (Eds.), *Children's early understanding of mind* (pp. 235–239). Hove, UK: Lawrence Erlbaum.

Harris, P. L. (2000). *The work of the imagination.* Oxford, UK: Blackwell.

Harris, P. L. (2007). Hard work for the imagination. In A. Göncü & S. Gaskins (Eds.), *Play and development: Evolutionary, sociocultural and functional perspectives* (pp. 205–225). Hillsdale, NJ: Lawrence Erlbaum.

Harris, P. L., Brown, E., Marriot, C., Whittall, S., & Harmer, S. (1991). Monsters, ghosts and witches: Testing the limits of fantasy–reality distinction in young children. *British Journal of Developmental Psychology, 9,* 105–123.

Hartup, W. W. (1996). The company they keep: Friendships and their developmental significance. *Child Development, 67,* 1–13.

Hass, C. C., & Jenni, D. A. (1993). Social play among juvenile bighorn sheep: structure development, and relationship to adult behaviour. *Ethology, 93,* 105–116.

Hawkes, K., O'Connell, J. F., Blurton Jones, N. G., Alvarez, H., & Charnov, E. L. (1998). Grandmothering, menopause, and the evolution of human life histories. *Proceedings of the National Academy of Sciences, USA, 95,* 1336–1339.

Hayes, C. H. (1951). *The ape in our house.* New York: Harper & Row.

Heinrich, B., & Smolker, R. (1998). Play in common ravens *(Corvus corax).* In M. Bekoff & J. A. Byers (Eds.), *Animal play: Evolutionary, comparative, and ecological perspectives* (pp. 27–44). Cambridge: Cambridge University Press.

Hellendoorn, J. (1994). Imaginative play training for severely retarded children. In J. Hellendoorn, R. van der Kooij, & B. Sutton-Smith (Eds.), *Play and intervention* (pp. 113–122). Albany: State University of New York Press.

Herrman, E., Call, J., Hernandez-Lloreda, M. V., Hare, B., & Tomasello, M. (2007). Humans have evolved specialised skills of social cognition: The cultural intelligence hypothesis. *Science, 317,* 1360–1366.

Hetherington, E. M., & Parke, R. D. (1979). *Child psychology: A contemporary viewpoint* (2nd ed.). New York: McGraw-Hill.

Hewes, J. (2007). The value of play in early learning: Towards a pedagogy. In T. Jambor & J. van Gils (Eds.), *Several reflections on children's play* (pp. 119–132). Antwerp-Apeldoorn: Garant.

Hines, M., & Kaufman, F. R. (1994). Androgen and the development of human sex-typical behaviour: Rough-and-tumble play and sex of preferred playmates in children with Congenital Adrenal Hyperplasia (CAH). *Child Development, 65,* 1042–1053.

Hole, G. J., & Einon, D. F. (1984). Play in rodents. In P. K. Smith (Ed.), *Play in animals and humans* (pp. 95–117). Oxford: Blackwell.

Holland, P. (2003). *We don't play with guns here.* Philadelphia: Open University Press.

Howe, N., Petrakos, H., & Rinaldi, C. M. (1998). "All the sheeps are dead. He murdered them": Sibling pretense, negotiation, internal state language, and relationship quality. *Child Development, 69,* 182–191.

Howes, C. (1994). *The collaborative construction of pretend.* Albany, NY: State University of New York Press.

Howes, C., & Matheson, C. C. (1992). Sequences in the development of competent play with peers. Social and social pretend play. *Developmental Psychology, 28,* 961–974.

Howes, C., Unger, O., & Matheson, C. C. (1992). *The collaborative construction of pretend.* Albany: State University of New York Press.

Hrdy, S. B. (1977). Infanticide as a primate reproductive strategy. *American Scientist, 65,* 40–49.

Hughes, B. (2007). Do locomotor play levels change following environmental modification? In T. Jambor & J. van Gils (Eds.), *Several reflections on children's play* (pp. 193–202). Garant: Antwerp-Apeldoorn.

Humphreys, A. P., & Smith, P. K. (1984). Rough-and-tumble play in preschool and playground. In P. K. Smith (Ed.), *Play in animals and humans* (pp. 241–266). Oxford: Blackwell.

Humphreys, A. P., & Smith, P. K. (1987). Rough and tumble, friendship and dominance in school children: Evidence for continuity and change with age. *Child Development, 58,* 201–212.

Hutt, C. (1966). Exploration and play in children. *Symposia of the Zoological Society of London, 18,* 61–81.

Hutt, C. (1970). Curiosity in young children. *Science Journal, 6,* 68–72.

Hutt, C., & Bhavnani, R. (1972). Predictions from play. *Nature, 237,* 171–172.

Hutt, S. J., Tyler, S., Hutt, C., & Christopherson, H. (1989). *Play, exploration and learning: A natural history of the pre-school child.* London: Routledge.

Huxley, J. S. (1942). *Evolution: The modern synthesis.* London: Allen & Unwin.

Isaacs, S. (1929). *The nursery years.* London: Routledge & Kegan Paul.

Jarrold, C. (2003). A review of research into pretend play in autism. *Autism, 7,* 379–390.

Jarrold, C., Boucher, J., & Smith, P. K. (1993). Symbolic play in autism: A review. *Journal of Autism and Developmental Disorders, 23,* 281–307.

Jarrold, C., Boucher, J., & Smith, P. K. (1996). Generativity deficits in pretend play. *British Journal of Developmental Psychology, 14,* 275–300.

Jarrold, C., Carruthers, P., Smith, P. K., & Boucher, J. (1994). Pretend play: Is it metarepresentational? *Mind and Language, 9,* 445–468.

Jarrold, C., Smith, P. K., & Boucher, J. (1994). Comprehension of pretense in children with autism. *Journal of Autism and Developmental Disorders, 24,* 433–455.

Jarvis, P. (2006). "Rough and tumble" play: Lessons in life. *Evolutionary Psychology, 4,* 330–346.

Jersild, A. T. (1955). *Child psychology* (4th ed.). London: Staples Press.

Johnson, J. E. (1978). Mother–child interaction and imaginative behavior of preschool children. *Journal of Psychology, 100,* 123–129.

Johnson, J. E., Ershler, J., & Lawton, J. T. (1982). Intellective correlates of preschoolers' spontaneous play. *Journal of Genetic Psychology, 106,* 115–122.

Kahen, V., Katz, L. F., & Gottman, J. M. (1994). Linkages between parent–child interaction and conversations of friends. *Social Development, 3,* 238–254.

Kamei, N. (2005). Play among Baka children in Cameroon. In B. S. Hewlett & M. E. Lamb (Eds.), *Hunter-gatherer childhoods: Evolutionary, developmental and cultural perspectives* (pp. 343–359). New Jersey: Transaction Publishers.

Kaplan, H. S., Lancaster, J. B., Hill, K., & Hurtado, A. M. (2000). A theory of human life history evolution: Diet, intelligence, and longevity. *Evolutionary Anthropology, 9,* 156–183.

Karmiloff-Smith, A. (1992). *Beyond modularity.* Cambridge, MA: MIT Press.

Kaufmann, J. H. (1974). Social ethology of the whiptail wallaby, *Macropus parryi,* in northeastern New South Wales. *Animal Behaviour, 22,* 281–369.

Kavanaugh, R. D., & Engel, S. (1998). The development of pretense and narrative in early childhood. In O. N. Saracho & B. Spodek (Eds.), *Multiple perspectives on play in early childhood education* (pp. 80–99). Albany: State University of New York Press.

Kelly, R. (2006). An exploration of the role of executive functions in the symbolic play of children with high-functioning autism, children with Asperger's disorder, and typically developing children. Unpublished doctoral thesis, LaTrobe University, Australia.

Kline, S. (1995). The promotion and marketing of toys: Time to rethink the paradox? In A. D. Pellegrini (Ed.), *The future of play theory* (pp. 165–185). Albany, NY: State University of New York Press.

Kline, S. (1997). *Out of the garden: Children's culture in the age of advertising.* Toronto: Garamond.

Konner, M. (1972). Aspects of the developmental ethology of a forging people. In J. S. Bruner, A. Jolly, and K. Sylva (Eds.) (1976), *Play: Its role in development and evolution*, Harmondsworth, Penguin.

Konner, M. J. (1976). Relations among infants and juveniles in comparative perspective. *Social Sciences Information, 15,* 371–402.

Kramer, L., & Schaefer-Hernan, P. (1994). Patterns of fantasy play engagement across the transition to becoming a sibling. *Journal of Child Psychology and Psychiatry, 35,* 749–767.

Kramer, R. (1976). *Maria Montessori: A biography.* Oxford: Basil Blackwell.

Krasnor, L. R., & Pepler, D. J. (1980). The study of children's play: Some suggested future directions. In K. Rubin (Ed.), *Children's play* (pp. 85–95). San Francisco: Jossey-Bass.

Kuczaj II, S. A. (1986). Language play. In P. K. Smith (Ed.), *Children's play: Research developments and practical applications.* London: Gordon and Breach.

Lancaster, J. B. (1971). Play-mothering: The relations between juvenile females and young infants among free-ranging vervet monkeys (*Cercopithecus aethiops*). *Folia Primatologica, 15,* 161–182.

Lancaster, J. B., & Lancaster, C. S. (1987). The watershed: Change in parental-investment and family-formation strategies in the course of human evolution. In J. B. Lancaster, J. Altmann, A. S. Rossi, & L. R. Sherrod (Eds.), *Parenting across the lifespan: Biosocial dimensions* (pp. 187–205). New York: Aldine.

Lancy, D. F. (1980). Play in species adaptation. *Annual Review of Anthropology, 9,* 471–495.

Lancy, D. F. (1996). *Playing on the mother ground: Cultural routines for children's development.* New York: Guilford Press.

Lancy, D. (2007). Accounting for variability in mother–child play. *American Anthropologist, 109,* 273–284.

Landreth, G. L., & Sweeney, D. S. (1997). Child-centered play therapy. In K. J. O'Connor & L. M. Braverman (Eds.), *Play therapy: Theory and practice* (pp. 17–45). New York: Wiley.

Larson, R. W., & Verma, S. (1999). How children and adolescents spend time across the world: work, play, and developmental opportunities. *Psychological Bulletin, 125,* 701–736.

Lawick-Goodall, J. van (1968). The behaviour of free-living chimpanzees in the Gombe Stream Reserve. *Animal Behaviour Monographs, 1,* 161–311.

Leacock, E. (1978). At play in African Villages. In J. S. Bruner, A. Jolly, & K. Sylva (Eds.), *Play—Its role in development and evolution* (pp. 466–473). Harmondsworth: Penguin Books.

Leevers, H. J., & Harris, P. L. (1999). Persisting effects of instruction on young children's syllogistic reasoning with incongruent and abstract premises. *Thinking and Reasoning, 5,* 145–173.

Leslie, A. M. (1987). Pretense and representation: The origins of "theory of mind". *Psychological Review, 94,* 412–426.

Lever, J. (1978). Sex differences in the complexity of children's play and games. *American Sociological Review, 43,* 471–483.

Levy, G. D. (1994). Aspects of preschooler's comprehension of indoor and outdoor gender typed toys. *Sex Roles, 30,* 391–405.

Lewis, C., Freeman, N. H., Kyriakidou, C., Maridaki-Kassotaki, K., & Berridge, D. M. (1996). Social influence on false belief access: specific sibling influences or general apprenticeship? *Child Development, 67,* 2930–2947.

Lewis, K. (2005). Social play in great apes. In A. D. Pellegrini & P. K Smith (Eds.), *The nature of play: Great apes and humans* (pp. 27–53). New York: Guilford.

Lewis, K., & Barton, R. A. (2004). Playing for keeps: Evolutionary relationships between social play and the cerebellum in nonhuman primates. *Human Nature, 15,* 5–21.

Lewis, K., & Barton, R. A. (2006). Amygdala size and hypothalamus size predict social play frequency in nonhuman primates: A comparative analysis using independent contrasts. *Journal of Comparative Psychology, 120,* 31–37.

Li, A. K. F. (1978). Effects of play on novel responses in kindergarten children. *Alberta Journal of Educational Research, 24,* 31–36.

Liebermann, J. N. (1977). *Playfulness: Its relationship to imagination and creativity.* New York: Academic Press.

Lillard, A. S. (1993). Pretend play skills and the child's theory of mind. *Child Development, 64,* 981–993.

Lillard, A. S. (1994). Making sense of pretence. In C. Lewis & P. Mitchell (Eds.), *Children's early understanding of mind* (pp. 211–234). Hove: Lawrence Erlbaum.

Lillard, A. S. (1999). Pretending, understanding pretense, and understanding minds. In S. Reifel (Ed.), *Play and culture studies, Vol. 3: Theory in context and out* (pp. 233–254). Norwood, NJ: Ablex.

Lloyd Morgan, C. (1896). On modification and variation. *Science, 5,* 139–155.

Loizos, C. (1967). Play behaviour in higher primates: A review. In D. Morris (Ed.), *Primate ethology* (pp. 176–218). Chicago: Aldine.

Lorenz, K. (1956). Play and vacuum activites. In M. Autuori (Ed.), *L'instinct dans le comportement des animaux et de l'homme* (pp. 633–645). Paris: Masson.

Lovejoy, C. O. (1981). The origin of man. *Science, 211,* 341–350.

Lussier, L., & Buskirk, E. R. (1977). Effects of an endurance training regimen on assessment of work capacity in pre-pubertal children. *Annals of the New York Academy of Sciences, 301,* 734–747.

Maccoby, E. E. (1990). Gender and relationships. *American Psychologist, 45,* 513–520.

Maccoby, E. E. (1998). *The two sexes: Growing up apart, coming together.* Cambridge, MA: Harvard University Press.

MacDonald, K. (1993). Parent–child play: An evolutionary perspective. In K. MacDonald (Ed.), *Parent–child play* (pp. 113–143). New York: State University of New York Press.

MacDonald, K., & Parke, R. (1986). Parent–child physical play. *Sex Roles, 15,* 367–378.

MacWhinney, B. (2005). Language evolution and human development. In B. J. Ellis & D. F. Bjorklund (Eds.), *Origins of the social mind* (pp. 383–410). New York and London: Guilford Press.

Majors, K. (2007). Children's imaginary companions and the purposes they serve: An interpretive phenomenological analysis. Unpublished PhD thesis, Institute of Education, University of London, England.

Manning, K., & Sharp, A. (1977). *Structuring play in the early years at school.* London: Ward Lock Educational.

Manwell, E. M., & Mengert, I. G. (1934). A study of the development of two- and three-year-old children with respect to play activities. *University of Iowa Studies in Child Welfare, 4,* 69–111.

Martin, P. (1984). The time and energy costs of play behaviour in the cat. *Zeitschrift für Tierpsychologie, 64,* 298–312.

Martin, P., & Bateson, P. (1994). *Measuring behaviour: An introductory guide* (2nd ed.). Cambridge: Cambridge University Press.

Martin, P., & Caro, T. (1985). On the function of play and its role in behavioural development. In J. Rosenblatt, C. Beer, M.-C. Bushnel, & P. Slater (Eds.), *Advances in the study of behaviour* (Vol. 15, pp. 59–103). New York: Academic Press.

Martini, M. (1994). Peer interactions in Polynesia: A view from the Marquesas. In J. L. Roopnarine, J. E. Johnson, & F. H. Hooper (Eds.), *Children's play in diverse cultures* (pp. 73–103). Albany: State University of New York Press.

Matevia, M. L., Patterson, F., & Hillix, W. A. (2002). Pretend play in a signing gorilla. In R. W. Mitchell (Ed.), *Pretending and imagination in animals and children* (pp. 285–304). Cambridge: Cambridge University Press.

Mather, J. A., & Anderson, R. C. (1999). Exploration, play, and habituation in octopuses (*Octopus dofleini*). *Journal of Comparative Psychology, 113,* 333–338.

Maudin, T., & Meeks, C. B. (1990). Sex differences in children's time use. *Sex Roles, 22,* 537–554.

Maybury-Lewis, D. (1956). *The savage and the innocent.* Boston: Beacon Press.

McGrew, W. C. (1972). *An ethological study of children's behavior* (pp. 149–173). New York and London: Academic.

McLoyd, V. C. (1982). Social class differences in sociodramatic play: A critical review. *Developmental Review, 2,* 1–30.

McLoyd, V. C., & Ratner, H. H. (1983). The effects of sex and toy characteristics on exploration in preschool children. *Journal of Genetic Psychology, 142,* 213–224.

Meins, E. (1997). *Security of attachment and the social development of cognition.* Hove: Psychology Press.

Mendoza, D. L., & Ramirez, J. R. (1987). Play in kittens (*Felis domesticus*) and its association with cohesion and aggression. *Bulletin of the Psychonomic Society, 25,* 27–30.

Michelet, A. (1986). Teachers and play. *Prospects, 16,* 113–122.

Mitchell, P. (1997). *Introduction to theory of mind.* London: Arnold.

Mitchell, R. W. (2007). Pretense in animals: The continuing relevance of children's pretense. In A. Göncü & S. Gaskins (Eds.), *Play and development: Evolutionary, sociocultural and functional perspectives* (pp. 51–75). Hillsdale, NJ: Lawrence Erlbaum.

Mitchell, R. W., & Neal, M. (2005). Children's understanding of their own and others' mental states. Part A. Self-understanding precedes understanding of others in pretense. *British Journal of Developmental Psychology, 23,* 175–200.

Morais, M. L. S. (2004). *Conflitos e(m) brincadeiras infantis: Diferenças culturais e de gênero* [Cultural and gender differences in children's play and conflicts]. Unpublished doctoral thesis, Instituto de Psicologia da Universidade de São Paulo, Brazil.

Morais, M. L. S., & Carvalho, A. M. A. (1994). Faz-de-conta: Temas, papéis e regras na brincadeira de crianças de quatro anos. [Make-believe: Themes, role play, and rules in 4-year-old children's play] *Boletim de Psicologia, 100/101,* 21–30.

Morais, M. L. S., & Otta, E. (2003). Entre a serra e o mar. [In between the mountains and the sea] In A. M. A. Carvalho, C. M. C. Magalhães, F. A. R. Pontes, and I. D. Bichara (Eds.), *Brincadeira e cultura: viajando pelo Brasil que brinca* (Vol. I, pp. 126–156). São Paulo: Casa do Psicólogo.

Morelli, G. A., Rogoff, B., & Angelillo, C. (2003). Cultural variation in young children's access to work or involvement in specialized child-focused activities. *International Journal of Behavioral Development, 27,* 264–274.

Morris, D. (1962). *The biology of art.* London: Methuen.

Morris, D. (1969). *The human zoo.* London: Cape.

Nabuzoka, D., & Smith, P. K. (1999). Distinguishing serious and playful fighting by children with learning disabilities and nondisabled children. *Journal of Child Psychology and Psychiatry, 40*, 883–890.

Nakken, H., Vlaskamp, C., & van Wijck, R. (1994). Play within an intervention for multiply handicapped children. In J. Hellendoorn, R. van der Kooij, & B. Sutton-Smith (Eds.), *Play and intervention* (pp. 133–143). Albany: State University of New York Press.

National Children's Bureau (2008, February). Play England. *Play Today, 61*, 6–7.

National Conference on the Vital Role of Play in Learning, Development and Survival (1979). Washington, DC.

Neill, S. R. St. J. (1976). Aggressive and non-aggressive fighting in twelve-to-thirteen year old pre-adolescent boys. *Journal of Child Psychology and Psychiatry, 17*, 213–220.

Newson, J., & Newson, E. (1968). *Four years old in an urban community*. London: Allen and Unwin.

Nicolopoulou, A. (2006). The interplay of play and narrative in childen's development: Theoretical reflections and concrete examples. In A. Göncü & S. Gaskins (Eds.), *Play and development: Evolutionary, sociocultural and functional perspectives* (pp. 247–273). Hillsdale, NJ: Lawrence Erlbaum.

Nielsen, M., & Christie, T. (2008). Adult modelling facilitates young children's generation of novel pretend acts. *Infant and Child Development, 17*, 151–162.

Nielsen, M., & Dissanayake, C. (2000). An investigation of pretend play, mental state terms and false belief understanding: In search of a metarepresentational link. *British Journal of Developmental Psychology, 18*, 609–624.

Norsworthy, N., & Whitley, M. T. (1937). *The psychology of childhood*. New York: Macmillan.

Nunes, A. (2002). No tempo e no espaço: brincadeiras das crianças A'uwe-Xavantes. [In time and space: A'uwe-Xavante children's play] In A. L. Silva, A. Nunes & A. V. L. S. Macedo (Eds.), *Crianças indígenas: ensaios antropológicos* (pp. 64–99). São Paulo: Global.

Oakley, F. B., & Reynolds, P. C. (1976). Differing responses to social play deprivation in two species of macaque. In D. F. Lancy & B. A. Tindall (Eds.), *The anthropological study of play: Problems and prospects* (pp. 179–188). Cornwall, NY: Leisure Press.

O'Brien, J., Boatwright, T., Chaplin, J., Geckler, C., Gosnell, D., Holcombe, J., & Parrish, K. (1998). The impact of positioning equipment on play skills of physically impaired children. In M. C. Duncan, G. Chick, & A. Aycock (Eds.), *Play and Culture Studies* (Vol. 1, pp. 149–160). Greenwich: Ablex.

O'Connor, K. J., & Braverman, L. M. (Eds.) (1997). *Play therapy: Theory and practice*. New York: Wiley.

Orme, N. (2002). *Medieval Children* (Rev. ed.). New Haven & London: Yale University Press.

Oswald, H., Krappmann, L., Chowduri, F., & Salisch, M. (1987). Gaps and bridges: Interactions between boys and girls in elementary schools. *Sociological Studies of Child Development, 2*, 205–223.

Overton, W. F., & Jackson, J. P. (1973). The representation of imagined objects in action sequences: A developmental study. *Child Development, 44*, 309–314.

Paley, V. G. (2004). *A child's work: The importance of fantasy play*. Chicago & London: University of Chicago Press.

Panksepp, J. (1980). The ontogeny of play in rats. *Developmental Psychobiology, 14*, 327–332.

Panksepp, J. (1993). Rough and tumble play: A fundamental play process. In K. MacDonald (Ed.), *Parent–child play* (pp. 147–184). New York: State University of New York Press.

Panksepp, J. (1998). *Affective neuroscience: The foundations of human and animal emotions*. New York: Oxford University Press.

Parke, R. D., Cassidy, J., Burks, V. M., Carson, J. L., & Boyum, L. (1992). Familial contribution to peer competence among young children: The role of interactive and affective processes. In R. D. Parke & G. Ladd (Eds.), *Family-peer relationships* (pp. 107–134). Hillsdale, NJ: Erlbaum.

Parke, R. D., & Suomi, S. J. (1981). Adult male infant relationships: Human and nonhuman primate evidence. In K. Immelman, G. W. Barlow, L. Petronovitch, & M. Main (Eds.), *Behavioural development* (pp. 700–725). New York: Cambridge University Press.

Parten, M. (1932). Social participation among preschool children. *Journal of Abnormal and Social Psychology, 27*, 243–269.

Patterson, E. (1980). Innovative uses of language by a gorilla: A case study. In K. Nelson (Ed.), *Children's Language* (Vol. 2, pp. 497–561). New York: Gardner Press.

Patterson, E., & Linden, E. (1981). *The education of Koko*. New York: Holt.

Peisach, E., & Hardeman, M. (1986). Imaginative play and logical thinking in young children. *Journal of Genetic Psychology, 146*, 233–249.

Pellegrini, A. D. (1988). Elementary school children's rough-and-tumble play and social competence. *Developmental Psychology, 24*, 802–806.

Pellegrini, A. D. (1993). Boys' rough-and-tumble play, social competence and group composition. *British Journal of Developmental Psychology, 11*, 237–248.

Pellegrini, A. D. (1994). The rough play of adolescent boys of differing sociometric status. *International Journal of Behavioral Development, 17*, 525–540.

Pellegrini, A. D. (1995a). *School recess and playground behavior*. Albany, NY: State University of New York Press.

Pellegrini, A. D. (1995b). A longitudinal study of boys' rough-and-tumble play and dominance during early adolescence. *Journal of Applied Developmental Psychology, 16*, 77–93.

Pellegrini, A. D. (2002). Rough-and-tumble play from childhood through adolescence: Development and possible functions. In P. K. Smith & C. Hart (Eds.), *Blackwell handbook of social development* (pp. 438–453). Oxford: Blackwell.

Pellegrini, A. D., & Bjorklund, D. F. (1997). The role of recess in children's cognitive performance. *Educational Psychologist, 31*, 181–187.

Pellegrini, A. D., & Bjorklund, D. F. (2004). The ontogeny and phylogeny of children's object and fantasy play. *Human Nature, 15*, 23–43.

Pellegrini, A. D., & Davis, P. (1993). Relations between children's playground and classroom behaviour. *British Journal of Educational Psychology, 63*, 86–95.

Pellegrini, A. D., Dupuis, D., & Smith, P. K. (2007). Play in evolution and development. *Developmental Review, 27*, 261–276.

Pellegrini, A. D., & Galda, L. (1993). Ten years after: A re-examination of symbolic play and literacy research. *Reading Research Quarterly, 28*, 162–177.

Pellegrini, A. D., & Gustafson, K. (2005). Boys' and girls' uses of objects for exploration, play, and tools in early childhood. In A. D. Pellegrini & P. K. Smith (Eds.) *The nature of play: Great apes and humans* (pp. 113–138). New York: Guilford.

Pellegrini, A. D., Huberty, P. D., & Jones, I. (1995). The effects of recess timing on children's playground and classroom behaviors. *American Educational Research Journal, 32*, 845–864.

Pellegrini, A. D., & Long, J. D. (2003). A sexual selection theory longitudinal analysis of sexual segregation and integration in early adolescence. *Journal of Experimental Child Psychology, 85*, 257–278.

Pellegrini, A. D., & Perlmutter, J. C. (1989). Classroom contextual effects on children's play. *Developmental Psychology, 25*, 289–296.

Pellegrini, A. D., & Smith, P. K. (1998a). Physical activity play: The nature and function of a neglected aspect of play. *Child Development, 69*, 577–598.

Pellegrini, A. D., & Smith, P. K. (1998b). Physical activity play: Consensus and debate. *Child Development, 69*, 609–610.

Pellegrini, A. D., & Smith, P. K. (2003). Children's play: A developmental and evolutionary orientation. In J. Valsiner & K. Connolly (Eds.), *Handbook of Developmental Psychology* (pp. 276–291). London: Sage.

Pellegrini, A. D., & Smith, P. K. (Eds.) (2005). *The nature of play: Great apes and humans*. New York: Guilford.

Peller, L. E. (1954). Libidinal phases, ego development and play. *Psychoanalytic Study of the Child, 9*, 178–198.

Pellis, S. M. (1981). A description of social play by the Australian magpie *Gymnorhina tibicen* based on Eshkol-Wachman notation. *Bird Behavior, 3*, 61–79.

Pellis, S. M. (1983). Development of head and foot coordination in the Australian magpie *Gymnorhina tibicen*, and the function of play. *Bird Behaviour, 4*, 57–62.

Pellis, S. M., & Pellis, V. C. (1987). Play-fighting differs from serious fighting in both target of attack and tactics of fighting in the laboratory rat. *Aggressive Behavior*, 13, 227–242.

Pellis, S. M., & Pellis, V. C. (1991). Role reversal changes during the ontogeny of play-fighting in male rats. *Aggressive Behavior*, 17, 179–189.

Pellis, S. M., & Pellis, V. C. (1998). The structure–function interface in the analysis of play fighting. In M. Bekoff & J. A. Byers (Eds.), *Animal play: Evolutionary, comparative, and ecological perspectives* (pp. 115–140). New York: Cambridge University Press.

Pereira, M. E. (1993). Evolution of juvenile period in mammals. In M. E. Pereira & L. A. Fairbanks (Eds.), *Juvenile primates* (pp. 17–27). Oxford: Oxford University Press.

Perner, J., Ruffman, T., & Leekam, S. R. (1994). Theory of mind is contagious: You catch it from your sibs. *Child Development*, 65, 1228–1238.

Piaget, J. (1936/1952). *The origin of intelligence in the child*. London: Routledge and Kegan Paul.

Piaget, J. (1951). *Play, dreams, and imitation in childhood*. London: Routledge & Kegan Paul.

Piaget, J. (1966). Response to Brian Sutton-Smith. *Psychological Review*, 73, 111–112.

Plotkin, H. (2004). *Evolutionary thought in psychology: A brief history*. Malden, MA: Blackwell.

Poirier, F. E., & Smith, E. O. (1974). Socializing functions of primate play. *American Zoologist*, 14, 275–287.

Pollock, L. (1983). *Forgotten children: Parent–child relations from 1500 to 1900*. Cambridge: Cambridge University Press.

Poole, T. B., & Fish, J. (1975). An investigation of individual, age and sexual differences in the play of *Rattus norvegicus* (Mammalia: Rodentia). *Journal of Zoology*, 179, 249–260.

Porter, M. L., Hernandez-Reif, M., & Jessee, P. (2009). Play therapy: A review. *Early Child Development and Care*, 179, in press.

Potegal, M., & Einon, D. (1988). Aggressive behaviours in adult rats deprived of playfighting experience as juveniles. *Developmental Psychobiology*, 22, 159–172.

Power, T. G. (2000). *Play and exploration in children and animals*. Mahwah, NJ: Erlbaum.

Preissler, M. A. (2006). Play and autism: Facilitating symbolic understanding. In D. Singer, R. Golinkoff, & K. Hirsh-Pasek (Eds.), *Play=Learning* (pp. 231–250). Oxford: Oxford University Press.

Punch, S. (2003). Childhoods in the majority world: miniature adults or tribal children? *Sociology*, 37, 277–295.

Rae, W. A., Worchel, F. F., Upchurch, J. L, Sanner, J. H., & Daniel, C. A. (1989). The psychosocial impact of play on hospitalized children. *Journal of Pediatric Psychology*, 14, 617–627.

Rakoczy, H., Tomasello, M., & Straino, T. (2006). The role of experience and discourse in children's developing understanding of pretend play actions. *British Journal of Developmental Psychology, 24,* 305–335.

Ramsey, J. K., & McGrew, W. C. (2005). Object play in great apes. In A. D. Pellegrini & P. K. Smith (Eds.), *The nature of play: Great apes and humans* (pp. 89–112). New York: Guilford Press.

Rasa, O. A. E. (1977). The ethology and sociology of the dwarf mongoose *(Helogale undulate rufula). Zeitschrift fur Tierpsychologie, 43,* 337–406.

Rasa, O. A. E. (1984). A motivational analysis of object play in juvenile dwarf mongooses *(Helogale undulate rufula). Animal Behaviour, 32,* 579–589.

Ray, D. C., Schottelkorb, A., & Tsai, M-H. (2007). Play therapy with children exhibiting symptoms of attention deficit hyperactivity disorder. *International Journal of Play Therapy, 16,* 95–111.

Renfrew, C. (2007). *Prehistory: The making of the human mind.* London: Weidenfeld and Nicolson.

Ridgers, N. D., Stratton, G., Fairclough, S. J., & Twisk, J. W. R. (2007). Children's physical activity levels during school recess: a quasi-experimental intervention study. *International Journal of Behavioral Nutrition and Physical Activity, 4,* www.ijpna.org/content/4/1/19.

Roggman, L., & Langlois, J. (1987). Mothers, infants, and toys: Social play correlates of attachment. *Infant Behaviour and Development, 10,* 233–237.

Roopnarine, J. L., Hooper, F. H., Ahmeduzzaman, M., & Pollack, B. (1993). Gentle play partners: Mother–child and father–child play in New Delhi, India. In K. MacDonald (Ed.), *Parent–child play* (pp. 287–304). New York: State University of New York Press.

Roopnarine, J. L., Hossain, Z., Gill, P., & Brophy, H. (1994). Play in the East Indian context. In J. L. Roopnarine, J. E. Johnson, & F. H. Hooper (Eds.), *Children's play in diverse cultures* (pp. 9–30). Albany: State University of New York Press.

Roopnarine, J. L. & Johnson, J. E. (1994). The need to look at play in diverse cultural settings. In J. L. Roopnarine, J. E. Johnson, & F. H. Hooper (Eds.), *Children's play in diverse cultures* (pp. 1–8). Albany: State University of New York Press.

Roper, R., & Hinde, R. (1978). Social behavior in a play group: Consistency and complexity. *Child Development, 49,* 570–579.

Rosen, C. S., Schwebel, D. C., & Singer, J. L. (1997). Preschoolers' attributions of mental states in pretense. *Child Development, 68,* 1133–1142.

Rosenblatt, D. (1977). Developmental trends in infant play. In B. Tizard & D. Harvey (Eds.), *Biology of play* (pp. 33–44). London: SIMP/Heinemann.

Rosenthal, M. K. (1994). Social and non-social play of infants and toddlers in family day care. In H. Goelman & E. V. Jacobs (Eds.), *Children's play in child care settings* (pp. 163–192). Albany: State University of New York Press.

Roskos, K., & Christie, J. (Eds.), (2007). *Play and literacy: Research from multiple perspectives* (2nd edition). Hillsdale, NJ: Lawrence Erlbaum.

Routh, D., Schoeder, C., & O'Tuama, L. (1974). Development of activity levels in children. *Developmental Psychology, 10*, 163–168.

Rubin, K. (2001). *The play observation scale*. University of Maryland. Retrieved November 26, 2008 from http://www.rubin-lab.umd.edu/Coding%20Schemes/POS%20Coding%20Scheme%202001.pdf

Rubin, K. H., & Howe N. (1985). Toys and play behavior: an overview. *Topics in Early Childhood Special Education, 5*, 1–9.

Rubin, K. H., Watson, K. S., & Jambor, T. W. (1978). Free play behaviors in middle-and-lower-class preschoolers: Piaget revisited. *Child Development, 47*, 534–536.

Ruffman, T., Perner, J., Naito, M., Parkin, L., & Clements, W. A. (1998). Older (but not younger) siblings facilitate false belief understanding. *Developmental Psychology, 34*, 161–174.

Rusk, R. R. (1967). *A history of infant education*. London: University of London Press.

Salmon, J., Booth, M. L., Phongsavan, P., Murphy, N., & Timperio, A. (2007). Promoting physical activity participation among children and adolescents. *Epidemiologic Reviews, 29*, 144–159

Savage-Rumbaugh, E. S. (1986). *Ape language: From conditioned response to symbol*. New York: Columbia University Press.

Saylor, C. F., Swenson, C. C., & Powell, P. (1992). Hurricane Hugo blows down the broccolli: Preschoolers' post-disaster play and adjustment. *Child Psychiatry and Human Development, 22*, 139–149.

Schafer, M., & Smith, P. K. (1996). Teachers' perceptions of play fighting and real fighting in primary school. *Educational Research, 38*, 173–181.

Schwartzmann, H. (1978). *Transformations: the anthropology of children's play*. New York: Plenum.

Schwebel, D. C., Rosen, C. S., & Singer, J. L. (1999). Preschoolers' pretend play and theory of mind: The role of jointly constructed pretence. *British Journal of Developmental Psychology, 17*, 333–348.

Serbin, L. A., Moller, L. C., Gulko, J., Powlishta, K. K., & Colburne, K. A. (1994). The emergence of gender segregation in toddler playgroups. *New Directions for Child Development, 65*, 7–17.

Sharpe, L. L. (2005a). Play fighting does not affect subsequent fighting success in wild meerkats. *Animal Behaviour, 69*, 1023–1029.

Sharpe, L. L. (2005b). Play does not enhance social cohesion in a cooperative mammal. *Animal Behaviour, 70*, 551–558.

Sharpe, L. L., & Cherry, M. I. (2003). Social play does not reduce aggression in wild meerkats. *Animal Behaviour, 66*, 989–997.

Shostak, M. (1981). *Nisa: the life and words of a !Kung woman*. Harmondsworth: Penguin Books.

Simon, T., & Smith, P. K. (1983). The study of play and problem-solving in preschool children: have experimenter effects been responsible for previous results? *British Journal of Developmental Psychology, 1*, 289–297.

Simon, T., & Smith, P. K. (1985). Play and problem-solving: a paradigm questioned. *Merrill-Palmer Quarterly, 31*, 265–277.

Simons-Morton, B.G., O'Hara, N. M., Parcel, G. S., Huang, I. W., Baranowski, T., & Wilson, B. (1990). Children's frequency of participation in moderate to vigorous physical activities. *Research Quarterly for Exercise and Sport, 61*, 307–314.

Singer, D. G., & Singer, J. L. (1990). *The house of make-believe: Play and the developing imagination.* Cambridge, MA: Harvard University Press.

Sinker, M., Brodin, J., Fagundes, V., Kim, F., Helberg, G., Linberg, M., Trieschmann, M., & Björck-Akesson, E. (1993). *Children's concept of play: A study in four countries.* Women Researchers in Play and Disabilities. Sweden: Samhall Kalmarsund Repro.

Slaughter, D., & Dombrowski, J. (1989). Cultural continuities and discontinuities: Impact on social and pretend play. In M. N. Bloch & A. D. Pellegrini (Eds.), *The ecological context of children's play* (pp. 282–310). Nowood, NJ: Ablex.

Sluckin, A. (1981). *Growing up in the playground: The social development of children.* London: Routledge and Kegan Paul.

Sluss, D. J. (2002). Block play complexity in same-sex dyads of preschool children. In J. L. Roopnarine (Ed.), *Conceptual, social-cognitive, and contextual issues in the fields of play. Play and Culture Studies, Vol. 4* (pp. 77–91). Westport, CT & London: Ablex Publishing.

Smilansky, S. (1968). *The effects of sociodramatic play on disadvantaged preschool children.* New York: Wiley.

Smilansky, S., & Shefatya, L. (1990). *Facilitating play: A medium for promoting cognitive, socio-emotional and academic development in young children.* Gaithersburg, MD: Psychosocial and Educational Publications.

Smith, E. O. (Ed.) (1978). *Social play in primates.* New York: Academic Press.

Smith, P. K. (1970). *Social play and behaviour of preschool children.* Unpublished doctoral dissertation, University of Sheffield, Sheffield, UK.

Smith, P. K. (1977). Social and fantasy play in young children. In B. Tizard & D. Harvey (Eds.), *Biology of play* (pp. 123–145). London: SIMP/ Heinemann.

Smith, P. K. (1982). Does play matter? Functional and evolutionary aspects of animal and human play. *The Behavioural and Brain Sciences, 5*, 139–184.

Smith, P. K. (1988). Children's play and its role in early development: A re-evaluation of the "Play Ethos". In A. D. Pellegrini (Ed.). *Psychological bases for early education* (pp. 207–226). Chichester and New York: John Wiley & Sons Ltd.

Smith, P. K. (1994). The war play debate. In J. H. Goldstein (Ed.), *Toys, play, and child development.* (pp. 64–84). Cambridge: Cambridge University Press.

Smith, P. K. (1996). Language and the evolution of mindreading. In P. Carruthers & P. K. Smith (Eds.), *Theories of theories of mind* (pp. 344–354). Cambridge: Cambridge University Press.

Smith, P. K. (1997). Play fighting and real fighting: Perspectives on their relationship. In A. Schmitt, K. Atswanger, K. Grammar, & K. Schafer (Eds.), *New aspects of ethology* (pp. 47–64). New York: Plenum Press.

Smith, P. K. (2000). Why I study . . . bullying. *The Psychologist, 13*, 348–349.

Smith, P. K. (2004). Play: Types and functions in human development. In B. J. Ellis & D. F. Bjorklund (Eds.), *Origins of the social mind: Evolutionary psychology and child development* (pp. 271–291). New York: Guilford Publications.

Smith, P. K. (2005). Social and pretend play in children. In A. D. Pellegrini & P. K. Smith (Eds.), *The nature of play: Great apes and humans* (pp. 173–209). New York: Guilford Press.

Smith, P. K. (2007). Evolutionary foundations and functions of play: An overview. In A. Göncü & S. Gaskins (Eds.), *Play and development: Evolutionary, sociocultural and functional perspectives* (pp. 21–49). Hillsdale, NJ: Lawrence Erlbaum.

Smith, P. K., & Connolly, K. (1972). Patterns of play and social interaction in pre-school children. In N. Blurton Jones (Ed.) *Ethological studies of child behaviour* (pp. 65–95). Cambridge: Cambridge University Press.

Smith, P. K., & Connolly, K. (1980). *The ecology of preschool behaviour.* Cambridge: Cambridge University Press.

Smith, P. K., Cowie, H., & Blades, M. (2003). *Understanding children's development.* Oxford, Blackwell.

Smith, P. K., & Daglish, L. (1977). Sex differences in parent and infant behavior in the home. *Child Development, 48*, 1250–1254.

Smith, P. K., Dalgleish, M., & Herzmark, G. (1981). A comparison of the effects of fantasy play tutoring and skills tutoring in nursery classes. *International Journal of Behavioural Development, 4*, 421–441.

Smith, P. K., & Dutton, S. (1979). Play training in direct and innovative problem solving. *Child Development, 4*, 830–836.

Smith, P. K., & Hagan, T. (1980). Effects of deprivation on exercise play in nursery school children. *Animal Behaviour, 28*, 922–928.

Smith, P. K., Hunter, T., Carvalho, A. M. A., & Costabile, A. (1992). Children's perceptions of playfighting, playchasing and real fighting: a cross-national interview study. *Social Development, 1*, 211–229.

Smith, P. K., & Lewis, K. (1985). Rough-and-tumble play, fighting, and chasing in nursery school children. *Ethology and Sociobiology, 6*, 175–181.

Smith, P. K., & Sharp, S. (Eds.) (1994). *School bullying: Insights and perspectives.* London: Routledge.

Smith, P. K., & Simon, T. (1984). The study of play and problem-solving in preschool children: methodological problems and new directions. In P. K. Smith (Ed.), *Play in animals and humans,* (pp. 199–216). Oxford: Blackwell.

Smith, P. K., Simon, T., & Emberton, R. (1985). Play, problem-solving and experimenter effects: a replication of Simon and Smith (1983). *British Journal of Developmental Psychology, 3*, 105–107.

Smith, P. K., Smees, R., & Pellegrini, A. D. (2004). Play fighting and real fighting: Using video playback methodology with young children. *Aggressive Behavior, 30,* 164–173.

Smith, P. K., Smees, R., Pellegrini, A. D., & Menesini, E. (2002). Comparing pupil and teacher perceptions for playful fighting, serious fighting and positive peer interaction. In J. L. Roopnarine (Ed.), *Conceptual, social-cognitive, and contextual issues in the fields of play. Play and Culture Studies, Vol. 4* (pp. 235–245). Westport, CT & London: Ablex Publishing.

Smith, P. K., & Syddall, D. (1978). Play and non-play tutoring in preschool children: Is it play or tutoring that matters. *British Journal of Educational Psychology, 48,* 315–325.

Smith, P. K., & Vollstedt, R. (1985). Defining play: an empirical study of the relationship between play, and various play criteria. *Child Development, 56,* 1042–1050.

Smith, P. K., & Whitney, S. (1987). Play and associative fluency: Experimenter effects may be responsible for previous findings. *Developmental Psychology, 23,* 49–53.

Snow, E. (1997). *Inside Bruegel: The Play of Images in Children's Games.* New York: North Point Press.

Spencer, H. (1898 [1878]). *The principles of psychology.* New York: Appleton.

Špinka, M., Newberry, R. C., & Bekoff, M. (2001). Mammalian play: Training for the unexpected. *Quarterly Review of Biology, 76,* 141–168.

Stamps, J. (1995). Motor learning and the value of familiar space. *American Naturalist, 146,* 41–58.

Stearns, S. C. (1976). Life-history tactics: A review of the ideas. *Quarterly Review of Biology, 51,* 3–47.

Stevenson, H. W., & Lee, S. Y. (1990). Contexts of achievement. *Monographs for the Society for Research in Child Development, 55,* (1–2, serial no. 221).

Suddendorf, T., Fletcher-Flinn, C., & Johnston, L. (1999). Pantomime and theory of mind. *Journal of Genetic Psychology, 160,* 31–45.

Sutton-Smith, B. (1966). Piaget on play: A critique. *Psychological Review, 73,* 104–110.

Sutton-Smith, B. (1986). *Toys as culture.* New York: Gardner.

Sutton-Smith, B. (1997). *The ambiguity of play.* Cambridge, MA: Harvard University Press.

Sutton-Smith, B., & Kelly-Byrne, D. (1984). The idealization of play. In P. K. Smith (Ed.), *Play in animals and humans,* (pp. 305–321). Oxford: Blackwell.

Sylva, K. (1977). Play and learning. In B. Tizard & D. Harvey (Eds.), *Biology of play* (pp. 59–73). London: SIMP/Heinemann.

Sylva, K., Roy, C., & Painter, M. (1980). *Child watching at playgroup and nursery school.* London: Grant McIntyre.

Symons, D. (1974). Aggressive play and communication in Rhesus monkeys (*Macaca mulatta*). *American Zoologist, 14,* 317–322.

Symons, D. (1978). *Play and aggression: A study of rhesus monkeys.* New York: Columbia University Press.

Tajfel, H., & Turner, J. C. (1985). The social identity theory of intergroup behavior. In S. Worchel & W. G. Austin (Eds.), *Psychology of intergroup relations* (pp. 7–24). Chicago: Nelson-Hall.

Takeuchi, M. (1994). Children's play in Japan. In J. L. Roopnarine, J. E. Johnson, & F. H. Hooper (Eds.), *Children's play in diverse cultures* (pp. 51–72). Albany: State University of New York Press.

Takhvar, M., & Smith, P. K. (1990). A review and critique of Smilansky's classification scheme and the "nested hierarchy" of play categories. *Journal of Research in Early Childhood, 4,* 112–122.

Taylor, M. (1999). *Imaginary companions and the children who create them.* New York: Oxford University Press.

Taylor, M., & Carlson, S. M. (1997). The relation between individual differences in fantasy and theory of mind. *Child Development, 68,* 436–455.

Taylor, M., Cartwright, B. S., & Carlson, S. M. (1993). A developmental investigation of children's imaginary companions. *Developmental Psychology, 29,* 276–285.

Teti, D. M., Bond, L. A., & Gibbs, E. D. (1988). Mothers, fathers, and siblings: A comparison of play styles and their influence upon cognitive level. *International Journal of Behavioral Development, 11,* 415–432.

Thelen, E. (1979). Rhythmical stereotypies in normal human infants. *Animal Behaviour, 27,* 699–715.

Thelen, E. (1980). Determinants of amounts of stereotyped behaviour in normal human infants. *Ethology and Sociobiology, 1,* 141–150.

Tinbergen, N. (1951). *The study of instinct.* Oxford: Clarendon Press.

Tomasello, M., Carpenter, M., Call, J., Behne, T., & Moll, H. (2005). Understanding and sharing intentions: The origins of cultural cognition. *Behavioral and Brain Sciences, 28,* 675–735.

Torigoe, T. (1985). Comparison of object manipulation among 74 species of nonhuman primates. *Primates, 26,* 182–194.

Trevathan, W. (1987). *Human birth: An evolutionary perspective.* New York: Aldine de Gruyter.

Trivers, R. L. (1974). Parent–offspring conflict. *American Zoologist, 14,* 247–262.

Tudor-Hart, B. (1955). *Toys, play and discipline in childhood.* London: Routledge & Kegan Paul.

Ustinov, P. (1977). *Dear Me.* Harmondsworth: Penguin.

Uzgiris, I. C. (1967). Ordinality in the development of schemas for relating to objects. In J. Hellmuth (Ed.), *Exceptional Infant* (Vol. 1, pp. 317–344). Seattle: Special Child Publications.

Vandenberg, B. (1981). The role of play in the development of insightful tool-using strategies. *Merrill-Palmer Quarterly, 27,* 97–109.

Van der Voort, T. H. A., & Valkenburg, P. M. (1994). Television's impact on fantasy play: a review of research. *Developmental Review, 14,* 27–51.

Van Lawick-Goodall, J. (1968). The behaviour of free-living chimpanzees in the Gombe Stream Reserve. *Animal Behaviour Monographs*, *1*, 161–311.

Verstraete, S. J. M., Cardon, G. M., De Clercq, D. L. R., & de Bourdeaudhuij, I. M. M. (2006). Increasing children's physical activity levels during recess periods in elementary schools: the effects of providing game equipment. *European Journal of Public Health*, *16*, 415–419.

Vygotsky, L. S. (1966 [1933]). Play and its role in the mental development of the child. *Voprosy Psikhologii*, *12*, 62–76.

Waddington, C. H. (1957). *The strategy of the genes*. London: Allen & Unwin.

Watson, M. W., & Peng, Y. (1992). The relation between toy gun play and children's aggressive behavior. *Early Education and Development*, *3*, 370–389.

Weir, R. H. (1962). *Language in the crib*. The Hague: Mouton.

Weisler, A., & McCall, R. B. (1976). Exploration and play: Resumé and redirection. *American Psychologist*, *31*, 492–508.

Wemmer, C., & Fleming, M. J. (1974). Ontogeny of playful contact in a social mongoose, the meerkat, *Suricata suricatta*. *American Zoologist*, *14*, 415–426.

West, M. (1974) Social play in the domestic cat. *American Zoologist*, *14*, 427–436.

Wheeler, O. A., & Earl, I. G. (1939). *Nursery school education and the reorganization of the infant school*. London: University of London Press.

Whitbread, N. (1972). *The evolution of the nursery–infant school*. London: Routledge & Kegan Paul.

Whitney, I., & Smith, P. K. (1993). A survey of the nature and extent of bully/victim problems in junior/middle and secondary schools. *Educational Research*, *35*, 3–25.

Wilson, E. O. (1975). *Sociobiology: the new synthesis*. Cambridge: Belknap Press.

Wilson, E. O. (1978). *On human nature*. Cambridge, MA: Harvard University Press.

Wilson, S. C., & Kleiman, D. G. (1974). Eliciting play: A comparative study *(Octodon, Octodontomys, Pediolagus, Choeropsis, Ailuropoda)*. *American Zoologist*, *14*, 341–370.

Wing, L., & Gould, J. (1979). Severe impairments of social interaction and associated abnormalities in children: Epidemiology and classification. *Journal of Autism and Developmental Disorders*, *9*, 11–29.

Wohlwill, J. F. (1984). Relationship between exploration and play. In T. D. Yawkey & A. D. Pellegrini (Eds.), *Child's play: Developmental and applied* (pp. 143–170). Hillsdale, NJ: Lawrence Erlbaum Associates.

Wolff, R. J. (1981). Solitary and social play in wild *Mus musculus* (Mammalia). *Journal of Zoology*, *195*, 405–412.

Woolley, J. D. (1997). Thinking about fantasy: Are children fundamentally different thinkers and believers from adults? *Child Development*, *68*, 991–1011.

Woolley, J. D., & Wellman, H. H. (1990). Young children's understanding of realities, nonrealities, and appearances. *Child Development*, *64*, 1–17.

Yarrow, L. J., McQuiston, S., MacTurk, R. H., McCarthy, M. E., Klein, R. P., & Vietze, P. (1983). Assessment of mastery motivation during the first year of life: Contemporaneous and cross-age relationships. *Developmental Psychology, 19,* 158–171.

Youngblade, L. M., & Dunn, J. (1995). Individual differences in young children's pretend play with mother and sibling: Links to relationships and understanding of other people's feelings and beliefs. *Child Development, 66,* 1472–1492.

Zigler, E. F., & Bishop-Josef, S. J. (2005). Play under siege. In E. F. Zigler, D. G. Singer, & S. J. Bishop-Josef (Eds.), *Children's play: The roots of reading* (pp. 1–13). Washington, DC: Zero to Three Press.

Author Index

Subject Index